AMERICAN DREAMS

AMERICAN DREAMS

A STUDY OF AMERICAN UTOPIAS

BY

VERNON LOUIS PARRINGTON, JR.

/1

SECOND EDITION, ENLARGED

WITH A POSTSCRIPT

NEW YORK / RUSSELL & RUSSELL

BROWN UNIVERSITY STUDIES

VOLUME XI

Americana Series No. 2

TO
JULIA PARRINGTON

PREFACE

From the very beginning Americans have dreamed of a different, and usually of a better world. So many of these dreams have achieved reality that it is almost a commonplace to say, as does Alfonso Reyas, Mexican humanist, that "America is a Utopia. . . . It is the name of a human hope."

Many of us are quick to forget how much of America has been built on promises. We pretend, rather, that a hard-headed materialism has been our single standard of accomplishment. Our last adventure in world war has left a bitter taste in our mouths. We feel that we have been pursuing some utopian will-o-the-wisp, and that the statesmen of other nations, who cherish a more pragmatic sense of values, have imposed upon us. In our disillusion we are inclined to look back at our traditions, to re-examine the perennial spirit of optimism which has characterized even the darkest years. We still sympathize, however, with Eric Sevareid's conviction that planning for a better world is "not so wild a dream."

The initial impetus for this study was the unfinished third volume of my father's *Main Currents in American Thought*. At the time of his death he had completed only one chapter, dealing with Edward Bellamy, of a section entitled "The Quest for Utopia." My investigation began with the writers mentioned in that chapter, and expanded to include Bellamy's predecessors, as well as some of those who have come after.

The men discussed have in common only their interest in outlining a different government, or a better way of life. Some of them were wise, some were foolish, and a few, simply ignorant. The ideas which seem the most foolish to us now have not always seemed so. In large measure these books are a record of our taste, and of the reforms which have so consistently appealed to us. Their prescriptions for economic, political, social, intellectual and religious change have differed widely. Each generation has worked out formulas which seemed to solve the problems of the day. Each generation has looked for reassurance and been satisfied by different promises. In prosperous years the old ways have been good enough; in times of depression we have turned to the new. As a people we have dreamed of a better world—but we have probably been more ready to believe in charlatans than in utopias.

Some years ago Oscar Wilde said that "A map of the world that does not include Utopia is not worth glancing at, for it leaves out the one country at which Humanity is always landing. And when Humanity lands there, it looks out, and seeing a better country, sets sail. Progress is the realization of Utopias." Contemporary concepts of "progress" are not always the same as those suggested by these utopians. Some of their "maps" do make sense, however—even in our present world.

Many libraries have not bothered to save utopian novels or any of the casual political protests which were widely distributed at the end of the last century. This study was aided by the excellent collection of such material in the Brown University Library. Another major source of material was The New York Public Library.

In its original form this book was submitted to Brown University as a doctoral thesis in American Literature. The work was made easier by the help and encouragement of Dr. Randall Stewart, Professor of English Literature in Brown University.

VERNON L. PARRINGTON, JR.

Seattle, Washington
April, 1947

TABLE OF CONTENTS

America was always promises.
From the first voyage and the first ship there were promises—
ARCHIBALD MACLEISH in
America Was Promises

CHAPTER ONE

THE NEW WORLD AND UTOPIA

PLANNING a better world has always been a pleasant occupation. Many men have tried to be specific about their plans, and the plans have been as unlike as they were themselves. Sometimes the world of imagination takes the form of a New Jerusalem, and an attempt to rationalize Christianity with the historical role of the Jews. Sometimes, too, it gets mixed up with our notion of Heaven. And like Heaven the directions for getting there have been no more specific than the program of entertainment promised upon arrival. Some men have visualized the perfect world as a creation of the past. They have followed Plato's concept of a Golden Age, an age which even in his own day depended for authority on the Hebrew tradition of a descent from grace. And they have taken pleasure in his fabric of the lost Atlantis, which he evolved as a pseudo-historical justification for his Golden Age.

Few men now believe in the glories of a lost world. Anthropologists have dissipated most of our illusions. We must look to the future, instead, and since most of us accept some theory of progress, we are usually optimistic. There would be little satisfaction in such a jaundiced prediction as Mother Shipton's, who wrote, in 1488,

> The world shall get rich and dirty
> And come to an end in nineteen thirty.

The same prophecy mentioned the discovery of a new land. In that she was on much more sure ground, for explorers were already sailing new channels, and the reports of their journeys which sifted down to the people were being discussed with enthusiasm.

From the very beginning this new land was a symbol for man's aspirations. America was a new continent where there was neither tradition nor authority to make men conform to any set rules. The new world made men dream, and some of them put their dreams on paper. Sir Thomas More's dream of a perfect government caught men's fancy. The name he gave to his own dreams came to be accepted. *Utopia* literally means *nowhere,* but that is no more than to say that perfection in matters of government is always relative. No government will ever be perfect, and no one will ever think that his own plan for a government is perfect, except when it is only a dream. People with imagination are never satisfied, and it is good that they should not be. Whatever progress has been made in the world has been the result of dissenting opinion. Utopias are largely the expression of those dissents, the comparison of what is with what could be. It is inevitable that many utopian novels should be satiric, for satire is the easiest way of pointing out the absurdities of the present. It is only when the present is attacked that a better future can be conceived. It is inevitable that many should be naive, for when men are concerned with dreams, they do not balk at little obstacles. It is inevitable that many should seem silly, for men differ sharply as to the means of fulfilling these dreams and aspirations.

The shores of utopia have long been littered with the attacks of those men who think of themselves as practical, and the utopian as a fickle and immature dreamer who is either unable or unwilling to compete in the world he finds about him. But there is more to be said for utopia than that. New concepts set men to thinking, to working out their own plans. Many of the men who have been scornfully called utopians might more accurately be called social planners.

Their plans carry no guarantee that they will attract every reader, for they have not all been generous with their citizens. The inhabitants of Campanella's *City of the Sun,* 1623, for example, would have had their lives regulated to the smallest detail—even to matters of diet and reproduction.

The traditions of utopia have become so numerous that it is not always easy to be specific about what the word itself means. Utopia has become much more than the ideal world located in some strange new land. Some utopian plans have been religious quackery, some have been outlines of specific social or economic reforms, and some have simply been the lush promises of politicians designed for the confusion of the gullible. Since most American utopias have dealt with the reorganization of society, they serve as an accurate reflection of the changing pattern of men's ambitions. That pattern has been kaleidoscopic, for America has always been a fertile soil for new ideas—the result of a mixture of races and the absence of any single set of fixed traditions.

In 1659 John Eliot dreamed of a government following the exact and written word of God. Since then many other men have outlined an ideal government, and their plans have all been different. There has always been an American dream, and its greatest charm has been that it was variable, and not bound to a single doctrine. Americans still disagree on the prescription for an ideal life, and *utopia* is still *nowhere.*

The romantic lure of the new world was exaggerated in the accounts of returned travelers. Often the men had seen what they described; just as often they had not—but always the unknown land was wonderful, and whether the "descriptions" were colonization tracts or not, the accounts were heavily loaded with lush descriptive phrases. Daniel Denton's *A Brief Description of New York* contains this passage:

The Fruits natural to the Island, are *Mulberries, Pesimons, Grapes* great and small, *Huckelberries, Cramberries, Plums* of several sorts, *Rasberries* and *Strawberries,* of which last is such abundance in June, that the Fields and Woods are died red.

The greatest part of the Island is very full of Timber, as Oaks white and red, Walnut-trees, Chesnut-trees, which yield store of Mast for Swine, and are often therewith sufficiently fatted with Oat-Corn: as also Maples, Cedars, Saxifrage, Beach, Birch, Holly, Hazel, with many sorts more.

The Herbs which the Countrey naturally afford, are Purslain, White Orage, Egrimony, Violets, Penniroyal, Alicampane, besides Saxaparilla very common, with many more. Yea, in *May* you shall see the Woods and Fields so curiously bedecke with Roses, and an innumerable multitude of delightful Flowers, not only pleasing the eye, but smell, that you may behold Nature contending with Art, and striving to equal, if not excel many Gardens in *England:* nay, did we know the vertue of all those Plants and Herbs growing there (which time may more discover) many are of opinion, and the Natives do affirm, that there is no disease common to the Countrey, but may be cured without Materials from other Nations.[1]

---

[1] The original edition was published in London in 1670. The quotations are from the Facsimile Text Society edition, 1937, pp. 3, 4.

The accounts of other colonies are equally lush, particularly the tracts issued to encourage settlement in Newfoundland and Maryland. It is not unreasonable, then, to call these advertising pamphlets utopian. Men first became interested in colonial enterprises for a number of reasons, both economic and religious—but the interest soon became fascination, and the new world utopia. Some men thought of the new colonies as sanctuary for persecuted sects, others as the solution for the unemployment problem in England—but, once involved, the lure of the new country was all powerful. Father Andrew White intended to write a religious tract which would explain the possibilities of the Maryland colony, but he actually wrote a glowing, utopian account of the fertility and lushness of the territory.[2]

The new world could not live up to its early promise, simply because it had seemed to promise too much. James Oglethorpe, for instance, was quickly disappointed in his hopes for Georgia; the experiment was not the religious asylum he had hoped it might be; it did not "relieve domestic unemployment"; it did not immediately promote "imperial trade and navigation." Oglethorpe was really a utopian who tried to put his dreams into practice. Others found an answer to some of their problems in the new world, only to discover that religious freedom or economic security did not inevitably produce a private world without worries. After the first period of colonizing zeal, there was a long and drab period of adjustment. Many men found their private solution in drink; some, of a more saintly disposition, found a more full and complete answer in the word of God. John Eliot would have been unhappy if he had been labeled a utopian, for he thought of himself as a practical man of God, who knew how to take positive action in his relations with his fellow man. But regardless of what he would have admitted himself, his *Christian Commonwealth* was designed to serve as a handbook of government. The book shows his faith and his goodness; it also shows that he was under the spell of the new country. Its vastness, its beauty, its emptiness made him want to plan for a better world. His solution is much the same as the solution of Charles Sheldon some

[2] Andrew White, *A Brief Relation of the Voyage unto Maryland*, 1634.

two hundred and forty years later. Both wanted to follow "In His Steps." Sheldon left the interpretation of what that would be up to the individual; John Eliot tried to provide for every circumstance. Since Eliot's thinking is so completely typical of his age, his blueprint for a *Christian Commonwealth* is worth considering in detail.

In his own day Eliot had a tremendous reputation, the result of his work with the Indians, his piety, and the force of his ecclesiastical rhetoric. Cotton Mather praised him extravagantly both as minister and man. "We had a tradition among us," he wrote, " 'that the country could never perish, as long as *Eliot* was alive.' "[3] Eliot knew Roger Williams well, and once in a flurry of enthusiasm went so far as to subscribe to his attack against the Commonwealth of Massachusetts.[4] In the light of *The Christian Commonwealth* it seems incredible that Eliot should ever have sympathized with any argument for the separation of church and state. Once he understood the implication of that point of view, once his waywardness had been pointed out to him, he changed his mind and again became comfortably orthodox.

Eliot's labors with the Indians were prodigious. He worked among them, believing that since they were the descendants of the lost tribes of Israel, there would be no question about his reward in heaven. In addition to the Bible, he translated into the Algonquian a psalter, a catechism, Baxter's *Call to the Unconverted,* a grammar, a logic primer, Bayly's *The Practice of Piety,* and Shepard's *The Sound Believer,* and *The Sincere Convert.* But this wasn't enough: Eliot convinced himself that since the Indians were "a people without any forme of government"[5] they would want to adopt a government based on the word of God. His attitude is implicit in the Calvinistic point of view, but it is not an attitude which shows any real appreciation of the Indian way of life. With such men as Eliot for missionaries, it is little wonder that the Puritan Theocrats were unsuccessful in their dealings with the tribes. They could not learn

---

[3] Cotton Mather, *Magnalia Christi Americana,* Hartford, 1820, Vol. I, p. 528.
[4] See James E. Ernst, *Roger Williams: New England Firebrand,* New York, 1932.
[5] John Eliot, *The Christian Commonwealth,* London, 1659, Preface.

the wisdom of moderation; they could not adjust the means to the end as did the Jesuits.

Having convinced himself that the Indians needed a government based on the word of God, Eliot set about discovering and analyzing God's specific instructions. This was no new game, of course; the Puritans were accustomed to such intellectual play, but none of the others hoped to govern mankind by their scheme. Eliot supplied text and verse for every argument. He was sure of his reasoning.

His ideal Christian Commonwealth is based on two assumptions: first, that Christ is King of Kings; and, second, that all laws must "arise and flow from the Word of God."[6] There can be no question about any of God's ordinances, he reasoned, provided only that individuals have faith. "Faith can see beauty, power and glory in any divine institution, when Human Wisdom may think it weak and contemptible."[7]

Since the Bible was to be the only source of law, there was no need for a legislative body. Obviously, man, corrupt by nature, could not hope to improve upon any of God's decrees. There remained, then, only to provide a system of magistrates. Eliot finds his cue in Exodus, 18:25: "And Moses chose able men out of all Israel, and made them heads over the people, rulers of thousands, rulers of hundreds, rulers of fifties, and rulers of tens." Ten, he decided, was the magic number. Groups of ten should live together under a leader, and so on in an ascending scale for groups of 100, 1000, 10,000 and 50,000—the system could expand indefinitely. Rulers are elected "by all the people, over whom they are to rule."[8] Once the people have elected their rulers they have no more voice in affairs. Presumably the rulers continue in power until death. They must "govern the people in the orderly and seasonable practice of God. . . . Rulers are eminently concerned to maintain the purity of religion . . ." and so ". . . they must read and meditate in the . . . [scriptures] all the daies of their life. . . ."[9]

This superior order of rulers is a divine institution. In this, reason justifies his faith, for, he explains, the "over-burdensomeness of governments by one man"[10] is a major cause of difficulty in administra-

[6] *Ibid.*, p. 3.   [7] *Ibid.*, Preface.   [8] *Ibid.*, p. 35.
[9] *Ibid.*, pp. 21, 22.   [10] *Ibid.*, p. 19.

tion. With his system responsibility is divided, but there is always a superior body to review decisions. At the top of the structure is a Supreme Council made up of "a convenient number of the most holy and able men"[11] whose duty it is "to supervise all rulers"[12] and to serve as a supreme court of interpretation. Eliot gave no thought to difficulties which might arise from varying interpretations of the Scriptures.

Before entering upon the new form of government, men would covenant together, confessing "their corruption by nature,"[13] acknowledging "the free grace of God, in their redemption"[14] and promising "to give up themselves unto him to be forever his"[15] and to receive from the Lord "both the platform of their Civil Government as it is set down in the holy Scripture; and also all their Laws,"[16] making the word of God "their only Magna Charta."[17] With such a covenant, and with the word of God to be interpreted only by the rulers, the individual would need a deep and abiding faith in God and in his immediate rulers. But, of course, this is a Christian utopia wherein only Christians might dwell, and Christians according to his lights. There would be no Catholics, for instance. He wanted no contact with "that dirty Romish religion."[18] Given the conditions he envisioned, given a body of Christians believing in his beliefs and not zealous enough to question them, such a system might work. It might have worked, for example, with Father Rapp's brow-beaten believers at New Harmony.

Eliot wasn't content with outlining a utopia; he actually suggested his scheme as a practical idea for England. Since England "by a wonderful work of God" is "in a capacity to chuse . . . a new government," he beseeches the "holy and faithful Saints . . . to . . . set the Crown of England upon the head of Christ," for "Christ is the only right heir of the Crown of England." "Let him be your JUDGE, Let him be your LAWGIVER, Let him be your KING! take the pattern and form of your government, from the word of his mouth."[19] The result will be "a sweet harmony and subjection to Christ." A government so instituted will "suit the present con-

[11] *Ibid.*, p. 17. [12] *Idem.* [13] *Ibid.*, p. 2.
[14] *Idem.* [15] *Idem.* [16] *Ibid.*, p. 3.
[17] *Idem.* [18] *Ibid.*, Preface. [19] *Idem.*

ditions of England, Scotland, and Ireland, or any other religious
people in the World. . . ."[20]

Eliot made one serious mistake. He questioned the divine right
of Kings. His book, as a result, was heretical, and was banned—
even in New England. The officials could not allow such treasonable
suggestions to remain uncensored. In Boston, at a session of the General Court for 1661, it was ordered

. . . that all persons whatsoever in this jurisdiction that have any of the
said Bookes in theire Custody shall on theire perrills within fowerteene
dayes after publication hereof either cancel or deface or deliver them unto
the next Magistrate or to the Secretary, whereby all farther divulment and
improovement of the said offensive Booke may be prevented.[21]

New England Puritans would have sympathized with Eliot's
philosophy of Scripture, but they would also have reasoned that
he had pushed faith too far, and had become impractical. The New
England of 1659 was no longer a place for utopians. Early dreams
had faded. Even the most idealistic had been forced to abandon
cherished projects. Although *The Christian Commonwealth* is in
the direct line of Puritan tradition, Eliot had forgotten that he was
not the only interpreter of the Bible, and that others would be sure
to disagree with his findings. New England's Saints were united only
in their intolerance and in their insistence upon a strict observance
of Scripture—they could never agree on what that observance should
be.

John Eliot was a true "dreamer in Israel," a good man, a devout
man, but not an intelligent man. He represents the extreme development of theocratic thought. Some two hundred years later Sylvester
Judd was to compose another religious utopia, one based on the
saving grace of Unitarianism, and the difference between the two
represents the changes in New England life. *The Christian Commonwealth* is the product of a new society in which the struggle
for existence left small place for tolerance. Sylvester Judd's *Margaret*
is the utopia of New England's golden age, when tolerance, good
will and human love seemed able to create a heaven on earth, a heaven
not supervised by a rigid system of magistrates.

[20] *Idem.*
[21] Quoted in V. L. Parrington, *The Colonial Mind,* New York (1927) p. 81.

CHAPTER TWO

EARLY SATIRISTS

AFTER this first flurry of utopianism, Americans were too busy with practical matters to be much concerned about dreams. Since most literate men were relatively prosperous, there seemed no need to outline a better society. After the war of 1812, however, political and economic uncertainties made men more articulate, and *utopia* provided a yardstick with which to measure the stupidities of the present.

The three volumes discussed in this chapter are satires, but one of them, George Tucker's *A Voyage to the Moon,* devotes several chapters to a superficial, but thoroughly utopian analysis of an ideal community.

The first of the satires is Ezekiel Sanford's *The Humours of Eutopia,* 1828, an extremely witty attack on the foibles of theocratic government. The opening sentences reveal the tone:

Weathersfield, in Connecticut, now only noted, I believe, for its fecundity in onions, was once the prolific source, whence issued many congregations of *Withdrawers,* to people the fair land of Steady Habits. The original settlers, being purely a theological community, having pitched their tents in the wilderness for no other purpose than to think and talk as much and as freely as they pleased on matters of religion, spent the chief part of their time in handling doctrines of faith and practice.[1]

As the story begins the community was at odds over the problem of baptism. Those who were not members of the church wanted to have their children baptized. "But the Pupils of the old school said, no: none but the *saints,* as they termed the actual members of the church, can have any voice in its government; and none but the seed of saints are fit subjects of baptism."[2] Since they couldn't have

---

[1] [Ezekiel Sanford], *The Humours of Eutopia; a Tale of Colonial Times.* By an Eutopian. Philadelphia, 1828, Vol. I, p. 1.
[2] *Ibid.,* p. 8.

their own way, the rebels decided to found a new colony, Eutopia. "The policy of Eutopia was, at first, extremely simple. The congregation enacted that the divine word should be the rule of action; and appointed Parson Steel as their judge in all cases, whether religious, civil, or criminal."³ Rebels soon found voice, however, even in Eutopia. Some of the young men protested against the necessity of wearing shaven crowns. To the Parson's citation of the biblical edict, "Doth not even nature itself teach you, that, if a man hath long hair, it is a shame unto him?" (1 Cor., xi, 14) the dissidents countered with the command, "Ye shall not round the corners of your heads, neither shalt thou mar the corners of thy beard." (Levit., xix, 27) Men could not or would not agree about hair, and finally the whole idea of relying upon the Divine Word had to be abandoned.

Having set his stage with some care, and having explained "Eutopia" in such fashion as to make it seem a mockery of John Eliot's *Christian Commonwealth,* Sanford plunges into an involved plot. The story proper, which deals with some extremely interesting Eutopians, need not be considered except so far as it involves an Indian chief, Skenedo. Skenedo was a Dartmouth man, and at Dartmouth he had learned many things touching religion and civilization, and he had hoped to teach these things to his tribe. Somehow the theories didn't work. He first discovered that he couldn't change his fellow tribesmen. New ideas, in other words, are no more acceptable in an Indian village than they are in Eutopia.

The thread of romance is light and witty. Sanford laughs at Eutopians, and he laughs at the pretentiousness of his own New England. The story is vigorous, interesting, and amusing, and that is a great deal to say about any American novel of 1828.

The second volume, Jonas Clopper's *Fragments of the History of Bawlfredonia,* 1819, relates the history of the original American colonies in caricature. The histories of the United States and Bawlfredonia turn out to be similar. Bawlfredonia is the older nation, but it was long isolated from the rest of the world. The country was rediscovered by Fredonious, but Bawlfredonious made so much money

³ *Ibid.,* p. 30.

that people came to know the continent by his name. From the first Puritanville was the most prosperous of the colonies. "Religion and religious topicks were discussed among them with as much interest as political questions in Blackmoreland. Swearing, drunkenness, gaming and debauchery, was scarcely known in that coloney; cheating was not so rare, especially amongst the dealers in notions."[4] But their prosperity was not so much due to their peculiar virtues as to their appreciation of the commercial value of stinkum-puff, "a kind of poison, of the most disagreeable taste and smell."

The satire is thinly disguised. Tom Paine becomes Tom Anguish. Thomas Jefferson becomes Thomas Tammany Bawlfredonious. Clopper makes fun of our patriotic attempts to exalt the revolution. He takes the revolution out of the realm of the holy. He questions the great virtue and complete patriotism of some of our heroes. He wonders about the honesty and methods of some of our early business men. For the most part, his satire is good natured, but there are many sharp digs. He has used a utopian technique, but he has turned it into an elaborate device for debunking tradition.

George Tucker, lawyer, political economist, and first Professor of Moral Philosophy at the University of Virginia, is a much more competent writer. His *Voyage to the Moon*, 1827, a satirical romance, contains some convincing satire on manners, and, mixed in with the pseudo-science, a superficial discussion of a utopian community. The story tells the adventures of Joseph Atterley, a gentlemen of Long Island, who finds himself wrecked on the Burmese Coast and taken captive by the natives. Eventually he is given some freedom, and he comes to know a learned Brahmin who proposes a trip to the moon. Atterley jumps at the chance, for a trip to the moon was, at the least, escape. They prepare their airship with great care. Motive power is achieved by means of a miraculous metal, lunarium, which serves to counteract the effect of gravity. The trip is successful; they land and begin to explore the mysteries of another planet.

Atterley is continually amazed by the customs of the Lunarians, and yet he shouldn't have been, for their customs are those of his

[4] [Jonas Clopper], *Fragments of the History of Bawlfredonia* . . . By Herman Thwackius [pseud.] Baltimore? 1819, p. 78.

own people. Their religious customs are strange; their philosophies are strange, their laws are strange, their clothes are strange. Their women wear dresses which resemble mainsails spread full to the wind. They deck themselves with the feathers of exotic birds. Their fortune tellers determine character by the finger nails and by the hair. Their physicians busy themselves with the theory of disease rather than with curing patients. Prize fights determine law cases according to rules which only the judges understand. Men live by quirks of fancy. One gentleman, for instance, spent years breeding over-sized cattle, but the animals cost so much to raise that they were less profitable than normal animals. Morosofians seem queer, in other words, because their follies are so familiar.

In sharp contrast to the Morosofians are the Okalbians, "a tribe or nation, who live separated from the rest of the Lunar world, and whose wise government, prudence, industry, and integrity, are very highly extolled by all, though, by what I can learn, they have few imitators."[5] The whole surface of the valley is "like a garden, interspersed with patches of wood, clumps of trees, and houses standing singly or in groupes."[6] The settlement had its beginnings in a time of religious fervor; a new sect desired to govern itself according to its own tenets. "At first, the new settlers divided the land equally among all the inhabitants, one of their tenets being, that as there was no difference of persons in the next world, there should be no difference in sharing the good things of this."[7] Eventually faith gave way to necessity; the property was divided, and, in the course of time, came into fewer and fewer hands. But the temper of the people is so remarkable that such concentration of property has no evil results.

"As the soil is remarkable fertile, the climate healthy, and the people temperate and industrious, they multiplied very rapidly until they reached their present numbers, which have been long stationary, and amount to 150,000, that is, about four hundred to a square mile. . . ."[8] When Atterley expressed interest in the static population, his guide explained in some surprise:

[5] [George Tucker], *A Voyage to the Moon.* . . . By Joseph Atterley [pseud.], New York, 1827, p. 184.
[6] *Ibid.,* p. 185. [7] *Ibid.,* p. 186. [8] *Ibid.,* pp. 186, 187.

Nothing is more easy. No man has a larger family than his land or labour can support, in comfort; and as long as that is the case with every individual, it must continue to be the case with the whole community. We leave the matter to individual discretion. The prudential caution which is thus indicated, has been taught us by our own experience. . . . It is now a primary moral duty, enforced by all our juvenile instructors with every citizen, to adapt his family to his means; and thus a regard which each individual has for his offspring, is the salvation of the State.[9]

Atterley seeks to discover the secret of the controlled birth rate, but the Brahmin suggests that in the United States it would do more harm than good to remove "one of the checks of licentiousness, where women are so unrestrained as they are with you."[10]

Magisterial corruption is solved by an ingenious system. Only the most modest men can become office holders, for moderation and disinterestedness are the two major qualifications of candidacy. As a final check "on the immoderate zeal of friends," the expense of maintaining officials is defrayed by those who vote for them, on the theory that "those who carry their point, and have the power, should also bear the burden: besides, in this way the voices of the most generous and disinterested prevail."[11]

There is no capital punishment in Okalbia, for "it is not more efficacious in preventing crime, than other punishments which are milder; and we prefer making the example to offenders a lasting one. But we endeavor to prevent offences, not so much by punishment as by education; and the few crimes committed among us, bring certain censure on those who have the early instruction of the criminal."[12]

Civil cases are determined by arbitration rather than by trial, and "each party is permitted to state his case, to examine what witnesses and ask what questions he pleases."[13] Atterley protests against this examination of interested witnesses, and seeks to explain how such things are done in the United States. His guide remains unconvinced. "It seems to me," he replies, "that your extreme fear of hearing falsehood, must often prevent you from ascertaining the truth. Then I think you often exclude a witness who is under a small bias, and admit another who is under a great one. You allow a man

---

[9] *Ibid.*, pp. 188, 189. [10] *Ibid.*, p. 190. [11] *Ibid.*, p. 193.
[12] *Ibid.*, p. 197. [13] *Ibid.*, p. 198.

to give testimony in a case in which the fortune or character of his father, brother, or child is involved, but reject him in a case in which he is not interested to the amount of a greater sum than he would give to the first begger he met."[14] Atterley is forced to agree, for he is unable to justify the legal theory of his own country.

Government is simple. Every man has his proper sphere of influence.

No qualification of property is required either to vote, or to be eligible to either house of the legislature, as they believe that the natural influence of property is sufficient, without adding to the influence by law; and that the moral effects of education among them, together with a few provisions in their constitution, are quite sufficient to guard against any improper combination of those who have small property. Besides there are no odious privileges exclusively possessed by particular classes of men, to excite the envy or resentment of the other classes, and induce them to act in concert.[15]

The valley of the Okalbians is properly utopian. By a happy combination of physical and intellectual activity, men are content within the narrow confines of their existence, content with honest government, modest officials, just laws, and the simple life. The Okalbians are civilized in the best sense; they have learned to appreciate simplicity.

For the rest, the novel tells of their hurried departure from the moon, and of Atterley's return to the United States where he is not given a hero's welcome. No one believes his account of the voyage to the moon. This volume is supposed to be the final refutation of the mockers.

Tucker is more satirist than utopian. It is obvious that the stupidities of the Lunarians are not confined to the inhabitants of the moon. But it is the two chapters dealing with the Happy Valley which one remembers. Tucker doesn't label the valley "utopia," but the description reveals him as a wistful, utopian dreamer.

[14] *Ibid.*, pp. 198, 199.   [15] *Ibid.*, pp. 200, 201.

CHAPTER THREE

TWO REBELS—MRS. MARY GRIFFITH AND COOPER

BOTH Mrs. Griffith and Fenimore Cooper thought that the world could be run efficiently, and both were positive that it was run very badly. Mrs. Griffith thought that the answer was to give women a greater sphere of influence. They wouldn't tolerate such stupidities as war. In many ways she was the intellectual kin of such women as Amelia Bloomer and Mary Ellen Lease. Cooper, by contrast, was an intellectual "sport." His reforms were emotional protests. As far as he was concerned, a better world would have been a world in which he was properly appreciated. They were both primarily rebels, but the reforms they suggest are the products of very different motivations.

Mrs. Mary Griffith must have been a very capable woman, a woman of determination, tact and imagination. She ran a farm, reared a family and wrote two pleasant volumes dealing with horticultural problems and women's rights. Her two volumes were published anonymously, but the introduction to the second, *Camperdown: or News from Our Neighborhood,* 1836, which included her utopian venture "Three Hundred Years Hence," explains that this is by the author of *Our Neighborhood.* Her identity is disclosed by a letter in the *New England Farmer* of May 4, 1831, a letter she had written to the Massachusetts Horticultural Society on presenting them with a copy of *Our Neighborhood.* In the same column, by way of reply, Mrs. Griffith is characterized as a brave woman, who, widowed in the "prime of life . . . boldly entered the career of rural industry with the hardy cultivators of the soil."[1] Her farm was in Charles Hope, New Jersey, but the Massachusetts Horticultural Society thought enough of her to make her a member and to

[1] *Colophon, New Series,* Vol. I, No. I, 1935, p. 124.

record her death in 1877. Beyond this, there is no evidence con-
cerning her life. She must have had to work very hard to keep her
farm profitable and her children fed and clothed. What she could
do she felt other women could do. Perhaps this was the result of
exposure to women's rights talk, or perhaps she thought well of
Godwin's doctrine. At any rate, she believed that if women were
given more influence, great blessings would result. She did not, however, demand the franchise. Women's influence, she felt, need not
be direct to be effective.

Her utopia is the story of Edgar Hastings and the world he discovers "three hundred years hence." Here is the dream technique,
much the same as in *Looking Backward,* but more simply done. Her
hero, Edgar Hastings, a young man of wealth and education, with
an excellent new house, and an excellent wife, baby and father-in-law,
dreams that the farmhouse, in which he is dozing, is buried under
a terrific avalanche and that he is preserved in cold storage for
three hundred years—to be welcomed to this new world by his distant
descendants. They explain his fate, and after the first shock Edgar
is ready to see what time has made of his country.

The country is still democratic, but it is democratic in fact as
well as in theory. Women have equal rights with men. There are
"no monopolies of soil, or air, or water."[2] Taxation is equitable,
for there is "but one tax, and each man is made to pay according
to the value of his property, his business, or his labour. A land-
holder, a stock-holder and the one who has houses and lands and
mortgages, pays so much per cent on the advance of his property,
and for his annual receipts—the merchant, with a fluctuating capital
pays so much on his book account of sales—the mechanic and
laborer, so much on their yearly receipts, for we have no sales on
credit now—that demoralizing practice has been abolished for up-
wards of a century."[3] "This direct tax includes all the expenses of the
general and state governments, and it operates so beautifully that
the rich man now bears his full proportion toward the support of the
whole as the poor man does. . . . The direct tax includes the poor

[2] Mrs. Mary Griffith, "Three Hundred Years Hence," first story in *Camperdown;
or, News from Our Neighborhood,* Philadelphia, 1836, p. 54.
[3] *Ibid.,* p. 66.

man's wealth, which is his labour, and the rich man's wealth, which is his property."[4] Such a taxation would certainly have benefited agrarians over city folks, for the one is taxed on land only, and the other on land in addition to income. If retarding the growth of cities is a sure road to utopia, as she believed, then her program has merit.

A large share of the country's new prosperity would seem to have been women's work. They abolished war one hundred and twenty years before Edgar was revived. As soon as women "were considered as of equal importance with their husbands—as soon as they were on an equality in money matters, for after all, people are respected in proportion to their wealth, that moment all the barbarisms of the age disappeared."[5] Once women had the power which comes with the purse they could organize to exterminate "that system which fastened the disgrace of a blow on the one who received it."[6] They taught their children not to kill; they taught them the true meaning of religion—and so made war impossible.

The government is concerned with the real problem of the people. The railroads, for instance, are handled jointly by the federal government and the several states. The great national road was founded in 1900, "the grand route from one extreme of the country to the other. Cross roads, leading from town to town and village to village, are under the control of the state governments."[7] A good Jeffersonian, Mrs. Griffith has been careful to give each community a route to market, as well as local control over the system. She wanted no all-encroaching central power.

The government provides a form of compulsory fire insurance, for which the fees are collected with the taxes in a singularly painless fashion. Since houses are fireproofed by a solution which impregnates the wood, and since the government is not trying to make a profit, rates can be very low.

Prohibition protects the women against drunken husbands. Liquor, except for cider and wine, has been banned for two hundred years. And if a woman is unfortunate enough to have a husband who can get drunk on these beverages, she is entitled to a divorce. The use of tobacco has been banned, on the theory, it would seem, that smoking

---

[4] *Idem.*   [5] *Ibid.,* p. 68.   [6] *Idem.*   [7] *Ibid.,* p. 55.

is not only wasteful but a dirty habit, and that husbands are more desirable without even the petty vices.

Several of the reforms show her country background. She doesn't like crowded buildings, and so it seems reasonable to have buildings limited to three stories in height—as a protection against unwise concentration and dangerous fires. The government calls for and delivers the mail, once every day. Rates are low. As a country dweller Mrs. Griffith realized the value of a regular mail service. And as a democrat and a farmer, she realized the futility of the protective tariff. Her new government thrives on complete free trade, and the advantages of that free trade reach over the country.

The streets of Philadelphia have become very clean; numerous fountains purify the air. The public markets are arranged to suit the most fastidious housewife. "On the ground floor, in cool niches, under which ran a stream of cold, clear water, were all the variety of vegetables; and there, at this early season, were strawberries and green peas, all of which were raised in the neighborhood."[8] Everything was agreeable: there were "no rotten vegetables or leaves."[9] There was "no mud, no spitting."[10] Mrs. Griffith must have had a vision of the vegetable department of a modern chain store.

Edgar is greatly surprised by the new college system. At Princeton the students "worked during leisure hours, everyone learning some trade or some handicraft, by which he could earn a living if necessity required it. Large gardens lay in the rear, cultivated entirely by the labor of the students, particularly by those intended for clergymen, as many of this class were destined to live in the country."[11] "It was able to maintain and educate three . . . hundred boys . . . the children of the rich and the poor."[12] The Princeton of today would have to face many changes to resemble the Princeton of Mrs. Griffith's dreams.

The countryside has changed as much as the city. Machines have greatly simplified farming. Edgar was amazed to find that they "mowed the grass, raked the grass, spread it out, gathered it and brought it to the barn—the same power scattered seeds, ploughed, hoed, harrowed, cut, gathered, threshed, stored and ground the

[8] *Ibid.,* p. 42.　　　　[9] *Ibid.,* p. 43.　　　　[10] *Idem.*
[11] *Ibid.,* p. 57.　　　　[12] *Idem.*

grain—and the same power distributed it to the merchants and small consumers."[13] These machines sound almost as wonderful as diesel caterpillars. They do everything: "they fill up gullies, dig out the roots of trees, plough down hills, turn water courses—in short, they have entirely superseded the use of cattle of any kind."[14] Mrs. Griffith doesn't explain the motive power of these new vehicles: she only suggests that they were "moved by some internal machinery."[15]

Women are no longer contented with the role of housekeeper. They are trained in business. There is no mention of the extent of this training, but the results must have been excellent, for they conduct "all the retail and detail of mercantile operations."[16]

Women engineered the transformation to the new way of life. The first step was education—a modest attempt to found a college for orphan girls. "From this moment a new era took place with regard to women, and we owe the improved condition of our people entirely to the improvement in the education of the female poor."[17] Property in marriage became "as much the woman's as the man's."[18] Other changes followed rapidly. Women followed up this opening thrust; their influence increased, and always for good. "In every plan for meliorating the condition of the poor, and improving the morals, it was woman's influence that promoted and fostered it. It is to that healthy influence that we owe our present prosperity and happiness."[19]

For the rest, Mrs. Griffith suggests some strangely assorted reforms, including perpetual copyright, the abolition of the death penalty, and the freeing of negroes. She abolishes the death penalty because it is not severe enough, and substitutes a combination of solitary confinement and hard labor, a punishment which effectively limits the number of murders. Her solution of the negro problem was the one popular in her day—emigration to Liberia and other healthy colonies." The slave-holders were satisfied with such a solution, for the government indemnified them out of proceeds from the sale of public lands. Once freed, the negroes prospered: ". . . their minds became inlightened, and, as their education advanced, they

[13] *Ibid.,* p. 34.   [14] *Ibid.,* p. 35.   [15] *Ibid.,* p. 33.
[16] *Ibid.,* p. 85.   [17] *Ibid.,* p. 42.   [18] *Ibid.,* p. 85.
[19] *Ibid.,* p. 87.

learned to appreciate themselves properly."[20] And when they appreciated themselves properly they refused to intermarry with whites, for they wanted to keep their distinctive negroid qualities.

Her attitude towards ministers would seem to indicate that her district church had difficulty in supplying the pulpit. She does not like the practice of bidding for the services of teachers and ministers. "A clergyman is selected with great care for his piety and learning—but principally for his piety; and, in consequence of there being no old clergymen out of place, he is a young man, who comes amongst us in early life, and sees our children grow up around him, he becomes acquainted with their character, and he has a paternal eye over their eternal welfare."[21] "He is our pastor, and we should never think of dismissing him because he had not the gift of eloquence, or because he was wanting in grace of action."[22] Mrs. Griffith evidently thought that serving the Lord was enough material reward for any man.

Her artistic prophecies are surprising. Portrait painting, she says, has long been out of fashion: people didn't want to look at ancestors when all of their thoughts were for the present and future. She lets actors become respectable members of society, for their productions are eminently moral and respectable. Shakespeare is still played, but a much improved Shakespeare. He "wrote as the times then were."[23] "Vulgarity" was not essential to his genius, and so the plays are produced in carefully edited versions.

"Three Hundred Years Hence" is something more than a curiosity. The story is pleasant and the ideas reflect the variety of interests in an active mind. A woman's utopia, it reflects a woman's dreams. An agrarian utopia, it reflects the rural, Jeffersonian point of view. The composition becomes more significant when contrasted with Cooper's utopia, *The Crater,* the outgrowth of a completely different background. Mrs. Griffith's work is interesting rather than important, surprising rather than revealing, but it does fill a niche in the history of American utopias.

Cooper was a thorough democrat, but he disliked the practices of

[20] *Ibid.,* p. 89.   [21] *Ibid.,* p. 60.   [22] *Ibid.,* p. 62.   [23] *Ibid.,* p. 79.

coonskin democracy so violently, and he attacked them so consistently that his faith has come under question. He insisted always that he was a true democrat: "This writer believes himself to be as good a democrat as there is in America. But his democracy is not of the impractical school. He prefers a democracy to any other system, on account of its comparative advantages, but not on account of its perfection. . . . He knows it has evils; great and increasing evils, and evils peculiar to itself; but he believes that monarchy and aristocracy have more."[24] Since he was conscious of abuses, he felt himself called upon to preach. And as a preacher he filled his later novels with moralizing on political and economic problems. *The Crater,* 1847, was a medium for airing some of his convictions.

The Crater is a utopian novel in the Robinson Crusoe tradition, but Cooper's hero is not content to leave his island; he wants to found a civilized colony. The colony which grows up is nominally democratic, except that power is lodged with those of birth and education. Democracy, Cooper felt, could work only so long as the aristocracy had the power. The decline of the colony begins with the immigration of lawyers, preachers, and newspapermen. These constitute a vocal and "unprincipled minority" who gain control and run things their own way. Finally, in desperation, Cooper has the Crater sink back into the sea, with the implication that this is the result of "popular government."

The story tells the adventures of Mark Woolston, a young man of education and breeding who has been trained to the sea. Shortly after his marriage, he sails as first mate of the *Rancocus,* on a voyage for sandalwood and tea. In the South Seas the *Rancocus* hits an uncharted reef and appears to be breaking up. The crew take to the boats and disappear. All are lost except Bob Betts and Mark, who have made their way to the Crater, the peak of an extinct volcano which has been forced above the sea. By some miracle the *Rancocus* is saved from destruction. She floats safely inside the reef. Bob and Mark ransack her and prepare to make their island habitable. Fortunately, the ship was well equipped: they find seeds of all kinds, clothing, wheelbarrows, the framework of a number of boats, and

[24] James Fenimore Cooper, *The American Democrat,* Introduction, New York, 1931.

a plentiful supply of trade goods for dealing with natives. Thus equipped, Bob and Mark have great success with the Crusoe game. The Crater is made fertile by means of sea weed and guano. Seed is sowed and the yield is beyond all expectation. Vegetables and melons of all kinds grow in profusion. They are able to find time for boat building, but just as their boat is launched, a sudden storm arises which carries off the boat and Bob Betts with it. Mark works on alone, and builds another boat. Eventually there comes a terrific eruption. The extent of the island is increased manyfold.

In his first extensive trip of exploration, Mark finds Bob Betts. Bob had sailed back to the States and had returned with Mark's wife, Bridget, with his sister and her husband, and with several other couples. They brought with them the material for colonizing. Here is the beginning of the ideal community, a community nourished by a fertile soil, a perfect climate and deep love. At first, everything is done together, but gradually, as more colonists arrive, responsibility as well as property is divided. Mark Woolston is elected Governor, with a council of the best educated men to advise him. The colony prospers: the colonists build houses, a brick kiln, a sawmill, a shipyard. Whaling becomes profitable, and also the traffic in sandalwood. Money is free, prices are low, and the merchants as well as the colonists are happy. Life is so easy that it is the Governor's great worry that the people lose their initiative.

The first serious difficulty springs from the activity of the Reverend Mr. Hornblower, the Episcopal minister. Those of other faiths grow restive under his too zealous ministrations. Men quarrel and bring in other ministers. They "began to pray at each other, and if Mr. Hornblower was an exception, it was because his admirable liturgy did not furnish him with the means of making those forays into the enemy camp."[25]

Finally there arrived in the colony a lawyer and a newspaper man:

Shortly after the lawyer made his appearance, men began to discover that they were wronged by their neighbors, in a hundred ways which they had never before discovered. Law, which had hitherto been used for the

[25] James Fenimore Cooper, *The Crater*, p. 452. Page references are to the volume in the Iroquois edition of Cooper's works, published by G. P. Putnam's Sons, New York and London.

purpose of justice, and of justice only, now began to be used for those of speculation and revenge.[26]

The influence of the press was equally demoralizing:

The press took up the cause of human rights, endeavoring to transfer the power of the state from the public departments to its own printing office; and aiming at establishing all the equality that can flourish when one man has a monopoly of the means of making his facts to suit himself.[27]

As a result of such ministration, "the people were soon convinced that they had been living under an unheard-of tyranny, and were invoked weekly to arouse in their might, and be true to themselves and their posterity."[28] They had not elected the present office holders; the office holders had been freely installed before the majority had arrived. Nevertheless, that was an injustice.

It was surprising how little the people really knew of the oppression under which they labored, until this stranger came among them to enlighten their understanding. Nor was it less wonderful how many sources of wrong he exposed, that no one had ever dreamed of having an existence. Although there was not a tax of any sort laid on the colony, not a shilling ever collected in the way of import duties, he boldly pronounced the citizens to be the most overburdened people in Christendom.[29]

Because the editor constantly talked reform, and emphasized man's natural rights, and because most of the people of the Crater thought that what appeared in print was true, a constitutional convention was held to establish a new government.

Thus fortified by the sacred principle of the sway of the majority, these representatives of a minority met in convention, and formed an entirely new fundamental law; one, indeed, that completely circumvented the old one, not only in fact but in theory. Two legislative bodies were formed, the old council was annihilated, and everything was done that cunning could devise, to cause power to pass into new hands. This was the one great object of the whole procedure, and, of course, it was not neglected.

When the new constitution was completed, it was referred back to the people for approval. At this third appeal to the popular voice, rather less than half of all the electors voted, the constitution being adopted by a majority of one third of those who did. By this simple, and exquisite

---

[26] *Ibid.*, p. 453.
[27] *Idem.*
[28] *Ibid.*, p. 453.
[29] *Ibid.*, p. 454.

republican process, was the principle of the sway of majorities vindicated, a new fundamental law for the colony provided, and all the old incumbents turned out of office. "Silence gives consent," cried the demagogues, who forgot they had no right to put the question.[30]

New men were elected to govern the Crater not because of any misconduct on the part of the old administrators, but because of the energy of a noisy and articulate minority. Many honest men stayed away from the polls because they were confused. Most of these had been satisfied with the Woolston regime, but since they didn't understand the trumped-up issues, they didn't vote.

The new government brought with it increasing discontent. Talk of equality changed the status of no one. Petty rivalries began to fester. The Crater was no longer utopia. When Mark realized this, he took his family and returned to Philadelphia. After a year he came back, but the Crater and the colony had disappeared, sunk beneath the sea, "and the labors and hopes of years had vanished in a moment."[31]

The *Crater* is a utopian novel, for Cooper does picture an ideal community, but it is a community which carries within itself the seeds of its own disintegration. In other words, Cooper stacks the cards against his own utopia, because he wants to point a moral. The moral is that man must be suspicious of those who talk too glibly about natural rights. Such men, he insists, are only interested in obscuring the real issues. Lawyers and editors deal in legal sophistry; legal sophistry leads to confusion; confusion leads to diffidence; and diffidence allows the minority to rule. And that condition, compounded with ignorance, provides the inevitable contradiction of democracy.

Cooper was too truculent and too honest for his own day. His political philosophy was discounted as the result of a brain confused by too many law suits. But his analysis of how an ideal state can be taken over by scoundrels is every bit as realistic as Sinclair Lewis's in *It Can't Happen Here*. And Cooper didn't have any obvious contemporary models.

[30] *Ibid.*, p. 462.
[31] *Ibid.*, p. 478.

CHAPTER FOUR

SYLVESTER JUDD—UNITARIAN

SYLVESTER JUDD's *Margaret*, 1845, pictures a New England utopia. The book takes this country as it emerges from the Revolution and carries it up "to what it is conceived should be."[1] Judd's thesis is simple. He reiterates the fact that a working Christianity would be utopia.

Judd's style, unfortunately, is not notable for clearness. According to Stanley Williams, "the latter part of the book is obscured in a fogland of transcendentalism."[2] It is not that bad. The fogland can be pierced by careful reading. The logic is clear, if one will see it, but transcendentalism and fogginess seem almost synonymous to the non-believer. As with so many kindred volumes, this is no utopia to satisfy later generations. In fact, to the casual reader it may appear no utopia at all.

Unitarianism was the key to a better world. The faith had solved Judd's own spiritual problem, and so it seemed reasonable that it should be the solution for others. His own "salvation" came after a long and difficult period of self-communion. He was reared in an orthodox home, and attended Yale, the center of Calvinism. During his college years, he was greatly concerned about the souls of the unconverted. Since Calvinistic doctrine insisted upon man's natural depravity and the necessity of an instantaneous conversion, Judd felt that it was his duty to work for a revival of religion among his fellows.[3] He came to have more and more doubts about Calvinism. His first teaching job after graduation brought him into contact with

---

[1] Sylvester Judd, *Margaret, a Tale of the Real and the Ideal, Blight and Bloom.* Preface, p. v. Page references are to the edition of 1882, published by Roberts Brothers of Boston.

[2] Article on Judd in the *Spirit of American Letters*, Vol. XI of *The Pageant of America.*

[3] See [Arethusa Hall] *Life and Character of the Rev. Sylvester Judd*, Boston, 1854, p. 71.

a number of Unitarians. Doubts disappeared. Unitarianism was the answer, for Unitarianism made the whole world good:

> I look upon the earth, and find it adapted to good: even its hurricanes, its earthquakes, its ocean storms are all for good. I find the beasts, the birds, the insects, all for good. I look upon man in his physical frame, and find all adapted to good. The eye is pleased with light, the ear with sound, the smell with odors: all senses have their appropriate objects; which objects, if rightly used, promote and are essential to our highest sensual happiness. I look upon the intellectual system, and find it adapted to good. It is surrounded by its appropriate objects, by which it is ever won to action, and with which it is ever delightfully engaged. So far, all conspires to good, and to the highest happiness of man and the glory of God.[4]

In 1840, after finishing the divinity course at Harvard, Judd entered upon his ministerial duties at Augusta, Maine, where he remained until his death in 1853. Those thirteen years were amazingly full. He wrote, in addition to *Margaret, Philo, An Evangeliad, Richard Edney,* a novel, and *The White Hills, An American Tragedy,* an unpublished drama in blank verse. In all of these books Judd's aim was moral, but the obviousness of his interest does not destroy their interest.

Judd's activity extended to participation in a number of reform movements. Unlike many ministers, he did not believe in denunciation as the best method of conversion. He believed, rather, in the power of love. In *Margaret* he sought to demonstrate that evil could be overcome by the example of good.

Judd was opposed to slavery. He recognized the evils of the system, but he did not believe that "slavery is going to be abolished by abusing the South. . . . As regards slaveholders, we might as well hang them all and have done with it. We make them guilty of all possible crimes."[5] In other words, he didn't know what could be done about slavery, and he was willing to let time take its course. The Indian question seemed to him even more troublesome than slavery. "I think," he writes, [that] "we have dealt worse by the Indians than by the Africans. We exterminate the former; we domesticate the latter. We find the black man a peck of corn a week; we curse the red men with whiskey."[6] For the rest, Judd is vastly concerned with the problem of intemperance, with prison reform,

---

[4] *Ibid.,* pp. 88, 89.   [5] *Ibid.,* p. 307.   [6] *Ibid.,* pp. 310, 311.

with women's rights, with plans for a better school system and more national holidays—but these are best considered along with the utopian scheme set forth in *Margaret.*

In 1845 *Margaret* was a seven-day sensation. Orestes Brownson fumed: ". . . we may dismiss the book, with sincere pity for him who wrote it, and a real prayer for his speedy restoration to the simple genus humanity, and for his conversion, through grace, to that Christianity which was given to men from above, and not, spider-like, spun out of his bowells."[7] Brownson had good reason for this violent reaction. The book typified the transcendental movement in its most virulent form, and transcendentalism, he thought, "is a much more serious affair than they would have us believe. It is not a simple 'Yankee notion,' confined to a few isolated individuals in a little corner of New England, as some of our Southern friends imagine, but is in fact the dominant error of our times. . . ."[8] Brownson was not alone in his condemnation. The orthodox called it "a weak and silly book," "too stupid to waste time upon," "sheer nonsense, from beginning to end." It was "rank heresy," "a strange production," "a dull attempt at a joke." Unitarians were equally quick to praise the volume as the "wonder of the age," and the "evidence that an American literature is possible." "We also find that 'it is a book not likely to be dismissed; that the author evidently has stuff in him, sterling metal, that rings as well as shines'; that it is 'the only American book that has ever been written'; that 'its descriptions are perfect as the paintings of Claude, the plot full of dramatic interest, the characters drawn with a Master's hand'; that it is 'an original book, full of beauty and power, with admirable fidelity to nature, having pages striking as Carlyle, quaint as Lamb, graphic as Washington Irving.' "[9]

Margaret was written as Unitarian propaganda. According to Judd,

. . . the book seems fitted partially to fill a gap, long left open in Unitarian literature,—that of imaginative writings. The Orthodox enjoy the works of Bunyan, Hannah More, Charlotte Elizabeth, the Abbots, &c., &c., But what have we in their place? The original design of the book was almost

---

[7] Orestes A. Brownson, *Essays and Reviews, Chiefly on Theology, Politics, and Socialism.* New York, 1852, p. 211.
[8] *Idem.*
[9] Hall, *op. cit.,* pp. 340, 341.

solely to occupy this niche. . . . It seems to me, that the book is fitted for a pretty general Unitarian circulation; that it might be of some use in the hands of the clergy, in our families, Sunday-school libraries, &c. . . . It aims to subject bigotry, cant, pharisaism and all intolerance. Its basis is Christ: him it would restore to the church, him it would enthrone in the world.[10]

Margaret is many things, but not a suitable volume for Sunday School children. The first edition is somewhat too earthy; the revised edition is simply too long. It has many faults as a novel. The major plot and the minor plot become confused. Antiquarian zeal crowds the story from many pages. Whole chapters are clumsy and inarticulate, and yet it is extremely readable. The book has the flavor of New England, a New England that has matured and grown mellow and lost its fanaticism. *Margaret* is the utopia of a wistful and good man.

James Russell Lowell praised Judd in his *Fable for Critics:*

> *Margaritas,* for him you have verified gratis:
> What matter his name? Why, it may be Sylvester
> Judd, Junior or Junius, Ulysses or Nestor,
> For aught I know or care; 'tis enough that I look
> On the author of 'Margaret,' the first Yankee book,
> With the *soul* of Down East in 't . . .
> 'T has a smack of pine woods, of bare field and bleak hill,
> Such as only the breed of the Mayflower could till . . .

Lowell comes very near the truth. The soul of "Down East" is there, but there is much more than that. The book is jammed with homely details—of food, liquor, amusements, medicines, jails, politics, the army, and the church. The faults of the Calvinistic creed are disclosed through the church's reaction to Margaret, a pure, sweet, innocent girl of the woods, almost too pure, too sweet, and too innocent. Judd wrote of his idea: "The plot of the book involved this—that while Margaret grew up in, or contiguous to, a religious and civilized community, she should remain for the most part unaffected by these influences; yet that she should not mature in ignorance, but should receive quite an amount of a species of erudition."[11] Margaret turns out to be much too well educated, much too refined and cultured a person to have been reared in the shiftless

[10] *Ibid.,* p. 354. [11] Judd, *op. cit.,* Preface, p. v.

fashion Judd describes. The New England soil possesses no such virtues.

Most of the book is concerned with Margaret's difficult youth. Finally she matures, she blossoms out, and one wonders about the cause, which turns out to be Mr. Evelyn, a lover of Christ, a lover of all things, a Unitarian. He and Margaret are married, and the utopian part of the book begins. Mons Christi, the center of their new world, and Livingston, the extent of it, are cast in the true utopian mold. A Christian utopia, it is moved and motivated by the love of Christ. The major helping agent is the wealth of Evelyn and Margaret. They seem to have unlimited funds at their disposal, and that, of course, made the task of rehabilitation relatively easy. Love was the cure-all, but it took Margaret to convince Mr. Evelyn that love was enough to produce reform. Mr. Evelyn explains the effect Margaret had on him:

When I first saw her, she was more purely in a state of nature than any civilized person I ever encountered. Neither internal sin nor external evil had deformed or diseased her, and she was prepared, like a new-born babe, to breathe the atmosphere of Christ the moment she came into contact with it, and to drink the sincere milk of the word. I once wholly despaired of seeing a Christian; she is one! I might say, I more than despaired of fulfilling my ideal in myself; she has aided me to do it! Christ pervades every corner and cranny of her being; she is filled with the fulness of God.

[She] gushes up like a fountain, and having supplied her home, she has enough wherewithal to overflow and run down the hill.[12]

The villagers were equally inspired by her example. They began to reform themselves, but Margaret and Evelyn helped: they paid mortgages; they gave men jobs; they provided amusements, dances, and spectacles; they rebuilt the church and made church service pleasant; they filled their new estate with Italian statuary; they held concerts; they rebuilt the jail; and most of all they gave men new hope. In modern terminology they were priming the pump. The priming was effective. The Livingston people must have amazed even themselves, for they had been "notorious for their indolence and dissipation." "Mr. Evelyn had their houses repaired and painted. . . . [He] planted a row of trees along the street, and had a beautiful

[12] *Ibid.*, p. 378.

statue of Diligence set up at the corner. He then assumed their debts, and said he would give no trouble for three years, provided they would pay the interest punctually. . . . [Results come quickly.] Old Mr. Tapley, a very sot, has labored unremittingly on his farm. When they had new door yards, the girls began to ornament them with flowers and shrubs. . . . The people, I think, do not drink any ardent spirits. . . . Many have abandoned drinking, and four distilleries have stopped. Esquires Beach and Bower say their duties, as Justices of the Peace, have greatly abated. Mr. Stillwater has converted his new bar-room into a reading room, and says his profits are nearly equal to what they were before."[13] Livingston became a clean, neat, tidy town, with every activity, from church to jail, conducted according to the spirit of Christ.

The fame of the township spread. A committee from the State legislature, sent to investigate the remarkable changes, was enthusiastic:

They say our roads are in fine order, in fact none are better in the State; that the whole town has a striking aspect of neatness and thrift; that during all the time of their visit they saw not one drunken man . . . ; that the consumption of intoxicating drinks has diminished from six or eight thousand gallons annually to a few scores; that the amount paid for schools has risen from three or four hundred dollars to two thousand; that all taxes . . . have been promptly paid; that our poor have lessened three-quarters; they say also that the value of real estate in Livingston has advanced twenty per cent, and that wholly exclusive of the improvement on Mons Christi; and that the mania for removing to the West, which prevails all over New England, has here subsided.[14]

There are no criminals, and not even any petty thieves.

They add, pleasantly enough, that, while they have been in a hundred houses, at all hours of the day, they have not heard a woman speak scandal or scold her children. They remark that a petition for divorce from Hope-still Cutts and his wife, formerly pending before the Legislature, had been withdrawn; and here, as all along, apprehensive of some collusion, they declare they made such an investigation as perfectly satisfied them these people were living in harmony and love.[15]

Patriotism is no longer expressed by military display. The men of Livingston have even refused to serve as soldiers. As good Christians

---

[13] *Ibid.*, pp. 350, 351.   [14] *Ibid.*, pp. 372, 373.   [15] *Ibid.*, p. 373.

they could not "conscientiously engage in taking, or preparing to take, the lives of their fellow beings, in pre-meditated battle." Livingston advanced materially as well as spiritually. The pecuniary ability of the people has kept pace with their moral excellence. Land has advanced in price, strangers are anxious to settle amongst us. The people have expended a good deal, and they have made money. Abstinence from ardent spirits, military duty, needless fashions, law-suits, have saved the town ten thousand dollars a year. . . . Add to this the recovery from idle habits, negligent dispositions and an unproductive uniformity, you will see our people are able to expend much in other ways.

Waste lands have been redeemed; sundry improvements in agriculture and mechanical arts adopted, whereby at once is a saving and a profit. Education, Literature, Religion, Recreation, Beauty, Music, Art, Morality, and General Happiness, are things the people enjoy, and for which they are able to pay. They have laid the foundation for a building to serve a composite purpose, of Library, Museum, Lecture Room, Reading Room.[16]

Women learned not to waste money, but to spend it wisely— for necessities, for objects of beauty, and for simple pleasures. "There are many common interests . . . , our Church, our Festivals . . . , Dances, Library, Schools, Music, Art, Love, Christ, Nature, God. . . ."[17] All these activities are a source of pleasure, and such pleasures can take the place of drinking. The puritan fathers, he thought, were such lamentably heavy drinkers because they had discarded all other forms of recreation.

Rum thus became the recreative element to our ancestors. If a man was tired, he drank rum; if he was disappointed, he drank rum; if he required excitement, he drank rum; the elders drank when they prayed, the minister when he preached. Rum . . . kindled alike the flames of devotion and the fires of revelry.[18]

Every month has its holiday. Holidays are based on the religious calendar, but dancing and gaiety are mixed in with church services. Dancing is everywhere encouraged.

We sometimes dance on the green, sometimes in our hall. It is enjoyed in all families. . . . It has supplanted many ridiculous games, and extirpated cruel sports. It has broken up drunken carousels, and neutralized the temptations to ardent spirits. . . . It brings the people together, interests strangers, and diffuses a serene, wholesouled harmony over the town. . . .
It embodies the recreative element in the healthiest and holiest forms.

[16] *Ibid.*, p. 386.   [17] *Ibid.*, p. 395.   [18] Hall, *op. cit.*, pp. 316, 317.

. . . We praise God in the dance: it is a hymn written with our feet. I would dance as I would pray, for its own sake, and because it is well-pleasing to God.[19]

Women advanced so far that they were no longer interested in changing fashions. There was one costume for every occasion; a simple, Grecian sort of garb.

Judd had no sympathy with the demand for women's rights. Like Mary Griffith, he believed that women's influence is indirect.

"As regards Woman, and her grievances and aspirations, . . . if she is not king, she is queen of home; she is mistress of a peculiar sphere; she is the head of a wonderful empire; and . . . in proportion as home is made attractive, men will stay at home, and women can in this way come to rule the men."[20]

In Philo he was even more definite:

> "Her effect
> Lies not in voting, warring, clerical oil,
> But germinating grace, forth putting virtue . . ."[21]

Even more amazing was the change in the legal profession: ". . . people come in from other towns and great distances to employ them. They say they can trust Livingston lawyers!"[22]

Sylvester Judd's utopia is definite enough, and easy enough to attain—given only one thing, Christians willing to abide by Christian ethics, in fact as well as spirit. If his ideal seems naive to us today, it is because we realize that there is a great difference between Christians and church-goers, between idealists and pragmatists. Judd had an idea, but he considered it from so many facets that the reader is likely to give up before he appreciates the thesis. Judd deserves to be remembered. His novels have many virtues, and they can well stand comparison with such books as Fenimore Cooper's *Crater*. Judd is interesting, colorful, picturesque, but he is also a moralist—and moralists are easy to neglect.

[19] *Ibid.*, p. 335.
[20] *Ibid.*, p. 320.
[21] *Ibid.*, p. 321.
[22] Judd, *op. cit.*, p. 397.

CHAPTER FIVE

FOUFOUVILLE, EXCELSIOR AND BLITHEDALE

WHOEVER Radical Freelance may have been, he was a man of many prejudices. Certainly he fancied himself a practical man of affairs. He knew very well that the world could not be reformed, and he had only scorn for those who thought it could. *The Philosophers of Foufouville,* 1868, is an indictment of long-haired reformers, but in the course of the novel it becomes pretty obvious that the author has a pet reform of his own. He wants to do away with the study of ancient languages. He wants children to study practical things, and not the wisdom of the ancients. He has his doubts about the wisdom and about the effect it would have on children if they actually studied the classics as carefully as they were supposed to. The solution of the problem of education is simply to eliminate the study of the classics.

The spirit of the novel is made clear by the definition of Foufouism as nonsense, hypocrisy, affectation, snobbery, and self-conceit. "Foufouites flock to mock auctions; they support astrologers, mediums, seventh daughters, and people whose 'sands of life have nearly run out'; they believe importers of all sorts of worthless foreign rubbish; they rail at democratic institutions; they invest in lotteries (in Wall Street, as well as elsewhere); lose their money in gambling halls; squander it in rum shops, and keep up the price of Greek and Latin dictionaries."[1]

The story concerns the utopian experiment of Dr. Goodenough at Harmony Hall, the phalanstery, a place large enough for a thousand members. There are only six inmates. The establishment is strictly vegetarian. There is no meat, and Dr. Goodenough is even pretty dubious about eggs. He can't quite make up his mind whether

[1] Radical Freelance [pseud.] *The Philosophers of Foufouville,* New York, 1868, pp. 295, 296.

the egg or the chicken came first. No fruit of the grape is permitted, and no tobacco, tea or coffee. Anything which can be labelled a stimulant is obviously bad. There is supposed to be perfect equality between the sexes and between all of the members. Both property and work are in common. Since marriage should only be for the purpose of breeding children, love is considered unnecessary. ". . . Husbands and wives will be kept rigidly separated from each other, excepting at such times as the laws of physiology teach us may be favorable to the attainment of the great end in view."[2]

Unfortunately, Dr. Goodenough's understanding of the laws of physiology wasn't clear enough to solve the problem of sex, even in his own Harmony Hall. One of the women, a mannish individual, who won't take her husband's name and who insists on being the boss and on wearing bloomers, tries to support Dr. Goodenough's position, but her perspective, too, is somewhat clouded. Charity Goodenough and Mr. Lovell, the youngest of the members, fall in love. Professor Malpest, Dr. Goodenough's chief aide, wants Charity for himself and tries to manipulate the ingenious laws of the place to bring about his purpose. But the Professor miscalculates and Mr. Lovell shows him to be a bigamist, a drunkard, and a forger. As a result the lovers are united and the colony disbands. It had failed because the members were not serious except in their separate purposes. None of them except Dr. Goodenough and the bloomer-wearing individual believed in celibacy, and they neither wanted to nor knew how to do any useful work. In other words, the Harmony Hall experiment, and all other Fourieristic experiments are ridiculous. They lack every ingredient essential to success, and no one but a determined Foufouite could possibly believe in them.

As one reads *The Philosophers of Foufouville*, one suspects that Radical Freelance must have participated himself in some such Fourieristic experiment. His irony has the bitter flavor of disillusionment. Hawthorne, by contrast, was not disillusioned; he was simply disappointed. For a time he had forgotten his natural skepticism— but he was in love, and the world seemed a very wonderful place. It was only in such a mood that he could have joined Brook Farm.

[2] *Ibid.*, p. 10.

Eventually he emerged from his dream world; eventually he realized that Brook Farm, Blithedale and Harmony Hall are pretty much the same place.

In 1835 Hawthorne suggested in his Journal that the modern reformer should provide good material for a sketch—"a type of the extreme doctrines on the subject of slaves, cold water, and other such topics. He goes about the streets haranguing most eloquently, and is on the point of making many converts, when his labors are suddenly interrupted by the appearance of the keeper of a mad-house, whence he has escaped. Much may be made of this idea."[3] Much was made of the idea, but Hawthorne would have been astounded if he could have realized that he would himself participate in a utopian venture. But the loss of his job at the Boston Custom House and the prospect of returning to Salem made "The Brook Farm Institute of Agriculture and Education" seem a glorious haven. He was doing his best to contemplate the world with colored lenses. He had visions of an idyllic existence with Sophia, lodged in their own cabin, and spending pleasant days in sunny fields.

At first Hawthorne was all enthusiasm. Even the New England climate didn't diminish his faith in the desirability of the rural life. After a day spent spreading manure, he could write to Sophia: "There is nothing so unseemly and disagreeable in this sort of toil as thou wouldst think. It defiles the hands, indeed, but not the soul. This gold ore is a pure and wholesome substance; else our Mother Nature would not devour it so readily, and derive so much nourishment from it, and return such a rich abundance of good grain and roots in requital of it."[4] This was May 4, 1841. On June 1, he wrote with less enthusiasm: "That abominable goldmine! Thank God, we anticipate getting rid of its treasures, in the course of two or three days! Of all hateful places, that is the worst; and I shall never comfort myself for having spent so many days of blessed sunshine there. It is my opinion, dearest, that a man's soul may be buried and perish under a dung-heap or in a furrow of the field, just as well as under a pile of money."[5]

[3] Nathaniel Hawthorne, *The Heart of Hawthorne's Journals,* Boston and New York, 1929, pp. 3, 4.
[4] *Ibid.,* p. 73.   [5] *Ibid.,* p. 74.

On September 3, after a few days away from the farm, he regards his own participation in the experiment with his old skepticism: "But really I should judge it to be twenty years since I left Brook Farm; and I take this to be one proof that my life there was an unnatural and unsuitable, and therefore an unreal one. It already looks like a dream behind me. The real Me was never an associate of the community; there has been a spectral Appearance there, sounding the horn at daybreak, and milking the cows, and hoeing potatoes, and raking hay, toiling and sweating in the sun, and doing me the honor to assume my name. But be thou not deceived, Dove of my heart. This Spectre was not thy husband."[6] On September 25, he wrote: ". . . One thing is certain. I cannot and will not spend the winter here."[7] At the end of October he departed from the farm and the life of that utopia.

Ten years and much of Hawthorne's best work intervened between the departure from Brook Farm and the picture of the experiment in *The Blithedale Romance*. Hawthorne acknowledges that he had Brook Farm in mind, but he qualifies his admission: "His whole treatment of the affair is altogether incidental to the main purpose of the romance; nor does he put forward the slightest pretensions to illustrate a theory, or elicit a conclusion, favourable or otherwise, in respect to socialism."[8] Hawthorne may well be perfectly sincere in this statement, but it is impossible not to read into the book a good deal of gentle satire. Undoubtedly it is not all directed at Brook Farm. Utopian experiments were making a great stir in the forties. The activities of the Perfectionists and the Icarians seemed particularly scandalous. The Fourieristic experiments at Redbank, at Skaneatales and at Sodus Bay had brought utopia squarely before the attention of the newspaper reading public. The time was right for a novel dealing satirically with these efforts. And Hawthorne could not possibly have dealt seriously with them. He had too keen an eye for human frailties and for the ironies of life.

The novel deals with a group of intellectuals who have gathered together at Blithedale in an effort to effect worthwhile reforms. Hawthorne has his hero explain their plans:

[6] *Ibid.*, p. 77.   [7] *Ibid.*, p. 79.
[8] Nathaniel Hawthorne, *The Blithedale Romance*, Preface.

It was our purpose—a generous one, certainly, and absurd, no doubt, in full proportion with its generosity—to give up whatever we had heretofore attained, for the sake of showing mankind the example of a life governed by other than the false and cruel principles on which human society has all along been based.

And, first of all, we had divorced ourselves from pride, and were striving to supply its place with familiar love. We meant to lessen the labouring man's great burthen of toil, by performing our due share of it at the cost of our own thews and sinews. We sought our profit by mutual aid, instead of wresting it by the strong hand from an enemy, or filching it craftily from those less shrewd than ourselves (if, indeed, there were any such in New England), or winning it by selfish competition with a neighbor. . . . And, as the basis of our institution, we purposed to offer up the earnest toil of our bodies, as a prayer no less than an effort for the advancement of our race.[9]

The story itself is of no particular concern here, but some of the characters are of interest because they are very definitely types. Zenobia is the vigorous, determined woman of wide abilities, who, having no family or other duties to occupy her mind, busies herself with reforms. She is a fascinating creature, but her mind is full of weeds.

It startled me, sometimes, in my state of moral as well as bodily faint-heartedness, to observe the hardihood of her philosophy. She made no scruple of oversetting all human institutions, and scattering them as with a breeze from her fan. A female reformer, in her attacks upon society, has an instinctive sense of where the life lies, and is inclined to aim directly at that spot. Especially the relation between the sexes is naturally among the earliest to attract her attention.[10]

The transcendental movement brought together a number of such women, well educated, able, industrious, and yet unable to concentrate on any single purpose—women of too many enthusiasms.

Hollingsworth is the prime mover at Blithedale. It is largely his idea and his money. But he doesn't stay interested. The pace is too slow. He begins to wonder whether he can reform the world. He decides finally to foresake Blithedale and to start an establishment for the reformation of criminals. Such men, Hawthorne decides,

. . . have no heart, no sympathy, no reason, no conscience. They will keep no friend unless he make himself the mirror of their purpose; they will

[9] *Ibid.*, pp. 19, 20. Page references are to the Everyman edition.
[10] *Ibid.*, p. 44.

smite and slay you, and trample your dead corpse under foot all the more readily if you take the first step with them, and cannot take the second and the third, and every other step of their terribly straight path. They have an idol, to which they consecrate themselves high-priest, and deem it holy work to offer sacrifices of whatever is most precious. . . . And the higher and purer the original object . . . the slighter is the probability that they can be led to recognize the process by which godlike benevolence has been debased into all-devouring egotism.[11]

Hawthorne realized, as most utopian visionaries have not, that it takes more than enthusiasm to establish a utopian community or even to bring about reforms. The hard-headed men who could run such a community as Brook Farm or Blithedale are the ones who would never be interested in such ventures, and who, if they were, would scarcely be acceptable to the enthusiasts.

Hawthorne intended, no doubt, to make of his story the same kind of romance that he had written before, but the material was so familiar that it is much more down to earth than most of what he has written. There is less other-worldliness and more matter-of-fact detail.

Hawthorne could contemplate Brook Farm wistfully: "Whatever else I may repent of, let it be reckoned neither among my sins nor follies that I once had faith and force enough to form generous hopes of the world's destiny,—yes!—and to do what in me lay for their accomplishment."[12] But in spite of his wistfulness he could not resist the temptation to make fun of Brook Farm and its inmates. It is not in the nature of a skeptic to be a utopian.

Alexander Lookup, in contrast to Hawthorne, was not a skeptic; he did not have the wit for such a reaction. He was something of a cynic, however, and he did realize that the gilded enthusiasm of the age must eventually become somewhat tarnished. It is conceivable that some of his nonsense may have seemed witty in 1860. His two volumes that appeared in that year were: *Excelsior: or, The Heir Apparent;* and *The Road Made Plain to Fortune for the Millions; or, The Popular Pioneer to Universal Prosperity.* They are not "poetical romances," as claimed by the publisher, but, rather, incredibly ex-

[11] *Ibid.,* pp. 71, 72.
[12] Quoted in Ludwig Lewisohn, *The Story of American Literature,* Modern Library edition [1939], p. 170.

travagant dramas, provided with a liberal quantity of bad doggerel, intended to satirize politicians and reformers. The satire is heavy-handed, however, and a good deal of it backfires.

Excelsior is presumably an attack on the banking structure of the country, with the implication that, if the people had their way, the banking system would be just, there would be no more foreclosures, business would be fair, and there would be a "Diamond United States," or utopia. "Excelsior" is the state baby, destined to free the people from the dictators, typified by Bigot and Despot, but before he is successful the dictators manage one last panic. Despot explains:

Unerring instinct guides me as certain as Nature's own favorite creature. We'll have a crash soon, a wild headlong panic that will topple over and engulph all the craft who have too much sail spread. Ay . . . the paper and credit bubbles, both are blown to their utmost tension.

And then comes the great harvest for our State Doctors and Undertakers.

Well, though the tradesmen and the millions may be swept down stream, it is in the muddy crisis that we make the greatest haul of the capital fish.[13]

The panic is such that Excelsior is enabled to lead a rebellion. The sovereign people awake to their sovereign rights and finally secure "Enlightened Law." The Despots and Bigots are consumed in flames by internal combustion and the "Diamond United States," becoming a "vitally consolidated Republic," is left to develop as a utopia, with only honorary governing offices. The people are supposed to have prevailed.

The Road Made Plain to Fortune for the Millions provides a different solution. There are two major evils which the people must fight, party and rent. "Party, an organized public plunderer, which usurps law and government in America, is not subject to the law of God. . . ."[14] To fight "Party," the people must remove the opportunities for plunder. They must attack "endless rent and taxation." "Endless rent and taxation are class legislation, creating a privileged, and irresponsible aristocracy. . . ."[15] The solution is ingenious:

[13] Alexander Lookup, *Excelsior, or The Heir Apparent,* New York and London, 1860, pp. 22, 23.
[14] Alexander Lookup, *The Road Made Plain to Fortune for the Millions,* New York and London: 1860, p. 99.
[15] *Ibid.,* p. 209.

"There is no other mode of bridling taxation than to universally plant yourself down to become your own landlords."[16] That is the first duty of the citizens; thereby "they inaugurate the Judgement Bar of God. . . ." Thus, the "Sovereign Citizen . . . can procure better than California, everywhere, over all the Continent."[17]

These two volumes are rhetoric and bombast rather than fiction, but they show how easy it was to make fun of utopian enthusiasm. They are by no means so skillful as *The Blithedale Romance* and *The Philosophers of Foufouville,* but there is the same rather sardonic appreciation of the antics of reformers.

[16] *Ibid.*, p. 22.
[17] *Ibid.*, p. 65.

CHAPTER SIX

EDWARD EVERETT HALE AND MARK TWAIN

EDWARD EVERETT HALE believed implicitly in the natural goodness of man. He pretended to have no doubts about man's impulses, and perhaps he did not have any for he was one of Boston's most respectable citizens. He was a successful writer and a successful minister. His South Church pastorate should have guaranteed both his respectability and his conservatism, and it was natural that Beacon Street should have accepted him at face value. But Beacon Street had cause to wonder occasionally about his conservatism. Many of his notions were heretical: "He defended the Rochdale cooperative system, the government ownership of coal-mines, old-age pensions, and he asked why all these measures were regarded as novel. Did not the people own the roads, the canals, aqueducts, school houses, light-houses? Did they not own the libraries, reservoirs, churches? . . . Had not the American genius always run in the line of the 'govern-ment ownership of the essentials'? Was the 'ownership of wealth in common' anything so odd?"[1]

The most remarkable thing about Hale is not that he could live down his heresies and become Beacon Street's "grand old man," but rather that he could have developed a social conscience in the first place. His enthusiasm bears the same stamp as that of Emerson and Bronson Alcott and Orestes Brownson and Sylvester Judd, but carried over to a later generation when reform was less popular. The post Civil War period was not one in which attacks on the established system were encouraged. There were so many "dangerous radicals" about, that men of means were always on guard to ward off fresh attacks. And they did not usually tolerate attacks from members of their own class. Hale would not have been tolerated, either, had he been considered more than an inconsequential dabbler whose work

[1] Van Wyck Brooks, *New England: Indian Summer*, New York, 1940, p. 419.

would have no real influence. Their judgment was right. His work didn't have any influence. Of his sixty-odd books, it was *The Man Without a Country* which was mentioned with pride by his fellow Bostonians. The volumes which reveal his social conscience have always been pretty thoroughly neglected.

Sybaris, 1869, is decidedly utopian. The story concerns the amazing adventure of a Colonel Ingham, who, in the course of a voyage in aid of Garibaldi, found himself wrecked on an island off the Italian Coast, an island which turned out to be the home of the modern Sybarites. And they were certainly not the luxury-loving, effeminate race discussed in Latin text books. After his week's visit, he realized that the reason Sybaris had remained unknown was that no one who had ever visited the place was willing to leave. In other words, Sybaris was utopia. "Here was a nation which believed that the highest work of a nation was to train its people. It did not believe in fight, like Milon or Heenan or the old Spartans; it did not believe in commerce like Carthage and England. It believed in men and women. It respected men and women. It educated men and women. It gave their rights to men and women."[2]

Colonel Ingham has a hard time convincing himself that the state is more concerned with its individuals than with augmenting its own power. His guide insists:

We consider the state to be made for the better and higher training of men, —much as your divines say that the church is. Instead of our lumping our citizens, therefore, and treating Jenny Lind and Tom Heenan to the same dose of public schooling,—instead of saying that what is sauce for the goose is sauce for the gander,—we try to see that each individual is protected in the enjoyment, not of what the majority likes, but of what he chooses, so long as his choice injures no other men.[3]

Consistent with this theory, the severest infraction of the criminal code is taking away from a citizen what cannot be restored. So, when someone built a row of tenement houses, it was ruled that the houses deprived the citizen of proper ventilation and light, and that they were dangerous to "health, growth, strength, and comfort." On this same principle, "an uninvited guest, who calls on another man on

[2] Edward Everett Hale, *Sybaris and Other Homes,* p. 26. References are to the edition published by Little, Brown & Co. in 1890.
[3] *Ibid.,* pp. 53, 54.

his own business, rises at the end of eleven minutes and offers to go. And the courts have ruled very firmly that there must be a *bona fide* effort."[4] The individual must be protected against bores; he must not be required to waste time, which is irreplaceable, simply out of a mistaken sense of politeness.

In Sybaris there is no such thing as crooked politics. If a man is to serve in an administrative position in the government, he must study the administrative systems of other countries. He is elected, finally, because he is well trained, not because he can make a good stump speech. The members of the school board have to know something about educational theory; it isn't enough that they publish school books or that their wives want public spirited husbands.

The election of officials is a very simple business. When an office is vacant, candidates' names are listed at a central place. There is no fixed time for voting. The books remain open for three months, and at the end of that time the man with the most votes is elected. Terms of office are indefinite. A man remains in office until he is too old for the job or until the majority of the voters decide that he ought to be removed.

All citizens must marry, on the theory that unmarried people are not normal and so will not be desirable citizens. No girl may marry before eighteen. If a girl doesn't marry before she is twenty-eight, she must travel abroad for thirty years, or until she marries. Men must marry between the ages of twenty-three and thirty or spend the same number of years abroad. Men are supposed to marry later than women to compensate for the fact that there are more men than women.

There is no servant problem in Sybaris, for there are no servants. Unmarried girls help with the work in large families, but they are not servants. Rather they are accepted as members of the family. As a result, there is no stigma attached to housework or to any other kind of physical labor.

It is perhaps natural that Sybarites should take religion seriously. The minister is much more than the man who delivers a sermon every Sunday. He is, literally, the shepherd of his flock. He must look after the physical welfare as well as the spiritual welfare of his

[4] *Ibid.*, p. 57.

flock. When a man commits a crime, the name of his minister is included in the report.

Sybaris is not a complete picture of utopia. It is a picture of an idealized New England community, without any of our glaring social evils. Hale is not a serious reformer. He is conscious of the necessity of adequate housing, and so he insists always that decent houses will make decent citizens. He sees the abuses of a corrupt legislator, and imagines a society where there could be no corruption. He dislikes the class feeling of the industrial areas, and he imagines a society in which all work is honorable, and in which every man and woman can feel pride in his work. In other words, Hale is pretty much a Sybarite himself. He wants to lead an agreeable life, but if he sees others suffering, his conscience won't let him alone.

He comes somewhat more to grip with reality in the two essays which are published with *Sybaris*—"How They Live in Vineland" and "How They Lived at Naguadavick." In these he is trying to show that slum areas can be eliminated only if better places to live are provided. The solution, he says, is properly laid-out suburbs. Man has a natural passion for holding land of his own. When a man can get into the open, when he can have his own cow and pig, when he can raise his own vegetables, then, says Hale, he becomes a good citizen. In other words, the way to clear slums is to give the slum dwellers, the recent immigrants, a chance at a decent life. They should be helped, not exploited.

Hale's *How They Lived in Hampton,* 1888, develops the same thesis about the necessity of decent working conditions and decent living conditions. But it is really an expression of his faith in the beneficent effects of Christianity and cooperation, which, with him, become almost synonymous. He tells the story of the Hampton woolen mills which had failed under private management and yet succeeded wonderfully when both labor and management had learned to cooperate. According to the Hampton plan, labor and management agreed to share equally the responsibility and the profits. Wages were lower than elsewhere, but the worker also received a share of the profits. The men tried always to find ways to save money and to improve the quality of the goods. As a result, the mill prospered, and with it, the town. Houses were better cared for. The schools were better taught. The books in the library were more frequently read. The churches were better attended. The store became a cooperative and sold at cost. The people even learned to entertain themselves. They learned to live the good, simple life which had been typical of New England towns before the rise of the factory system. In other words, Hale is trying to prove that the factory system and the democratic system are not incompatible. Our American workmen are the best in the world, he insists, but they cannot be treated like automatons. The greater their measure of responsibility, the greater their enthusiasm, and so the greater the return to capital. Intelligent management can profit from intelligent workmen. The solution is cooperation. Cooperation and a working democracy become the same thing. "The secret of Democracy," Hale wrote, ". . . is that everybody wants the machine to move, and so makes it move, and does his share."[5] "The people of the United States understand perfectly well that there must be order, there must be command, there must be authority. But, on the other hand, the people of the United States, from the circumstances which called them into existence, understand that they are the real fountain of authority, order, and command, and they like to be consulted before authority is asserted."[6]

E. E. Hale was not a practical man. His generalizations about the good life are pleasant, but they are not constructive. In effect, he is simply a yearner after the old days of a simple village economy, when inequalities weren't so obvious, and when there was no such thing as a class system. He was too good a man not to see that the economic structure was out of order. His solution, however, shows his goodness and not any economic or political astuteness.

Mark Twain fits into the same utopian niche as Edward Everett Hale. Even more than Hale he disliked the inequalities of the world about him, and felt the futility of his role as observer. "The Curious Republic of Gondour," his three page sketch of utopia, is not the sort of dream world pictured by the idealist who has faith in the democratic impulses of the people. The story shows a good deal of the same sardonic skepticism which is apparent in *The Gilded Age*. Mark Twain

---

[5] Edward Everett Hale, *How They Lived in Hampton*, p. 393. Page references are to Volume IX of the Little, Brown & Co. edition of Hale's works.
[6] *Ibid.*, pp. 454, 455.

was still reflecting on his disillusioning experiences in Washington a few years earlier.

The most remarkable thing about this utopian fragment is the name of the author and the fact that it was first published anonymously in *The Atlantic Monthly*. According to his biographer, Albert Bigelow Paine, no one suspected that he was the author. He withheld his name ". . . in the fear that the world might refuse to take him seriously over his own signature, or *nom de plume*."[7]

According to Paine, this was his third essay dealing directly with social criticism. "His paper on 'Universal Suffrage' had sounded a first note, and his copyright petitions were of the same spirit."[8] He exaggerates some for humourous effect, but it is not all humour. He believed in democracy, but he saw the country being exploited by men without conscience. And even universal suffrage, which had seemed to be an infallible safety valve, was not successful. He reflects on this in "The Curious Republic" and suggests that extra votes be given to those with education and property.

I found that the nation had at first tried universal suffrage pure and simple, but had thrown that form aside because the result was not satisfactory. It had seemed to deliver all power into the hands of the ignorant and non-tax-paying classes; and of a necessity the responsible offices were filled from these classes also.

A remedy was sought. The people believed they had found it; not in the destruction of universal suffrage, but in the enlargement of it. It was an odd idea, and ingenious. You must understand, the constitution gave every man a vote; therefore that vote was a vested right, and could not be taken away. But the constitution did not say that certain individuals might not be given two votes, or ten! So an amendatory clause was inserted in a quiet way; a clause which authorized the enlargement of the suffrage in certain cases to be specified by statute. To offer to "limit" the suffrage might have made instant trouble; the offer to "enlarge" it had a pleasant aspect. But of course the newspapers soon began to suspect; and then out they came! It was found, however, that for once—and for the first time in the history of the republic—property, character, and intellect were able to wield a political influence; for once, money, virtue, and intelligence took a vital and a united interest in a political question; for once these powers went to the "primaries" in strong force; for once the best men in the nation were put forward as candidates for that parliament whose business it should be to enlarge the suffrage. The weightiest half of the press quickly joined

[7] Albert Bigelow Paine, *Mark Twain: A Biography*, New York, 1912, p. 554.
[8] *Ibid.*

forces with the new movement, and left the other half to rail about the proposed "destruction of the liberties" of the bottom layer of society, the hitherto governing class of the community.

The victory was complete. The new law was framed and passed. Under it every citizen, howsoever poor or ignorant, possessed one vote, so universal suffrage still reigned; but if a man possessed a good common-school education and no money, he had two votes; a high-school education gave him four; if he had property likewise, to the value of three thousand *sacos*, he wielded one more vote; for every fifty thousand *sacos*, a man added to his property, he was entitled to another vote; a university education entitled a man to nine votes, even though he owned no property. Therefore, learning being more prevalent and more easily acquired than riches, educated men became a wholesome check upon wealthy men, since they could outvote them. Learning goes usually with uprightness, broad views, and humanity; so the learned voters, possessing the balance of power, became the vigilant and efficient protectors of the great lower rank of society.[9]

In the rest of the fragment he takes swipes at other phases of the Washington scene; at patronage, at the purchase of justice, at the aggressive selfishness of the period. The story ends on this note: "There was a loving pride of country about this person's way of speaking which annoyed me. I had long been unused to the sound of it in my own. The Gondour national airs were forever dinning in my ears; therefore I was glad to leave that country and come back to my dear native land, where one never hears that sort of music."

It would be fruitless to look for the sources of such an essay. Mark Twain's dissatisfaction with suffrage is not surprising at a time when the "spoils" system was in full swing. What he proposed is simply government by an intellectual aristocracy, and that idea goes back, at least, to Plato. It is his method of achieving such a government which is unusual.

Utopias were not as common in the seventies as they were after the publication of *Looking Backward*. Howells urged Twain to follow up the "Gondour" paper, and possibly he intended to. Other projects interfered, however, and his sketch was never finished.

Actually, the germinal idea of "Gondour" was not carefully thought out. It was the work of a few hours, and reflected a momentary bitterness. Had he tried to develop it in more detail, he would have found

[9] *The Atlantic Monthly,* October, 1875, 36:461-463.

that he was working at cross purposes with his own, more fundamental faith in democracy.

Howells' interest in the fragment is worth noting, for his own "Altruria" is at least similar to "Gondour." Both countries are laid in the present and both have a history close enough to that of the United States to illustrate contemporary social problems. By the time Howells was writing his own utopian novels, however, *Looking Backward* had stimulated such a rash of utopianism that he had a myriad of sources for his project.

CHAPTER SEVEN

RADICAL BACKGROUNDS

THE decades of the seventies and eighties were periods of increasing social consciousness. The farmers were organizing their
Granger societies and their National Alliances, but the change from
romanticism to realism was slow. Visions of prosperity lingered,
despite hard times. Agriculture had few leaders, but the growing
bitterness, the growing sense of inequality, the new perception of a
class struggle created a union among farmers which culminated in
the Populist revolt.

Farmers have never been good "joiners," good organizers, and
this, in itself, has been enough to insure that agriculture would be
subordinate, in political influence, to industry. The most remarkable
thing about the Populist movement was the sudden and enthusiastic
cooperation of the farmers, with each other and also with reform
groups. The consequence of this fusion was an organized reaction
against monopoly, against banks and the monetary system, against the
burden of taxation, against the tariff, against governmental policy—
against everything which was opposed to their immediate interests.

The labor unions were hard hit after the panic in 1873, but they
took shape again as effective secret societies: the Sovereigns of Industry, the Industrial Brotherhood, the Knights of Labor, and Molly
Maguires. Increasing unemployment forced labor to a more active
role. At times their activities got out of hand, as in the railroad strike
of 1877. The public reacted vigorously to all such extravagances; all
labor organizations became bad. Even so, the Greenback-labor movement of 1870 was more successful than any third party had ever been
before. More than a million votes were given to the party candidates.

The campaign of 1896 was the last determined stand of the various
reform groups. Despite the fact that the Populists and Democrats
were defeated, many of the reforms which they had fathered were

eventually enacted. It was Populist campaigning which secured the adoption of such measures as the initiative and the referendum, the recall, the Australian ballot, and the popular election of Senators.. And more important, it was the "hayseed economists" whose arguments led to the serious study of the monetary problem, and laid the groundwork for the later Federal Reserve banking system.

The rebellious spirit of the decades is expressed in a great many radical volumes. Three of these will be sufficient to illustrate the different channels of thought: *The Eden of Labor,* 1876; *Progress and Poverty,* 1879; and *A New Moral World,* 1885. Of these, only *Progress and Poverty* has any claim to recognition. The others had only an ephemeral interest. They can no longer be taken seriously, but they are interesting as an indication of the ideas about which men quarrelled.

The Eden of Labor; or, The Christian Utopia doesn't explain how to achieve an ideal state. It explains, rather, the development of the conflicts between capital and labor which have made the world so far from utopian. Collens has attempted to trace man's gradual assumption of economic bondage from a free state in the Garden of Eden to his position as a wage slave in industrial areas. His argument is buttressed with innumerable quotations from Scripture and with frequent references to Adam Smith and Quesnay. He acknowledges the countless abuses in the world, and he insists that "charity is the principle on which political economy should be based." But charity is impossible when the competitive spirit is necessary to success in business. Charity and practical Christianity are impossible in a capitalistic society. "To a *fundamental change of system* must, therefore, the world look for a restoration of the economic equilibrium; and there is no prospect of this but in one direction. If labor and capital were united in the same persons, and these were united by the law of love which is from our Lord Jesus Christ, there would be ABUNDANCE for all mankind."[1]

Collens' solution is not necessarily naive, and it is certainly not new. He almost seems to admit that there is no hope of any real reform, for he realizes that utopia requires a world of men who will take

[1] T. Wharton Collens, *The Eden of Labor; or, The Christian Utopia.* Philadelphia, 1876, p. 116.

seriously the injunctions of Christ which they profess to believe.
Progress and Poverty is an analysis of the economic framework of
society from a fresh point of view. Henry George is not content to
accept, without question, the theories of classical economists. He feels,
rather, that their insistence upon rationalizing the relationship of
capital and labor has resulted in an intensification of abuses, many
of which might otherwise have been avoided. He wants to re-define
and then to re-examine.

He emphasizes, for example, the falseness of the notion that wages
are drawn from capital. Wages, he says, come directly from the
product of the laborer's own work. The sum to be paid in wages is
not fixed. It depends on the number of men working and the amount
of work done. "Production is always the mother of wages. Without
production, wages would not and could not be. It is from the produce
of labor, not from the advances of capital, that wages come."[2]

His analysis of the function of rent is even more significant. "Rent,
in short, is the price of monopoly, arising from the reduction to
individual ownership of natural elements which human exertion can
neither produce nor increase."[3] And it is the capacity of yielding rent
which gives value to land. There is, he says, "no occupation in which
labor and capital can engage which does not require the use of land."[4]
In other words, land is the basis of all wealth.

George's most important contribution, the single tax, stems from
this conception of land and rent, and also from his belief that a state
may not justly take from an individual what he has himself created.
All personal taxes, then, are wrong; but since the value of land is
created by society, a single tax on land would be eminently fair, for
it would not deprive the individual of the fruits of his own labor. As
the property of society as a whole increased, however, so would the
income of the government.

This theory has had a tremendous appeal from the first—and the
reason is largely its equalitarianism. In the eighties and nineties, particularly, when men were always conscious of the extremes of wealth
and poverty, they needed faith in something which would seem to

[2] Henry George, *Progress and Poverty*, p. 56. Page references are to the Modern
Library edition.
[3] *Ibid.*, p. 167.   [4] *Ibid.*, p. 169.

promise better days ahead. The single tax became a symbol; it provided an answer to a problem which was obvious, but which otherwise seemed insoluble. Men wanted such an answer; they were ready to be convinced. Henry George had a tremendous influence during the last quarter of the century. The radical movement was greatly influenced by his thinking. And certainly a good number of the writers of utopian novels seemed to think that the single tax provided a solution for most of our economic problems.

A New Moral World, by James Casey of Providence, is devoted to the task, first, of demonstrating that money is the root of all evil, and second, of providing a satisfactory solution. It is the utmost folly, he says, to assume "that the present state of society is the best possible. . . . The world is yet in its infancy."[5] Our social structure provides an example of "the most heterogeneous mass of confusion and disorder that the mind can conceive."[6] No sane individual could propose that we try to keep static a social framework constructed with so many flaws. And no sane individual could assume that there is any just division of the fruits of labor. The land of the world should belong to all the people of the world for their united use. Instead there is the profiteer and the proletariat, the judge and the criminal. "With our present state of society we manufacture our criminals and then punish them for being so."[7] "When money is abolished, the occupation of the thief, the burglar, the money broker, the bank cashier, and the swindler will be gone."[8] Since money is obviously the cause of our misfortunes, we must reorganize society in such a way as to get along without it.

"Our new system of society provides for the happiness and comfort of everyone, and establishes universal friendship, fraternity, and the brotherhood of man, combined with the most complete, extensive system of education. . . ."[9] It will remove poverty, privation and crime from the world. It will erase the words "master" and "servant," "workman" and "thief" from the English language. It will change the earth from hell to heaven and people it with saints. That is no small order, but Casey says that this new system of education can effect the change.

[5] James Casey, *A New Moral World,* Providence, 1885, p. 9.
[6] *Idem.*   [7] *Ibid.,* p. 13.   [8] *Ibid.,* p. 14.   [9] *Ibid.,* p. 19.

In the late nineteenth century, education was usually considered as a great leveller and reformer. Just educate your men and women and their sins will disappear. The only trouble was that few people could agree on what constituted the right kind of education. Casey wasn't one to quibble about the meaning of education. As far as he was concerned, education meant college. Establish enough colleges for everyone, and provide instruction for life instead of for four years and the millennium will surely have been achieved.

There should be built enough colleges, with factories attached, to provide for everyone. Scholars would reside on the premises, in their own cottages, and with their own families. They would attend school three hours a day and work three hours a day. With no profiteering, the manufactured products would provide enough profits to support the college and the students, and also to undersell all competitors.

Outside manufacturing agencies would soon be taken over or forced to suspend operations—but the owners could then become scholars. In a few years more, money will not be worth anything except as a metal, so it will be useless for those who have it to hold on to it any longer, because this new system may become a government measure any day in this or some other country, for it is sure to be brought to the attention of every government on earth almost as soon as it is known. It is natural to expect that some governments will fight shy of it at first.[10]

The last sentence is typical of the blithe optimism which characterized so many reformers.

The establishment of the colleges is made to sound easy. First, of course, there must be a victory at the polls to provide a majority of legislators. The legislators will see the wisdom and simplicity of the plan and quickly enact the necessary measures. The plan can be financed either by surplus money or by fiat money. Fiat money is recommended, for that won't even have to be redeemed. Eventually there will be no need for money. Men will be provided with the necessities of life simply because they are students at a college. There will be nothing left to buy.

The system of representation should then be changed, he says, so that legislators are elected from the various colleges rather than from districts and states. The new college system should be made the basic

[10] *Ibid.*, p. 18.

law of the land. There should be no privileges for anyone. Churches should be allowed to continue operation, but the public should somehow be made to realize that no question of "human duty" is involved in church membership.

James Casey is certainly sincere. He lashes out at the abuses which were evident in industrial new England. Most of what he says is nonsense, but that isn't so important as the fact that he has an acute social conscience, and that, along with many others, he is insisting that something must be done. And at that time a social conscience was a relatively new phenomenon in the United States.

It is easy enough now to poke fun at the economic theory expounded in all three of these volumes, but then we have the advantage of some sixty years of changing interpretations. Collens and Casey were considered eccentric, perhaps, but not unbalanced. These and similar books were read and discussed in all seriousness. It was inevitable that the utopian novelist should deal with similar ideas. It was inevitable that political and economic theory should no longer be the exclusive property of the scholar and politician. Laborers and farmers came to think that they, too, knew something of these mysteries. Their grasp of the material was not always thorough, but it was thorough enough to give the politicians pause. Increasingly, in the last two decades of the century, the Republicans and the Democrats gave heed to the protests and reforms of the leftwing.

CHAPTER EIGHT

THE PRECURSORS OF BELLAMY

UTOPIAN novels were produced at intervals throughout the century, but it was not till the eighties that utopianism became the vogue. New ideas were in the air; men began to think and write and talk socialism. It was inevitable that some one book would catch the fancy of the public and become a symbol of this new enthusiasm. *Looking Backward*, 1888, became such a symbol for two reasons: it was skillfully written and it was published at just the right moment. Bellamy's thinking was exactly in tune with the thinking of his contemporaries. It is a mistake, however, to think of him as an innovator. In the five years preceding the publication of *Looking Backward*, there were three utopian novels which show points of similarity with Bellamy's work—*The Diothas; or, A Far Look Ahead*, by John Macnie; *The Republic of the Future*, by Anna Bowman Dodd; and *The Crystal Button*, by Chauncey Thomas. These novels are interesting in themselves, and also as a point of departure for studying Bellamy.

John Macnie had no great faith in the masses as did Bellamy. He did not foresee utopia as the result of education. The utopia which he portrays in *The Diothas; or, A Far Look Ahead*, 1883, is achieved after years of war have so weakened the countries of the world that they must concern themselves with the business of self-preservation. His new society is capitalistic, but it is rationally capitalistic. In large measure Macnie is interested in demonstrating that capitalism was not responsible for all the ills of the nineteenth century, and that communism would not provide a universal solution. He writes in the preface: "It will be seen that the author is not deeply imbued with the communistic ideas now so attractive to many. To become the well-fed slaves of an irresistible despotism, with the hierarchy of walking delegates, seems hardly the loftiest conceivable destiny for the human race."[1]

---

[1] [John Macnie], *The Diothas; or, A Far Look Ahead. . . .* By Ismar Thiusen [pseud.], New York and London, 1883, p. iv.

Macnie and Bellamy had probably known each other. There was a tradition at the University of North Dakota, where Macnie taught for many years, that the two of them ". . . had gone over the themes of their utopias a few years before the earlier one was published."[2] At any rate, the plot of *Looking Backward* is remarkably similar to *A Far Look Ahead.*

Ismar Thiusen, the hero, submits to an experiment in the nineteenth century and wakes up in the ninety-sixth century. The New York he had known was gone; it was no longer an area of rabbit warrens, slums, and super-slums. No one lived on Manhattan; the island was simply a huge warehouse. Men lived simple, well-ordered lives. They divided their time between profession, handicraft and leisure. It was not a communistic world, for individuals had a great deal of individual freedom and a man was able to own what he earned, but it had the one great virtue of communism, a classless society. Everyone belonged to the aristocracy. Everyone worked, and everyone felt that work was good. Idleness was esteemed the meanest of the vices.

The plot is concerned with Ismar Thiusen's adjustment to the ways of the new society. A great part of this adjustment revolves about his love affair with Reva Diothas. Ismar is somewhat confused when he discovers that, in addition to being Reva's lover, he is also her ancestor. He solves this dilemma by assuming that he must have been reborn. The idea of reincarnation was popular in the eighties; a good many novels based their plots on some phase of the idea. The romance of Ismar and Reva prospers, despite the confusion of being both ancestor and lover. Reva accepts him, and then, according to custom, he leaves her for a year. On their one visit during the year, they go rowing, get caught in the current, and are swept over some falls. Ismar wakes up in his previous world, to discover that his girl, Edith Alston, was really waiting for him, and that he was, after all, to become the ancestor of the lovely Reva.

The new world order had been achieved after years of bloody conflict. A military genius had almost conquered the world, but he had been defeated when he tried to subjugate America. With peace, men sought desperately for a final solution of national problems, and the

[2] Arthur E. Morgan, *Edward Bellamy*, New York, 1944, p. 241.

solution was "a sort of federal union . . . by which all become pledged
to preserve a republican form of government throughout the world,
and to guarantee to each nation the integrity of its territory, even
amicable arrangements for transfer or union being subject to the
approval of all."[3]

Macnie conjures up a good number of natural marvels for his
world of the future. Men had learned to control the rain supply, and
also to control the climate. The New York climate was mild the year
round. Men had learned not to waste sewage, but to use it to fertilize
the soil. Men had learned that "ersatz" goods and foods were better
than the natural product. "Our experts are able, not only to imitate
any definite compound known to exist in nature, but even to invent
others, some of the greatest value."[4] Family groups still ate together,
but men had learned that experts could prepare better meals, more
efficiently than could their wives. The telephone had become almost
as wonderful as it is today. It served as telephone, radio and dicta-
phone. Men had even learned a new system of mathematics, a duo-
decimal system based on the number twelve. Altogether, Macnie
imagines a good number of scientific changes. The inventions which
have been most commented upon in *Looking Backward* had been
imagined earlier by Macnie.

Education was regarded as the main business of life. Children
were taught practical subjects; they didn't waste years in the study of
dead languages. At fifteen boys began the study of their special handicraft; at sixteen, their professional or artistic pursuit. Young men and
women all over the country had equal opportunities for study, for
each district had its own institute of higher learning. Between seventeen and twenty-five, young men were members of the conscript labor
force. Their work took them to all parts of the world; these years
of work took the place of a grand tour, and served to put the finishing
touches on their education. In addition to the manual labor, they
studied part of each day. In the same fashion, after they were married,
both men and women divided their time between work with their
hands and work with their brains.

Girls spent these years of apprenticeship at home, but they worked

[3] Macnie, *op. cit.*, p. 113.
[4] *Ibid.*, p. 85.

alternate weeks at the central depots where they helped with cooking, baking, and laundry.

The new world's system for controlling marriage is almost as remarkable as the system for controlling the rain supply. The courtship follows a set routine: when a girl is first engaged she binds up her hair, thus warning off other males. For two months the man is allowed to enjoy as much of her company as is consistent with the "probationary nature of the relationship." If the girl wants to call the whole thing off, all she has to do is let down her hair. After these first two months, rings and kisses are exchanged, and the couple must spend a full year apart. At the end of the year, if they are still interested in each other, they can get married. The only other requirement is that all couples, immediately after marriage, must spend six months at a University.

Altogether, the state is a benevolent despotism. The state wants its citizens to live good lives, and, in consequence, so regulates their education, choice of handicraft and business, marriage, and behavior, that the citizens must inevitably conform to the predetermined pattern. Inheritance, for example, is controlled: and since a man can will only so much to his family, there is little incentive to pile up a vast fortune. In the same way, insurance is compulsory; all married couples must contribute to a fund which will protect them from accidental loss.

Macnie thought of his state as utopian because men and women were forced to live good lives. He was not particularly concerned about the fact that some people must have been forced into uncomfortable molds. Perfection is always a relative matter, and certainly the elements which go to make up any man's utopia depend completely on his environment. Macnie was rebelling against the poverty of his age, a poverty which economists, bred to Malthusian economics, insisted was an inevitable corollary of the capitalistic system of free enterprise. It was inevitable that he should envision his utopian state as a centralized, all engrossing power in which men had the opportunity to become neither wealthy beyond other men, nor poor beyond other men. Abstract freedom is important, he would have admitted, but much more important is freedom from want. Any government is a system of compromises, and guaranteeing security seemed more important to Macnie than guaranteeing the individual's right to be different. With Macnie utopia and the full dinner pail became pretty much the same thing. Eventually even this much liberalism seemed too strong; he felt the need to apologize for his work.

Anna Bowman Dodd's *The Republic of the Future* is a satiric utopia. Mrs. Dodd was evidently tired of hearing how marvelous the world of the future was going to be. She had evidently heard too much about reform. Perhaps she was annoyed by John Macnie's *A Far Look Ahead* or by the Fourieristic experiments. At any rate she had no faith in human perfectibility. *The Republic of the Future* is her answer to idealists. It was published in 1887 by Cassell's National Library, in a ten cent, paper-backed edition. With the single exception of Mrs. Dodd's volume, the Library was devoted to the classics. It would be interesting to know why such a volume was included. Since it cannot have been because of literary excellence, it must have been because the subject matter was considered timely. Perhaps the publishers were trying to nullify the effects of radical talk. For this purpose the volume came out a year or more too early. Had it been published as an answer to Edward Bellamy, it would have aroused vastly more interest. Some of her arguments could have been aimed at *Looking Backward* with good effect. As it is, though, she makes too many vague generalizations. No Nationalist would have had much trouble brushing aside her criticisms.

Everything in Mrs. Dodd's republic of the future is run by machinery. Men travel by pneumatic tubes. Men register at hotels which have mechanical hotel clerks. Mechanical devices show them to their rooms, and when they are hungry, they press a button and capsules of food appear miraculously before them. Machinery does many things which might more easily be done by hand, but since "labor of a degrading order is forbidden by law, machinery must be used as its substitute."[5]

Mrs. Dodd describes this new world through the eyes of a Swedish nobleman who is visiting socialistic New York for the first time. Sweden had retained the old competitive system, and so her traveller was constantly surprised. Utility, he reasons, must have been the only

[5] Anna Bowman Dodd, *The Republic of the Future*, New York, 1887, p. 18.

feature considered in the development of the new order. Every house is the same. The city "is as flat as your hand and as monotonous as a twicetold tale."[6] "The total lack of contrast which is the result of the plan on which this socialistic city has been built, comes, of course, from the principle which has been decreed that no man can have any finer house or better interior, or finer clothes than his neighbor. The abolition of poverty, and the raising of all classes to a common level of comfort and security, has resulted in the most deadening uniformity."[7] Even the shop windows are dull, since there is neither rivalry nor competition. Everything is too sensible. Even eating has become a matter-of-fact, dull business. State scientists examine people once a month and prescribe a diet. Food is shipped once a month from Chicago. Preparation is simple, for the food is either in pellets or condensed. "We take our food as we drink water, wherever we may happen to be, when it's handy, and when we need it."[8]

Women have become the dominant sex. "The perfecting of the woman movement was retarded for hundreds of years, as you know, doubtless, by the slavish desire of women to please their husbands by dressing and cooking to suit them. When the last pie was made into the first pellet, woman's true freedom began. She could then cast off her subordination both to her husband and to her servants. Women were only free, indeed, when the State prohibited the hiring of servants. Of course, the hiring of servants at all was as degrading to the oppressed class as it was a clog to the progress of their mistresses' freedom. The only way to raise the race was to put everyone on the same level, to make even degrees of servitude impossible."[9] The home became progressively less important. Housework, too, had to be done by machinery. And since it had been impossible to invent a machine which could dust, there were no gadgets, no pictures in the apartments—"only the necessary chairs and tables. If men want to see pictures, they can go to the museums."[10] Inevitably men became more and more indifferent to their wives. There was "a gradual decay of the erotic sentiment."[11]

As women came to feel themselves the dominant sex, they re-

[6] *Ibid.*, p. 19.   [7] *Ibid.*, p. 21.   [8] *Ibid.*, p. 30.
[9] *Ibid.*, pp. 31, 32.   [10] *Ibid.*, p. 33.   [11] *Ibid.*, p. 37.

belled more and more against the responsibilities of motherhood. They couldn't do anything about having children, but they did pass a law "providing that children, almost immediately after birth, should be brought up, educated and trained under state direction, to be returned to their parents when fully grown, and ready for their duties as men and women citizens."[12]

The words "home" and "wife" lost all real meaning. "Husband and wife are in reality two men having equal rights, with the same range of occupation, the same duties as citizens to perform, the same dreary leisure."[13] "How can a man get up any very vivid or profound sentiment or affection for these men-women—who are neither mothers nor housekeepers, who differ in no smallest degree from themselves in their pursuits and occupations? Constant and perpetual companionship, from earliest infancy to manhood and old age has resulted in blunting all sense of any real difference between the sexes."[14]

Women have been as successful in foreign affairs as in business. Diplomacy had become a relatively simple and speedy matter. Foreign statesmen were willing "to concede anything rather than to continue negotiations with women diplomatists."[15]

Mrs. Dodd doesn't quibble about the fact that a socialistic society is possible. She is concerned solely with demonstrating that no sensible person would want such a society. She is saying, in effect, that desire is more important than the fulfillment of desire, that working for possessions is more important than getting them. No one enjoyed life in her republic of the future. "To connect the word enjoyment with the aspect of these serious socialists is almost laughable. A more sober collection of people I never beheld." "They have the look of people who have come to the end of things and who have failed to find it amusing. The entire population appears to be eternally in the streets, wandering up and down, with their hands in their pockets, on the lookout for something that never happens. What indeed is there to happen? Have they not come to the consummation of everything, of their dreams and their hopes and desires? A man can't have his dream and dream it too. Realization has been found before now, to be exceedingly dull play."[16] "Ennui is the curse of the land. The

[12] *Ibid.*, p. 39.   [13] *Ibid.*, p. 40.   [14] *Ibid.*, p. 42.
[15] *Ibid.*, p. 44.   [16] *Ibid.*, pp. 22, 23.

arts languish because the arts depend on the imagination, and imagination has been declared illegal since all are not born with it. Your libraries and museums are open, but who sees them filled with readers and students? In other words, man having been born heir to all things has ceased to value them."[17]

The best that can be said for Mrs. Dodd's *Republic of the Future* is that it is amusing. The worst, that she expected her arguments to be taken seriously. She has tried to reduce to absurdity all notions of human equality, but she presupposes that because people have enough to eat and warm clothing and a house, all other desires will disappear. That is as silly as to assume that men and women could become completely sexless. The capitalistic system has many virtues, but it is a little too much to assume that capitalism is the sole explanation of the sexual impulse.

It is interesting to speculate on whether or not Edward Bellamy read Mrs. Dodd's little book. He may very well have done so. If he did, that may be the explanation of his insistence in *Looking Backward* on a system of state honors to take the place of monetary reward. More than any of the other utopian novels, *Looking Backward* is concerned with proving that economic and social equality will increase rather than diminish the number of human interests and enthusiasms.

The Crystal Button was published in 1891, three years after the publication of *Looking Backward*. It had been written earlier, between 1872 and 1878, but Thomas could not satisfy himself that the plot was carefully enough developed. There were too many technical details; there was not enough story. The success of *Looking Backward* convinced the publishers that a utopian novel wouldn't have to depend for success on literary excellence. *The Crystal Button* was revised in an effort to avoid duplication with Bellamy's book. The revision did not make it a good novel. The plot is more perfunctory even than that of *Looking Backward*, but it is a supremely good example of a novel by an engineer. Thomas let his imagination wander freely. Some of his suggestions seem obvious now, but others still seem like good material for an adventure serial.

The plot hinges on an accident which rendered Paul Prognosis, an

[17] *Ibid.*, pp. 84, 85.

engineer, unconscious for many years. His imagination remained active, however, and when he recovered he was able to relate a continuous story about Tone, the remarkable city of the future. Unlike most utopian novelists, Thomas does not moralize about the present. The future will be better, he thinks, simply because engineers will have had time to work out a more practical system.

As far as physical details are concerned, Tone represents a vast change. Buildings were all constructed in pyramid shape. These houses were so arranged that "each terrace was fifteen feet in height and depth, and . . . each dwelling had a frontage upon it of twenty feet. The flooring of each was four feet above the terrace, so that the door was reached by a few steps; and under the main windows of each were low, broad windows serving to light or ventilate the lower or basement room."[18] Glass was used freely. Architects wanted to achieve as large an area as possible "for the play of air and direct sunshine." In other words, the architects of the future were modernists. They were trying to do the same thing that our Frank Lloyd Wrights are trying to do.

Thomas's solution of the traffic problem sounds very much like an idealized version of New York's system. Traffic is run on two levels: local traffic on the street, through traffic in tunnels. The new Queens tunnel proves that the idea works and that people are willing to pay for uncongested traffic lanes. The subways of Tone are more efficient than New York's. The trains are run by compressed air and they never slow down or stop at way stations. Passengers are picked up and let off by a system of tenders. Thomas speaks of airplanes, too, but he was unable to foresee how greatly they would change transportation. Transcontinental traffic is handled by streamlined, light weight trains, which make the trip in twenty-four hours. We may still wonder about his assumption that trains will ever travel two hundred miles an hour, but he was certainly right in predicting that the way to speed up trains was to lighten them.

A great deal of *The Crystal Button* sounds like pages taken from *The Scientific American*. Thomas is full of Yankee ingenuity. Many of his suggestions are as plausible as they are ingenious. His city of

[18] Chauncey Thomas, *The Crystal Button*, Boston, 1891, pp. 79, 80.

Tone gets its power from wind generators which are based on the same principle as those sold by Sears Roebuck and used by farmers in the middle west. He visualizes an elaborate tube-delivery service, much as in *Looking Backward*. He imagines a mild climate in all of the United States, a climate secured by changing the course of the gulf stream. It is a fantastic notion, but it is a notion that continues to fascinate the editors of Sunday supplements. Even more fantastic is his idea of abolishing the alphabet and substituting symbols, "every one of which flashes a well-rounded idea, so that we are now able to present one of the largest histories . . . in a few-score pages."[19]

The new order of intelligent management was brought about through the vision of John Coster, who belived that the abolition of political deceit was the solution of all our ills. He organized a society, with the crystal button as the symbol, a symbol indicating that the wearer had taken an oath to "be true and honest in every act, word, and thought."[20] This is much the same method that is used in the religious novel *In His Steps*, wherein the members of the church group vow to ask themselves, when confronted with a problem, what Jesus would have done. John Coster's society grew and its influence grew. Politics gradually became honest. And once government was honest, the state gradually absorbed the public utilities, transportation facilities, insurance companies and land. There was no revolution, for property holders were dealt with honestly. Property owners were guaranteed interest on their holdings over a period of years. Along with this, the monetary system was inevitably changed. Money was no longer based on gold but rather on "the world's surplus of food products."[21] And with no gold, there was no longer speculation. Some men became rich, but they were not envied, for the money was returned, at death, to the government. Children were able to make their own way.

Gradually the complications of state ownership were eliminated. There was established the "Government of Settled Forms," a perfect system, in which public service was the highest honor. Perfection was attained because "waste, war, idleness, ignorance, and miserliness" were eliminated.

---

[19] *Ibid.*, p. 33.   [20] *Ibid.*, p. 158.   [21] *Ibid.*, p. 267.

The "Government of Settled Forms" is even more absurd than the idea for a new alphabet, but some of the things which he says are essential to a perfect government are far from absurd. He insists on preventive medicine. Consistent with this, he believes in strict laws governing marriage: "No diseased or deformed person who is liable to communicate serious infection of any kind to offspring is ever allowed to marry."[22] Criminals aren't punished; rather, they are hospitalized. Those with a "mental, physical, or moral taint are sterilized." The patent system was abolished. "Its usefulness vanished as soon as the age of science supplemented the age of guesswork and experiment."[23] The government was seriously concerned about soil conservation. An elaborate system of soil control was developed. Soil was even manufactured to insure a general fertility. It was expensive, at first, but not in the long run. Farmers were told what their soil could best grow, what was most needed. As a result, there was no such thing as over-production.

Thomas describes a technocratic, centralized state. Just as Thorstein Veblen does in *The Engineer and the Price System,* he visualizes the possibilities of scientific management. The engineer and the scientist, he understands, could exercise the dominant power in society simply because they control technological development. He is assuming that engineers and scientists could somehow develop enough solidarity and social conscience to realize their power and to use it for the greatest good of the greatest number.

His theory of perfect government is ridiculous. His citizens of Tone would have far too little individual freedom for our taste. His government is a dictatorship, but given honest, enlightened leaders, it is easy to argue that such a system could provide a more efficient government than a democracy.

Thomas absorbed many of the ideas that were popular in the seventies. His notions about government insurance come from the German socialists. He could scarcely have helped hearing a good deal about currency reform. The farmers were demanding a new system; western miners were demanding a new system. Currency reform was regarded as a universal palliative. The same point of view about treat-

[22] *Ibid.,* p. 68.
[23] *Ibid.,* p. 136.

ment of criminals was expressed frequently in contemporary journals. His scientific notions are more surprising, but they are usually rather common ideas given some ingenious twist. These ideas were all in the air. Thomas was aware of the intellectual fever of his generation before most other writers, and he was aware of this fever because he was an engineer turned writer, and not at all an idealist.

CHAPTER NINE

BELLAMY AND HIS CRITICS

EDWARD BELLAMY was an idealist; he had a deep faith in the natural goodness of man. He was not a politician, not an economist; he wanted, simply, to search out the responsibility for an economy which was producing so much poverty and suffering. He felt that man could not be as cruel and unjust as his competitive behavior made him seem, and partly as an intellectual problem, partly as a social problem, he set out to find the answer. The result was *Looking Backward,* a utopian novel which sold a million copies in a few years and which had a tremendous effect on the social thought of the day. Articles on the book filled the contemporary periodicals. It was enthusiastically praised and violently condemned. Serious novels supported his point of view; an equal number of almost more serious novels attacked him. Nationalist Clubs sprang up to preach the gospel which Bellamy had expounded, and for a time they created a great stir. The philosophy of Nationalism was idealistic in the extreme, but, in keeping with the times, Nationalists proposed a positive set of reform measures. They claimed a membership, in their clubs, of nearly a million, and threatened to form another third party movement. Had it not been for the immediate necessity of voting with the stronger party of opposition, they would have done so. After 1896, reform sentiment having been thoroughly depressed, and the reforms modified and adopted by the major parties, the movement gradually disappeared.

Bellamy was tremendously surprised to find that *Looking Backward* had made him a prophet of the masses. He thought of his work as being completely an intellectual protest. Despite the momentary success of the Nationalist movement, his work is not important as a political document, for it was not the embattled farmers or laborers who read it. The book appealed to the middle class, who are usually the last to realize the need for an alteration of the existing economic scheme. It served as a mirror for intellectual reactions already sowed by the widespread feeling of discontent.

Bellamy's early life was placid. He attended the village schools of Chicopee Falls, Massachusetts, where his father had long held a pastorate, and then spent two years at Union College. At the age of eighteen he had a year of travel and study abroad, spending most of the time in Germany. Speaking of this year he later wrote:

I well remember in those days of European travel how much more deeply that black background of misery impressed me than the palaces and cathedrals in relief against it. It was in the great cities of Europe and among the hovels of the peasantry that my eyes were first fully opened to the extent and consequences of "man's inhumanity to man."[1]

Bellamy seems to have heard nothing about Marx or the German socialists in this year. After the publication of *Looking Backward*, Bellamy wrote to Howells:

I have never been in any sense a student of socialistic literature, or have known more of the various socialist schemes than any newspaper reader might.[2]

On his return to this country he was admitted to the bar, but he never practiced. He worked, instead, as a journalist—first, for the *Springfield Union* and then for the *New York Evening Post*. In 1880 he and his brother founded the *Springfield Daily News*, which he edited until after the publication of *Looking Backward*, when Nationalist activity absorbed him.

Bellamy's, *The Duke of Stockbridge*, a romance of Shays's rebellion, is indicative of his sympathies. It is not a very good novel, but his analysis of the sources of economic discontent following the Revolution is exact and penetrating. The hero of the story, Perez Hamlin, returns from his service in the Continental army to find his brother in jail for debt, and his family and townspeople virtually the slaves of the landed gentry. Replying to a query as to whether he knew that some of the negroes had been set free, Perez exclaims bitterly:

Yes, I heard of that when I was away, but I didn't know the reason why they'd set them free till I got home. I see they've made slaves of the poor

[1] Edward Bellamy, *Equality*, Edition of 1934. Quoted in the Preface, p. iv.
[2] Morgan, *op. cit.*, p. 372.

folks, and don't need the niggers any more. . . . I find pretty nearly every rich man has a gang of debtors working for him, trying to work out their debts.[3]

The increasing despair and bitterness of the farmers is nicely contrasted with the disdain of their betters. The Parson seeks to quiet the people by suggesting that perhaps "these present calamities are God's judgment upon this people for its sins, seeing it is well known that the bloody and cruel war, now over, had brought in upon us all manner of new and strange sins, even as if God would have us advertized how easily that liberty which we have gained may run into licentiousness."[4] One of the Tory gentlemen in the novel declares:

That is the trouble nowadays . . . these numskulls must needs have matters of government explained to them, and pass their own judgment on public affairs. And when they cannot understand them, then, forsooth, comes a rebellion. I think none can deny seeing in these late troubles the first fruits of those pestilent notions of equality, whereof we heard so much from certain quarters, during the late war of independence. I would that Mr. Jefferson and some of the other writers of disturbing democratic rhetoric might have been here in the State the past winter, to see the outcome of their preaching.[5]

The Duke of Stockbridge has a bitter tone. There is not even a pleasant ending to take away the sting. The novel is important as a precursor of *Looking Backward,* and as one of the first American novels to deal realistically with American material.

Bellamy was a literary dabbler, and he spent a great deal of time experimenting with Hawthornesque fantasies. *Dr. Heidenhoff's Progress* is concerned with the possibility of forgetting some great sin and returning to normal life. It is a fantastic story, based on what seems today completely unreasonable psychological evidence. Even less interesting is his psychic effort, *Miss Ludington's Sister: A Romance of Immortality.* Both enjoyed an astonishing popularity, and in England Bellamy was hailed as "the lineal descendant of Hawthorne." At the time of his death it was prophesied that these would be the works for which he would be remembered, and that his social studies would soon be forgotten.

---

[3] Edward Bellamy, *The Duke of Stockbridge,* New York and Boston, 1900, p. 77. First published serially in 1879.

[4] *Ibid.,* p. 46.

[5] *Ibid.,* p. 349.

His abrupt change in subject matter from psychological studies to the economic analysis of *Looking Backward* can best be explained by a growing awareness of the political struggle which was taking shape in the country. He has this to say about the inspiration for *Looking Backward:*

According to my best recollection, it was in the fall or winter of 1886 that I sat down to my desk with the definite purpose of trying to reason out a method of economic organization by which the republic might guarantee the livelihood and material welfare of its citizens on a basis of equality corresponding to and supplementing their political equality.[6]

But regardless of what he says himself, the inspiration for *Looking Backward* did not come just from within himself. The whole of the nineteenth century was a period of utopian activity. In the period before the Civil War there had been literally hundreds of attempts to establish practical, working communities. "Communistic communities were founded in this country by Germans, Frenchmen, Englishmen, Austrians, Poles, and Russians, and a few even by Americans."[7] After the War, with the spread of railroads and the rise in land values, the organization of such communities became increasingly difficult. But even so, no intelligent human could have matured in the post Civil War period without some realization of the scope of these activities. In addition, Bellamy must have acquired some notions of utopianism from his days in Germany. And there had been several utopian novels published in America just preceding *Looking Backward,* novels which are remarkably similar in plot to Bellamy's.

It is not necessary to assume that Bellamy was a plagiarist. Most of the similarities are in the utopian tradition. There are only so many ways to set the stage for such a novel: One can establish his society in the past or in the future, below the earth or in the sky, or one can place it in the present by imagining some undiscovered land. Bellamy and Macnie both use the simplest and most credible technique. There are various ways to project the future: Mrs. Griffith has her hero come to life after being preserved by quick freezing; Chauncey Thomas gives his hero the ability to dream the future; Mrs. Dodd doesn't bother with difficulties of plot—she simply imagines a state

---

[6] *Equality,* p. iv.
[7] Frederick B. Adams, Jr., *Radical Literature in America,* Stamford, 1939, p. 7.

in the new world which has remained similar to our own, and, by comparison, points out the absurdities of the socialistic monster; both Bellamy and Macnie use the obvious device of hypnotism, obvious because hypnotism had became a fad in the eighties, and because people assumed that it had remarkable properties.

Looking Backward, 2000-1887, tells the story of Julian West, a young and wealthy Bostonian, who sleeps, hidden away from the world, for 113 years, and awakes still young and vigorous. West's amazement at the simplicity, efficiency and justice of the new system is so great that its workings have to be explained to him in great detail. It is this enumeration and discussion of the virtues of the new order, in contrast to the old, which constitutes the greater part of the volume. Bellamy was particularly proud of the psychology with which he handled Julian West's reaction to the new world. It is all managed ingeniously, but the characters have no personality; they are only puppets marched around in formation so that the scenery may be seen in perspective.

To illustrate the virtues of his ideal republic, Bellamy emphasizes the absurdity of the economic system of 1887. The parable of the stage coach is well known:

By way of attempting to give the reader some general impression of the way people lived . . . I cannot do better than compare society . . . to a prodigious coach which the masses of humanity were harnessed to and dragged toilsomely along a very hilly and sandy road. The driver was hungry, and permitted no lagging. . . . Despite the difficulty of drawing the coach at all along so hard a road, the top was covered with passengers who never got down, even at the steepest ascents. These seats on top were very breezy and comfortable. Well up out of the dust, their occupants could enjoy the scenery at their leisure, or critically discuss the merits of the straining team. Naturally such places were in great demand and the competition for them was keen, every one seeking as the first end in life to secure a seat on the coach for himself and to leave it to his child after him. . . .

I am well aware that this will appear to the men of the twentieth century an incredible inhumanity; but there are two facts, both very curious, which partly explain it. In the first place, it was firmly believed that there was no other way in which Society could get along, except the many pulled at the rope and the few rode; and not only this, but that no very radical improvement even was possible either in the harness, the coach, the roadway, or the distribution of the toil. . . . It had always been so. It was a pity, but it could not be helped, and philosophy forbade wasting compassion on what was beyond remedy.[8]

The key to the great and efficient United States of the year 2000 is the distribution of wealth and labor. The country had become completely socialized. Dr. Leete, Julian West's host, explains all the details of the new order in contrast to the old, but he is extremely vague in recounting the transitional stages from private capitalism. He is content to explain that the gradual revolution was simply the result of education. There was no violence, for people had so long been accustomed to vast corporations that the final merger was accomplished without trouble. With this assumption by the government of all utilities, of all production and service organizations, citizens automatically became government employees, to be distributed according to the needs of labor.

The perfectability of this new system which Bellamy outlines is the perfectability of the machine. The machine is pictured as the salvation of man and not as the force of destruction which Samuel Butler and Mrs. Dodd picture. The paternalism of the state is all inclusive, but it is a paternalism based on a universal salary of four thousand dollars a year, paid to the individual because of his needs as a man and not because of his capacity as a worker. Positions are determined by capacity, and since the monetary rewards are the same, hours and conditions of work are relative.

The labor army is modeled on army standards, but love of duty had become such a powerful force that men put their best energies into their work simply because it is for the common good.

Education, as much as work, is considered a state duty. After completing the equivalent of a college course, young women as well as young men enroll for a period of three years in the unclassified, rough labor army. After this period they are given every opportunity to transfer to the particular branch of trade or profession they prefer. And if gifted in any way they are given until the age of thirty to train themselves. Up to the age of forty-five men and women must serve the state. After that there is retirement on full pay, with the opportunity of living a life of leisure.

[8] Edward Bellamy, *Looking Backward, 2000-1887*, pp. 10, 12, 13. Page references are to Houghton Mifflin's Riverside Library edition, 1926.

Production and distribution are divided into ten departments, each a special industrial group. Each division estimates the year's demand upon its particular goods and services, and working on such estimates the labor supply is divided. "After the necessary contingents have been detailed for the various industries, the amount of labor left for other employment is expended in creating fixed capital, such as building, machinery, engineering works, and so forth."[9] Production automatically follows consumer demand. Any article is manufactured upon demand, and the price is determined solely by the cost of production.

The problem of distribution is solved by great sample stores where there is no selling, but only ordering from samples. The quality of every product is stated definitely, for unless there is demand, production is curtailed. Advertising has become a thing of the past. Meals, like goods, are prepared at central agencies. Each family has its own dining room, but the food is served and prepared in quantity by details of the labor army.

The system is perfect in mechanical provisions. Intellectually, socially, and physically, the system is minutely regulated. There are various allowances for the expression of individual views in newspapers and books, but the regimentation of the state is complete. There is need for safety valves which are not provided. In this respect *Looking Backward* suffers from the same inherent mistakes as all utopias. It assumes a perfectability in man. It assumes a race who could control and minister to a machine civilization, who could remain peaceable and contented with prosperity. Bellamy would not admit the extent of human failing, but that is why *Looking Backward* is an important book. The book is the result of honest idealism. Bellamy wanted everyone to be motivated by middle-class virtues. He wanted people to live simple, honest lives. He wanted public morality to be based on the same code as private morality. He wanted to do away with the artificiality and repression in human life. And the means was economic and social equality. It is futile to enumerate the fallacies inherent in his vision. The important thing is the effect that vision had on Bellamy's contemporaries.

Looking Backward was the immediate stimulus which led to the

[9] *Ibid.*, p. 183.

formation of the vast number of Nationalist Clubs. Bellamy was soon
drawn into active participation. As he became more and more involved in Nationalism, his attitude toward the reforms he had proposed changed, and he asserted positively that Nationalism was not
just a theory "dealing with the ultimate possibilities of human development," but rather "a proposition tending to immediate action or
practical results."[10] In an article entitled "The First Steps Towards
Nationalism," appearing in the *Forum* of October, 1890, Bellamy
explained in some detail the aspirations of the movement. "Stated in
general terms, the policy proposed by Nationalists is the successive
nationalizing or municipalizing of public services and branches of
industry, and the simultaneous organization of the employees upon a
basis of guaranteed rights, as branches of the civil service of the
country; this process being continued until the entire transformation
shall have been effected."[11] If these suggested reforms could be carried out, and Bellamy insists they are practical, there would be a
slow but definite approach to the ideal state of *Looking Backward*.
In other words, Nationalist reforms would be the means of transition
to the new order.

The first step in the program would be the nationalizing of telephone and telegraph facilities. Post Office duties would be extended
to include these functions as well as parcel post service. All communi-
cation services were essentially a government function, it was felt,
for there were so many possibilities of abuse by private corporations.
Nationalists as well as Populists and other reformers insisted upon
the necessity of railway reform. As spokesman for the group Bellamy
decried "the demoralizing effect upon our politics of the vast money
power of the railroad and of its unprincipled use to control legislation."[12] "Nationalists," he wrote, "are in complete agreement as to
the desirability of an immediate national assumption of control over
the railroads of the country."[13] He explains succinctly the other essential parts of the program.

Nationalists propose immediate legislation looking toward government
control of the coal mines of the country.[14]

[10] *Forum*, 10:174.   [11] *Idem.*   [12] *Ibid.*, p. 176.
[13] *Idem.*   [14] *Ibid.*, p. 180.

Nationalists everywhere are agitating in favor of the assumption and conduct by municipalities of local public services, such as transit, lighting, heating and water supply, which are now rendered by corporations; and they vehemently oppose the granting of any further franchises for such purposes.[15]

Nationalists advocate laws in every state making obligatory the education of children during the whole school year, up to seventeen years, forbidding their employment during the whole school year, and providing for the assistance, from public funds, of children whose parents are unable to support them during school attendance.[16]

When the businesses described shall have been nationalized or municipalized, there will be a body of nearly two million workers in the public service. Here will be consumers enough to support the beginnings of national productive industries, both manufacturing and agricultural, together with a system of distribution, for the exclusive supply of those in the public service.[17]

These were not revolutionary measures, he was sure, for there would be no hasty or ill-considered action, "no letting go of the old before securing a hold on the new. . . ."[18] Once such a program was adopted there would be a gradual and orderly progress toward the ideal society.

THE CRITICS

Looking Backward has been widely translated; there are editions in German, Polish, Russian, Dutch, and French, and, probably, in many other languages. Bellamy's audience kept increasing until the first World War, and the novel still sells five thousand copies a year in the United States. The volumes written in answer to Bellamy are a good indication of the extent of this increasing popularity. There would have been few attempts to answer him if he hadn't been considered dangerous. There were full length, satiric sequels in 1890, 1891, 1893, and 1896, in addition to some vitriolic attempts to prove that Bellamy was both fool and plagiarist. These volumes are well worth considering in detail, for they are interesting both as criticisms of Bellamy and as indications of the changing attitude to reform of the right wing.

Looking Within, 1893, by J. W. Roberts, is at once a satiric re-

Ibid., p. 181. [16] *Ibid.*, p. 182. [17] *Ibid.*, p. 183. [18] *Idem.*

interpretation of Bellamy's world and an attempt to reconstruct another ideal world on the basis of Bellamy's mistakes. Roberts was dismayed at the uncritical enthusiasm with which people were praising the Nationalist proposals. He explains his purpose in the preface:

The object of this work is . . . to warn fellow citizens of the danger that threatens them from the alluring delusion, which . . . is leading them along the slippery path of ruin, and prevent any such catastrophe ever overtaking our beloved country in the future.

Like most of Bellamy's critics he over-emphasizes Bellamy's influence:

"Looking Backward" has been the bane of this nation. It breeds a notion in the minds of thousands that somehow the government will be compelled by agitation to do for them what God, nature, and society demand they shall do for themselves. Its Utopian notions have taken root in many minds. Multitudes who never saw the book have received its teachings second-hand, and been poisoned by them.[19]

The story begins with the hero's education in the eighties and nineties. Always in this process of educating himself he is concerned with finding the proper relationship between farmer, laborer and capitalist. He finds no solution, but he is convinced that farmers and laborers demand everything and give nothing. "Every worthless, lazy, trifling pest wants the government to lift him into opulence. The wildest schemes are to be fathered by the government."[20] "If the republic is ever destroyed, it will be overthrown by the agitators who corruptly use labor as a cloak to cover their aims."[21]

Finally, the factory of his fiancée's father is burned by an agitator, simply because higher wages had been refused—at a time when there was no operating profit, and when the factory was kept open only to avoid putting men out of work. His fiancée must help her father. They cannot get married as they had planned. In desperation and disgust he swallows a potion which puts him to sleep for thirty-five years. He awakes in 1927, to find his girl beside him, and the country shaken by a violent struggle between capital and labor, or, as he puts it, between the anarchists, the discontented, and established authority. He and his fiancée decide against the world of 1927, and

[19] J. W. Roberts, *Looking Within, The Misleading Tendencies of "Looking Backward" Made Manifest,* New York, 1893, p. 64.
[20] *Ibid.,* p. 63.   [21] *Ibid.,* p. 62.

put themselves to sleep for a still longer period. This time they awake in the year 2000, and find that the world outlined by Bellamy has actually come to pass. They meet Julian West, Dr. Leete and Miss Leete, but they are not taken in by their blithe assumption that everything is for the best. They see the apathy with which people perform their daily tasks, the enthusiasm with which they turn to such diversions as drinking and gambling. One man may be conscientious, but most are slipshod. There is no need to hurry. The reward is the same. There is no incentive to excel in any way. Everything is at a dead level. "Such a system excludes emulation, shuts out ambition, abolishes hope of preferment or distinction." " 'Liberty, Equality, Fraternity' is the motto, and the effect is to make it a reality. That it fails in every way and at every point, except where the government dispenses to the people, is evident."[22] "The indolent, slothful, and careless fared as well as the most punctual and painstaking. This is, practically, offering a premium for laziness. The conscientious toiler gets nothing for his faithfulness; the sloth loses nothing by his delinquencies."[23]

The whole system gradually deteriorated. There were too few farmers: too many men discovered how easy, comparatively, was life in the city. There was, finally, not enough farm produce to go around. Choice of occupation was abolished, and hours of labor were extended. Energy filled men again; they worked with enthusiasm. Once the need was filled, however, men slipped back into their old, slothful ways.

Our hero decides that there can be no satisfaction in living in such a world. He reflects on the lessons of the system:

We have learned some things that ought to do us good. Among others we may name these: Paternalism does not promote industry. It does not promote morality. It is no aid to intellectual development. Its influence is paralyzing in all directions. It kills and does not make alive. It blights and never beautifies. It blotches and never adorns. It degrades labor. It debases manhood. It ends progress. It stifles enterprise. It destroys commerce. It estranges our people and makes aliens of brethren. It breeds discontent. ... It blots out all enthusiasm. It checks right-directed ambition. It develops a race of drones. It crystalizes injustice and inequality. It handicaps genius. It buries talent. It wastes energy. It despoils humanity. It produces no great men. It throttles improvement. Its unemployed time is devoted to evil

<hr>

[22] *Ibid.*, p. 169.   [23] *Ibid.*, p. 211.

rather than good. It is the promoter of material death. It is political malaria.[24]

They decide that it is time for another potion. This time they sleep for twenty-five years. Conditions are worse than ever. The country was just beginning to realize that the latest experiment in equality wasn't a success. Bodies and faces had been molded to a set pattern so that everyone looked alike—in addition to dressing alike, living in the same kind of houses, and working the same number of hours. They had secured equality, but the system was not widely approved. The women were particularly unhappy. They suspected the worst of their husbands, and they had reason to, for it was quite simple, in a crowd, for a man to go home with the wrong wife.

A governmental decree proclaimed the failure of the whole utopian experiment:

We have known for years that the present system of government is a failure. Any system which removes personal interest in what one does, or personal responsibility for the manner of doing it, and for actions in general, from the individual to a central power, must fail.[25]

Having no personal interest in and no acquaintance with each other, our people are fast losing the sense of nationality and the patriotic love of country as a whole so essential to stability and prosperity.[26]

There was no chance for any improvement without a fundamental change, and because men and women realized that they wanted to eat, they decided, enthusiastically, to return to the old constitution of the nineteenth century, only with certain modifications. First, the ownership of land should be restricted to twenty acres per family. Second, there should be a progressive income tax, beginning at one thousand dollars and working up so that at fifty thousand the state would take fifty per cent. Third, no man with a large income should be allowed to hold a responsible office. Fourth, parasitic idlers would not be tolerated.

The return to a modified capitalistic state worked. The people were happy again. They went to work with a new enthusiasm. "Torpor was turned into activity, indifference into energy. New life was infused into every department of industry. Business proper was

---

[24] *Ibid.*, pp. 232, 233.   [25] *Ibid.*, p. 265.   [26] *Ibid.*, p. 267.

born again."[27] Our hero and his girl are finally satisfied. They decide that this is a society in which they can live out their days in contentment.

Looking Within says all the usual things, but parts of the book are ingenious, particularly the idea of molding bodies to guarantee equality. For the rest, it is surprising how close in spirit are the reforms, designed to return the system to the nineteenth century order, to the programs of the Nationalists and the Populists of the same decade. Roberts was an idealist posing as a pragmatist, and he certainly was more radical than he knew.

Looking Further Backward, 1890, by Arthur D. Vinton, is an attempt to point out the weakness of Nationalism, to insist upon a more Machiavellian philosophy of history. Vinton is quick to acknowledge that the problems of the day are acute. And it is only, he says, because Bellamy in *Looking Backward*, and Laurence Gronlund in *The Cooperative Commonwealth* have dared to face these problems that their books have received so much attention. "The benefit which their books have done is very great; but the utopian schemes which they recommend as remedies for the evils which exist today are fraught with danger."[28]

This is the story of how Nationalism declined and was overthrown, taken from Julian West's diary. According to his analysis, there were two fundamental flaws in the system: There was no secrecy, even in matters of public interest, and the state had no way to defend itself. The state had failed even "to maintain a standing army large enough to enforce order, or to do police duty in times of local rebellion or disturbance." Professor West wrote in his diary:

We knew of course that the whole tendency of nationalism was to wipe out individualism and to train the individual to rely in all matters upon his rulers; but we had not expected that this loss of individualism would be so complete as to prevent our declaration of war from being considered as a matter of personal moment to each individual.[29]

War had come to Nationalist America because she was weak and because China was strong. The Chinese simply transported troops to

---

[27] *Ibid.*, p. 273.
[28] Arthur Dudley Vinton, *Looking Further Backward*, Albany, 1890, p. 6.
[29] *Ibid.*, p. 28.

our shores and the coastal cities surrendered with little more than a protest. No one had any initiative. Men didn't know how to think for themselves. Railroad officials kept sending war material to the enemy because no one had remembered to countermand an order. Without leaders the Nationalists were powerless. And there were no leaders: "Under Nationalism men had become mere routinists— theorists following a beaten track and blind to all things outside of it. Individual responsibility had received its death stroke when the rewards of individual initiative and execution had become equalized."[30]

The whole financial structure of the state collapsed. Local officials didn't know what to do, and the invaders did. They came prepared with their own paper money, in the best modern tradition. The country is taken over gradually; the invader leaves things much as they are, except that he ships many of the inhabitants to other parts of the world, so that there will be room for more Chinese.

At the time of the story, some parts of the Middle West were still unconquered, but it was just a matter of time. The invaders were consolidating the economics of each section they conquered. Julian West had been killed in battle, and a Chinese professor was using West's notes to drive home to his students the necessity of a Machiavellian rather than an idealistic government.

In spite of the fact that this is aimed at Bellamy, the real argument has to do with the folly of allowing Orientals to settle on the Pacific Coast. Vinton was not alone in his fear of the Orientals. Between 1880 and 1900 there were a number of other books saying much the same thing. A good example is Pierton W. Dooner's *Last Days of the Republic,* a bitter demand for a stronger army and for harsher treatment of the Orientals. Bellamy, however, did supply the framework of the story, and the reason is that Bellamy's popularity would guarantee Vinton an audience.

Mr. East's Experiences in Mr. Bellamy's World, 1891, is the most rational of the satires aimed at *Looking Backward.* Conrad Wilbrandt approaches the problem with typical German thoroughness, and attempts to demonstrate the superficiality with which Bellamy has outlined his new world order. The basis of his attack is illustrated by the following quotation:

[30] *Ibid.,* p. 97.

Socialism has a provision for everything. It conquers obstacles by simply pushing them aside. I believe, had social democrats lived before the discovery of navigation, they would have thought of draining the ocean before building ships. If house-keeping and rearing children are an obstacle to the equalization of the sexes, they abolish the duties of the housekeeper and the Mother. Family life is to be transferred to dining rooms and restaurants, and children are to be educated in government institutions.[31]

According to the fiction, the world of 2001 is organized as Bellamy pictures it, with the same institutions and the same people. But the world is examined through the eyes of a critic less credulous than Julian West. Freidrich Ost, the hero who is transplanted from the Germany of 1890, is a dabbler in Eastern mysteries. He becomes so interested in an East Indian's claims about suspended animation that he offers himself as a guinea pig. He is buried in a zinc box, and is supposed to be dug up in a month. Something goes wrong, however, and he eventually recovers in Bellamy's world.

Before the experiment, he had been vastly interested in Bellamy's program of reformation; and in spite of his skepticism he had great hopes for a new era. He rapidly becomes disillusioned. Dr. Leete, he learns, is not a reliable critic; in fact, he is such a complete idealist that no one takes him seriously. There is no general prosperity. Theft is common, especially at the end of the year when credit cards are running out. There is a constant temptation to be rashly extravagant, so that at the end of the year there is nothing to do but steal or go hungry. Eight hours of labor a day is compulsory. There is only slight choice as to jobs, for no one wants the unpleasant tasks. And there is no retirement at an early age. Labor service had been extended to the age of sixty-five—otherwise there would not have been enough workers. "Now, working men have not only made improvement in their condition impossible, but they have rendered their position worse in the exact proportion that the dimunition of socialistic production, the mistakes of the government, the lessening of the stimulus to labor, the deterioration of good—apart from all perils to society—restricted the number of their pleasures. And all this was purchased at the cost of personal liberty. Man in the Socialist State

---

[31] Conrad Wilbrandt, *Mr. East's Experiences in Mr. Bellamy's World.* . . . Translated from the German by Mary J. Safford. New York, 1891, p. 148.

has become a slave. Though society alone is ruler he is still a slave because he has no free will, free decision, free movement."[32]

People are largely discontented. There is nothing to look forward to. Everywhere are "the plainest signs that people had remained unaltered. It possessed all the qualities needed for an imperfect world, nothing which suited a Utopia."[33]

Even the simplest pleasures are difficult to obtain. There are no good wines or good cigars. And home life is non-existent. Men and women eat at central kitchens and the children are turned over to the state at the age of six—simply because it is cheaper for the state to raise them than to give an adequate credit card allowance to the parents.

All of the world, except for Central Asia, goes over to the new system, and Central Asia capitalizes on the benevolence of the system. She purchases vast quantities of manufactured goods from Germany, builds up her reserves of commodities, and then finally declares war on the socialized world. The socialist government collapses; Ost is swallowed up by the war and Wilbrandt is able to end his novel without tieing together the threads of romance which he had spun.

Wilbrandt says no more than countless other critics, but his work takes on added interest because he is a German. Here is evidence that *Looking Backward* was taken seriously abroad as well as at home. The novel is ingenious, but the arguments are commonplace. He produces all the conventiontal arguments against socialism: that the supply of labor would be inadequate, that the system of distribution and supply would break down, and that there were no adequate rewards for genius. All of these objections are pretty well answered in Bellamy's second book, *Equality,* or at least they are answered as well as they can be, theoretically.

Looking Further Forward, by Richard Michaelis, is supposed to be a continuation of Julian West's story, but a continuation written after he realized that Dr. Leete's account of life in the new world was completely dishonest. As the story opens, Julian West has just been appointed Professor of History at Shawmut College. His first lecture, which he has worked out carefully, is barely tolerated by the stu-

[32] *Ibid.,* p. 188.   [33] *Ibid.,* p. 184.

dents. He can't understand why they should treat him with such disdain; he had been led to believe that his lectures would be received enthusiastically. As he is leaving the lecture room, very much puzzled, he meets the janitor, Mr. Forrest, his predecessor as Professor of Nineteenth Century History. He discovers that Mr. Forrest had been demoted because he had been foolish enough to admit that he did not think that the new era was perfect. In fact, he thought that the nineteenth century's competitive system was far better. He explains his point of view to Julian West:

> We are not getting along in good style. We are not enjoying an unprecedented prosperity. . . . And so far as the annihilation of poverty is concerned, it amounts practically to nothing but the enrichment of the awkward, stupid, and lazy people, with the proceeds of the work of the clever and industrious women and men.[34]

Mr. Forrest assures Julian West that it is not stupidity which has left him so ignorant, but, rather, effective propaganda. The figures which Julian had studied were not accurate, for the sole purpose of the bookkeepers was to confuse the public. Washington, he says, is making corruption a fine art. "The lobby in the halls of Congress in your days is described as a bad crowd, but to compare it with the hustlers of our days, would be like comparing a Sunday school with pandemonium."[35]

The competitive system was bad in many ways, Mr. Forrest admits, but the individual always had some hope of bettering his lot. Now, he says, there is not even hope. Congress has little power. All real authority is vested in the hands of the President and the chiefs of the administrative bureaus. Men cannot rise in the government simply on the basis of ability. Favoritism and self-interest determine all matters of policy, and there is no appeal, for all protests are handled by judges who are themselves administrative appointees.

Dr. Leete's laboratory is cited as an instance of favoritism. He would never have been able to build a laboratory out of his credit card savings, for, after all, says Mr. Forrest, the average income is only $204.00 a year. The reason for such a low income level is the

[34] Richard Michaelis, *A Sequel to Looking Backward, or "Looking Further Forward,"* London. ca. 1890, p. 34.
[35] *Ibid.*, p. 52.

tremendous amount of wasted energy. The labor army was used more efficiently in 1880, despite the tremendous waste, than in the new society. And despite the waste of the competitive system, it provided some incentive for efficient production. There was not the constant slowing down of production that the new system seemed to enforce.

If only the statesmen of the nineteenth century had not junked their whole system, and had been content with moderate reforms, then, says Mr. Forrest, the United States would never have been faced with such a hopeless future. If only in the 1890's the reformers could have secured an accurate bureau of statistics to determine what was happening in economic matters; if only farm holdings had been limited, say to forty acres; if only the government had nationalized forest lands and mining properties; if only the government had nationalized public utilities, and particularly the railroad and tele-graph companies; and if only there had been a heavy inheritance tax to prevent the acquisition of huge fortunes—then discontent would have disappeared, and prosperity would have been a reality rather than a dream.

Julian West finally realizes that he has been duped, that the new world is not utopia. The final blow is his discovery that "marriage will be abolished, together with religion and all personal property; free love will be proclaimed and we will live together like a flock of rabbits."[36] He becomes a propagandist for a new order. *Looking Further Forward* is supposed to be the first effective blow for another new era. A hurriedly written and badly developed novel, it is never-theless an effective reply to Bellamy's idealism.

George Sanders is the most vitriolic of the Bellamy haters; he cares little how he tars Bellamy, provided only that the brush be full and black. Bellamy is a dreamer, and a dangerous one, he is a Socialist, and his plan is "the most anarchistical, world wide scheme of plunder ever suggested to the bewildered gaze of the people."[37] In fact, Bellamy's proposals are essentially sacrilegious, for any religious man would know that if God had intended man to live in the world of *Equality,* he would not have given him initiative and will power.

[36] *Ibid.,* p. 69.
[37] George A. Sanders, *Reality, or Law and Order vs. Anarchy and Socialism,* Cleveland, 1898, p. 210.

Sanders discloses his own political philosophy in every paragraph, but nowhere more clearly than when he explains that the trouble with democracy is stupid citizens and "that the elective franchise should have been limited by an educational and property qualification at least."[38] In other words, Sanders is a McKinley Republican, and Bellamy's work had aroused his indignation.

Bellamy, he charged, was so blind that he could not realize that "our people are the freest, most contented, and prosperous people on the face of the earth. They live contentedly in the sunshine; most of them have peaceful, happy homes and fully believe 'God's in his heaven, all's well with the world.' Most of them believe in the reply of old Dr. Lyman Beecher, who when asked how he was getting along in his old age said, 'Oh, I am doing a thousand times better than I used to, because I have made up my mind to let God manage his own universe.' "[39] To Sanders that was irrefutable logic. God has ordained that there should be private property, and therefore we must recognize it. (He forgets that Bellamy also acknowledges property rights.) To clinch his argument he explains that even pagans and savages recognize private property—which is by way of saying that if God and pagans agree, there can be no chance of error.

The poor have always existed and always will. Bellamy's dreams can change nothing. Even "if all wealth were equally distributed among the population today, tomorrow it would be found in practically the same hands it had been in before the distribution."[40]

Bellamy's schemes "offer neither temporary nor permanent relief for the poor and the laborers." He seeks "by every possible theory, argument, insinuation, ridicule, sarcasm, and the denial of statistics and indisputable facts to belittle all race progress; all civilization, and those who have perfected it; all principles and policies by which it has been obtained—and all because it has not been achieved through his theory of economic equality. . . . The spirit of the argument is one of hatred and uncompromising hostility towards capital, and all who labor for it, or possess it. It is an utter refusal to acknowledge it as anything else but an evil. . . ."[41]

There are, he admits, certain abuses fixed in the capitalistic system,

---

[38] *Ibid.*, p. 162.   [39] *Ibid.*, p. 69.   [40] *Ibid.*, p. 79.   [41] *Ibid.*, p. 21.

but "it may be reasonably expected that the advancement of the race . . . will soon check and forever wipe out any injustice that is now apparent."[42] It may even be that Bellamy's "views of perfected love will be reached and greatly surpassed in the next one hundred years; but along the lines of thought and action, science and love, now in full operation among the races of men."[43]

Bellamy, the idealist, who dreams of a perfect love was as respectable as Bellamy, the reformer, was dangerous. Sanders respects wistful idealists. He is pleased that there are "so many altruistic and purely benevolent organizations, supported by inspired, consecrated leaders, self-denying workers" concerned with "the uplifting of the poor and toiling masses . . . , the beautifying of home life, and the banishment of the dark shadows."[44] In other words, God is good, capitalism is good, the world is good—and everything is going to be better. The only rational course for the rational man is to believe in the American system, respect his betters, and remember that God is directing his destinies. Sanders prided himself on being a rational man.

Mrs. John B. Shipley's *The True Author of Looking Backward,* 1890, is largely nonsense. Mrs. Shipley was annoyed at Bellamy's reputation as the prophet of a new age. And she was annoyed because she thought that Bellamy was no better than a plagiarist, that he got most of his ideas from August Bebel's *Die Frau und der Sozialismus,* 1883, ideas which, she insists, are much more honestly treated in the original. Bellamy could not appreciate all of Bebel, she says, because he was not an economist, and because he was too good a Christian to be honest about Christianity. In spite of all the similarities between Bebel's work and Bellamy's, Mrs. Shipley has no justification for declaring that Bellamy was a plagiarist. It should be obvious that the two of them must have had many ideas in common. Bebel's volume is direct socialist propaganda. He is primarily concerned with demonstrating that the inequality of the sexes is a result of the capitalistic order. Along with this, he insists upon the stupidity of our system of distribution, and recommends, among other things, the efficiency of the centralized kitchen. And he explains that in a socialized state

[42] *Ibid.,* p. 67.   [43] *Ibid.,* p. 22.   [44] *Ibid.,* p. 114.

the first duty of the citizen must be to perform faithfully his own tasks. Bellamy had similar ideas, but what of it? Bebel's notions are good socialist doctrine, but he was only one of a number of nineteenth century socialists who believed in much the same sort of thing. He preceded Bellamy, but so did many other literate socialists. In other words, these ideas, whose similarity enraged Mrs. Shipley, were no more original with Bebel than they were with Bellamy. They were simply in the air; they were part of the intellectual ferment of the day; their source lies far back in Anglo-Saxon intellectual history. Bellamy may conceivably have read *Die Frau,* but if he did, it was only one of a number of volumes which stimulated his thinking. Bebel's position as leader of the German Socialist party would not necessarily have made his work known to Bellamy.

The True Author of Looking Backward is interesting only as an indication of the extent to which Bellamy was being read. Even cranks have no interest in sources until a book becomes famous.

THE ADMIRERS

Some of Bellamy's critics go off the deep end, but by contrast with Bellamy's too enthusiastic admirers, they are hard-headed, Machiavellian realists.

Perhaps the least effective of all the enthusiasts is Mrs. C. H. Stone. Her volume, *One of "Berrian's" Novels,* 1890, is an attempt to answer those who insist that life in utopia would be extremely dull. She hopes to convince of the fallacy of their reasoning those "who believe 'competition' to be the only incentive to progress."[45] In her story she attempts to indicate some of the motives that may animate a future society. She explains her point of view in the preface:

It is quite the fashion to insist that such [utopian] conditions [as described in *Looking Backward*] would necessitate "great monotony of character and incident, and a lack of all incentive to action" when really they would indicate just the opposite. In the first place such a state of society as Mr. Bellamy portrays would never be achieved without such strength of character as would of itself make monotony impossible; and though life will always contain all the grades of human nature that exist now, there will be also evolved a much higher grade that will make even this great change described in *Looking Backward* possible.[46]

[45] Mrs. C. H. Stone, *One of "Berrian's" Novels,* New York, 1890, Dedication.
[46] *Ibid.,* the Nineteenth Century Preface.

The novel itself pretends to be the work of Berrian, the most famous of the novelists of the year 2000. The story deals with the revolution of 1997, the last of the attempts to throw off the benevolent yoke of the new society. Casca, the villain, is still possessed of a primitive desire for personal freedom. He believes in the sanctity of the individual. He is an outright materialist. The point of the story is the necessity of emphasizing spiritual values as opposed to material values.

We have beaten back to its proper confines the purely physical ideal, and each age becomes more appreciative of the multitude of rare delights in store for natures which are responsive in every thought. . . .[47]

When spiritual values are properly appreciated and cultivated, then the new world must inevitably prosper in every phase.

The novel is an extremely incompetent example of writing. If we are to accept Mrs. Stone's fiction, she would prove the opposite of what she intended—not that life would never be dull in the new world, but rather that it would be all dullness.

Thomas Reynolds is an enthusiastic advocate of Edward Bellamy's ideas, but he suggests in his *Prefaces*[48] that his own novel, *Nonsecomnes,* published some thirty years earlier in *The Weekly Star,* a temperance and vegetarian journal, may well have had some influence on Edward Bellamy's thinking. It is a volume of notes which amplifies the provocative material in *Looking Backward.* He considers such matters as credit cards, the equality of the sexes, methods of guaranteeing opportunities for self-expression, the problem of human nature, and methods of insuring that people will do their just share of work. For the most part, he agrees with Bellamy, but he dissents violently on the question of credit cards. The credit cards are the same thing as money, he says, except that they would make bookkeeping incredibly difficult. Bellamy is right, he insists, in saying that money is the root of all evil, but *money* means our competitive system, rather than just the medium of exchange. While money remains "as it must . . . with our gradual reforms, all our efforts will be useless; or while we are laboriously sweeping away one abuse, money

[47] *Ibid.,* the Twentieth Century Preface.
[48] Thomas Reynolds, *Prefaces and Notes, Illustrative, Explanatory, Demonstrative, Augumentative, and Expostulatory to Mr. Edward Bellamy's Famous Book, "Looking Backward,"* London, 1890.

will be creating two others, equally bad or worse. Consequently, whenever the change of system is made, it must be thorough, complete—the total abolition of money being the first step."[49] The solution, he says, is a system of ration cards, and he is right in assuming that such a system would work.

Reynolds feels that the Bellamy system is eminently practical, and that, given popular support, the major changes could be instituted in six months. He goes so far as to draw up the outline of an act to be presented to Parliament for "the total abolition of all monetary transactions, and acts of barter, or remunerative exchange . . . and for the regulation of the community under these altered conditions."[50]

Thomas Reynolds is interesting as an example of how an idealist thinks, and as a testimonial to Edward Bellamy's influence. His book is evidence that *Looking Backward* was taken just as seriously abroad as it was in the United States, and that the translations into German and Russian, Czechoslovakian and Polish sold because of social idealism, and not because *Looking Backward* was a popular American novel. Europeans read Bellamy for the same reason that they read Upton Sinclair—economic problems are of vital importance to them, and whenever there is a provocative and interesting analysis, it will be widely read.

Solomon Schindler was an enthusiastic Nationalist. His religious liberalism caused him to emigrate from Germany. In Hoboken, first, and then in Boston he continued to develop his notions of a reformed Judaism. Gradually he developed a reputation as a religious and civic leader. He was elected to the Boston School Board as a fusion candidate. He organized the Boston Federation of Jewish Charities. He was long Superintendent of a Home for Infirm Hebrews. In Schindler's mind, religion was largely a question of social ethics. The greater part of his life he spent trying to convince people of the necessity of a realistic ethical standard. With him that meant a lively social conscience. He felt that the truly religious man must be concerned with ameliorating the diseases of society. "A child of the age of evolution and the glorification of science, he applied the theory of evolution to his religion more logically than psychologically. Though intellectually a pessimist, he was emotionally an optimist with

[49] *Ibid.*, p. 22.   [50] *Ibid.*, p. 54.

the heart of a poet, and the cynical, iconoclastic philosophy he preached
was tempered by a broad tolerance."[51] It was largely his optimism
which made him so enthusiastic about *Looking Backward*, which
caused him to do a German translation, *Ein Rückblick*, and which later
prompted him to write a sequel, *Young West*. *Young West* is full
of the enthusiasm for reform which characterized the intellectual
liberal. Schindler argues, in the volume, for vegetarianism, cremation, a simplification of the marriage ritual, and a communistic treatment of education. The book is printed with colored margins—blue,
green, and yellow—designed to allay the monotony of the printed
page. The publisher's notice explains:

Reliable medical authority informs us that the reading eye wearies mostly
from being compelled to gaze for a long time upon the sharp contrasts of
white and black, also that the strain thus brought upon the eye would be
materially lessened, if simultaneous with the printed page some colour
were brought within its focus.

The reader wonders about the medical authority, and he knows that
the colored margins make it more difficult to concentrate upon the
page, rather than less. The type does not stand out boldly enough.

   Young West tells the story of Julian West's son, a son who achieves
distinction as a citizen of the new world, and who undertakes to write
a biography of his famous father. He finds a confession written long
before:

I cannot deny that during my sleep the world has wonderfully progressed;
I found a haven of peace in place of a battlefield; I found a loving and
lovable brotherhood where I had left individuals fighting with individuals
for a crumb of bread; I found cleanliness where I had left squalor; order
where I had left confusion. . . .

I am morally compelled to acknowledge the present social order as perfect,
and yet my soul rebels against it. . . . I miss too many conditions that were
dear to me by force of habit. The very absence of worry, of care, oppresses
me like a calm on the ocean oppresses the sailor. I do not live—I vegetate.

After I have done my best I am no more than is my neighbor, who has
also done his best according to his abilities.

I yearn for death because I am not fit to live in the present age on account
of my early education, and unfit to live again in the past on account of the
lessons which the present has taught me.[52]

[51] Article on Schindler in the *Dictionary of American Biography*.
[52] Solomon Schindler, *Young West*, Boston, 1894, pp. 275, 277.

In these words Schindler has Julian West admit the validity of the most frequent argument against such a society, that it would be extremely dull, and that the lack of responsibility and the lack of rewards would breed apathy. The point which Schindler makes in refutation is that men must be educated to utopia by slow degrees. Life in any revolutionary period is hard. Education is the only key to a perfect or nearly perfect regime, and if one could only train people not to expect corruption, they would be ideally happy in a simple, well-ordered and honestly administered society.

Most of the book is an attempt to explain the new system of education, the system which makes it easy for Young West to be happy in nurseries, on the theory that a trained personnel can teach children better than their parents, who are inclined either to ignore children or to spoil them. The result is a perfect educational system. The children are taught to depend upon themselves, to do what they can for themselves, and to get along with their fellows. The system smacks of progressive school practice, for the child is encouraged to follow and develop his own interests. As he goes on from the nursery to primary school, high school and college, the student is constantly shifted to the school which best trains his particular talent. The task of these schools is simplified by hypnotism. Through hypnotism, mind-reading is made easy; there is never much question about directing a student's interests and talents. If reading the mind reveals an occasional evil impulse, then it is perfectly possible, by the same process, to substitute good impulses. There is no need to fumble with confusing and contradictory aptitude tests. The citizen is inevitably well trained to fulfill his duties. Schindler suggests that if contemporary educators knew what they were training for—if they knew whether they wanted to produce obedient citizens, good soldiers, religious men, or simply thinking men—our educational system might be effective. It is bad, he implies, because we are grasping for an unknown; our whole system reflects our uncertainty. Democracy, he is sure, is absolutely dependent upon an effective and universal system of education. As it is, however, majority rule becomes something of a joke. It is not the voice of the people which determines election; the cunning can always find a way to defeat the public will. A careful system of education, however, could make democracy an economic as well as a political ideal, could turn democracy into utopia.

Young West is trained as an engineer and architect. After college, and an unfortunate love affair of the sort that seems inevitable even in the best regulated utopia, he goes to work for the Tunnel Authority. He perfects a system of restoring to the soil, in the shape of sterile bricks, the fertility which had been drained from it. As a result he achieves fame and the office of president. Presidents are elected by popular vote, but they are elected because they happen to be qualified to carry on some project facing the government. Young West became president at a time when the sewer division of the government was about to be reorganized. His term as president is as placid as the rest of his life. He works hard, achieves some honor and success, and retires to write the biography of his father. It is in the course of this work that he discovers that his father had been unhappy, and that he begins to have doubts about the system. His doubts, however, are resolved. He sees that his father's attitude was inevitable, given his background and training.

Young West is full of the blithe optimism of the reformer who is convinced that a better world is an immediate possibility. Most of the ideas are inadequately developed, and most of them reflect current reform opinion. He acknowledges that the prison system is wrong, but he evades the problem by explaining that there can be no crime in the new order. The new hypnotism simply eradicates "brutal traits in our nurseries and primary schools by applying the hypnotic process." His suggested change of the marriage ritual, which is to be simply a matter of registration, is equally naive. The public is extremely slow to accept such changes.

Schindler was an extremely pleasant, well-meaning and intelligent idealist, with a highly developed social conscience. And yet, despite his political cynicism, he was too ready to accept reforms and reformers at face value. Young West shows his naïveté as well as his idealism.

THE REBUTTAL

Equality, 1897, came as an anti-climax, the result of Bellamy's participation in Nationalist activity, and of his attempts to defend the thesis of *Looking Backward.* It is a continuation of *Looking Backward,* an exposition in more detailed fashion of matters of economic arrangement. *Equality* is not a very good novel. Bellamy is no longer simply a dreamer; he is a preacher, and preaching is seldom pleasant. The Nationalist program seemed almost perfect in his own eyes, and he wanted to convince everyone that this was not just one way to bring about reform, but *the* way. His grasp of economic questions is much more solid, however, and he hammers away constantly at the contrast between the world as it is and the world as it could be. The result of his political experience is evident, for here far more than in *Looking Backward* he considers the virtues of most of the different reforms which filled the campaigns of the Populist period. Much more is made of the equal position of women in all fields of activity. The educational system is explained in greater detail. The new banking system is contrasted with the old, and the possibilities of centralized control are made evident. In this section is a definite reflection of the monetary agitation preceding the campaign of 1896, for there is the old reiteration of the damaging effect of mortgages, and of the necessity of an expanding currency to meet the needs of business. There is some consideration of technological unemployment. "The march of invention," Dr. Leete explained, "was white with the bleaching bones of innumerable hecatombs of victims."[53] And the reason, of course, was that "the net result of labor-saving machinery was to increase the difference between the production and consumption of the community which remained in the hands of the capitalists as profit."[54] Reforms extend to religion and food. There was no more sectarianism in religion. The bigotry and hypocrisy of petty cults disputing over minor points of theology had disappeared in a new perception of the meaning of faith. Meat was no longer considered an essential part of the diet. The people were all vegetarians, but it is insisted that this is not simply a fad, but rather a realization of the frequency with which animal flesh transmitted disease. Faddism, of course, disappeared with the old economic order. Even women had forgotten the necessity of ornament and changing fashions in dress. The new passion for exercise made comfortable clothes essential, and the natural color in women's cheeks made any kind of cosmetics unnecessary.

[53] Edward Bellamy, *Equality*, p. 224. Page references are to the Appleton-Century edition of 1934.
[54] *Ibid.*, p. 239.

Bellamy emphasizes constantly the relative rank of men and "things" in the two societies. Whereas the old democracy made men conform to "things," the new democracy made "things" conform to men. Economics had become the study not of property rights but of human beings.

The old ethics conceived of the question of what a man might rightfully possess as one which began and ended with the relation of individuals to things. Things have no rights as against moral beings, and there was no reason, therefore . . . why individuals should not acquire an unlimited ownership of things so far as their abilities permitted. But this view absolutely ignored the social consequences which result from an unequal distribution of material things in a world where everybody absolutely depends for life . . . on their share of those things. That is to say, the . . . so-called ethics of property . . . overlooked the whole ethical side of the subject—namely, its bearing on human relations. It is precisely this consideration which furnishes the whole basis of the modern ethics of property. All human beings are equal in rights and dignity, and only such a system of wealth distribution can therefore be defensible as respects and secures those equalities.[55]

His distinction between political democracy and pure democracy is reasonably accurate. The old system, he says, was not popular government at all, but only a mask for "plutocracy, under which the rich were the real though irresponsible rulers." Working people were little better than slaves under that system, for their only liberty was liberty to starve. In contrasting wage slavery and chattel slavery, the advantage was found to be mostly on the side of the latter, because "under the wage system the employer had no motive of self-restraint to spare life or limb of his employees, and he escaped responsibility by the fact of the consent and even eagerness of the needy people to undertake the most perilous and painful tasks for the sake of bread."[56]

Bellamy attacked the inequalities and the stupidities of his contemporary America in many ways. Even the eighth-grade school children of the new order have a better insight into economic problems than the great scholars of the nineteenth century. Bellamy's lack of respect for conventional economic dogma is illustrated by a teacher speaking to the children.

And yet . . . the only real fault of these so-called books on Political Economy consists in the absurdity of the title. Correct that, and their value as documents of the times at once becomes evident. For example, we might call them 'Examinations into the Economic and Social Consequences of trying

[55] *Ibid.*, p. 87.   [56] *Ibid.*, p. 85.

to get along without any Political Economy.' A title scarcely less fit would perhaps be 'Studies into the Natural Course of Economic Affairs when left to Anarchy by the Lack of any Regulation in the General Interest.' It is, when regarded in this light, as painstaking and conclusive expositions of the ruinous effects of private capitalism upon the welfare of communities, that we perceive the true use and value of these works.[57]

The title, *Equality*, illustrates the scope of Bellamy's idealism. Economic equality seemed to him the whole aim of democratic society, and in this cause he spent his best energies. But he was under few illusions as to the importance of his work. "Thirty years ago," he wrote, "*Looking Backward* would have fallen flat, and . . . the reason it has not done so today is that within this period a great revolution has taken place in the minds of reading men and women as to the necessity and possibility of radical social reform."[58] That is to say, the reading public had been prepared for *Looking Backward* by a long series of articles and novels dealing with similar problems.

As an idealist Bellamy reasoned that his work was to make thinking men and women more aware of the social order in which they lived. He wanted "to purge our legislative and congressional lobbies, to put an end to stock-gambling in its chief form, and to terminate the wholesale swindling of the investing public by railroad promoters, speculators, grabbers, and wreckers. . . ."[59] His idealism was a fresh current in a materialistic age.

Between 1888, the date of publication of *Looking Backward,* and 1900, there were published a surprising number of utopian novels. This vogue for utopianism was not the result of Edward Bellamy's work, but rather of an increasing social consciousness which resulted from the closing of the frontier, and from the increasing industrialism of the East. Very few of these novels can be classed as escape literature. The few that can be so classed are spiritualist as well as utopian. Edward Bellamy is the most literate and the most popular of the utopians, but his popularity is not entirely the result of his literary skill. It resulted, rather, from the fact that his ideas were so completely typical of the reform movement. He put into readable form many of the ideas which were in the air. He was taken seriously because so many other people were thinking the same things.

[57] *Ibid.*, p. 190.
[58] An article by Bellamy in the *North American Review,* 150:351.
[59] *Ibid.*, p. 363.

CHAPTER TEN

THE REFORMER AS HISTORIAN

M ANY of the utopian novelists who wrote after the publication of *Looking Backward* used Bellamy's trick of carrying American history into the future. Some of them, however, were more specific about the transition period. *Nequa* by A. O. Grigsby and *That Island* by Samuel Crocker dealt with the history of a utopia, and in both political developments in the utopia exactly paralleled developments in the United States. In other words, Grigsby and Crocker were political pamphleteers. They were insisting on the efficiency of their particular reforms, and on the necessity of action.

Nequa, or The Problem of the Ages is the stepchild of *Equity*, a weekly magazine, published in Topeka, Kansas, and "devoted to the discussion of fundamental economics and the higher ethics of business."[1] The problem of the ages, it soon becomes clear, is the political problem of the present. The plot depends on the usual devices, but utopia, this time, is in the inner world. Some explorers at the North Pole have their ship pulled slowly toward the inner core of the world. Eventually they are rescued and taken to Altruria, a thoroughly civilized country. Fortunately the natives understand English, so the explorers are able to appreciate the remarkable history of the country, a history which parallels, at every turn, the history of the United States. To begin with, Altruria had a republican form of government and the people were "more independent by far than the people of any other country ever had been, notwithstanding the fact that they were robbed unmercifully by the private banks which issued notes and then suspended so that the notes which the people had accepted for their property became worthless. At frequent intervals, these bank panics reduced thousands of people to bankruptcy. But the country was new and land could be had for the asking, so when pressed to the wall, as it were, in the more populous districts along the eastern

[1] [A. O. Grigsby], *Nequa, or, The Problem of the Ages*, by Jack Adams [pseud.], Topeka, 1900, Preface.

border, they came west on the public lands, made new homes and soon accumulated another competency. It is not strange that this international Gold Power of the world cast longing eyes upon a country that was so productive, and could recover so rapidly from industrial depressions and financial disasters."[2]

Eventually there was a war over chattel slavery, and afterwards the masses found themselves in debt "for all the expenses of the war INCLUDING THEIR OWN SERVICES, to an international money power. . . ."[3] Chattel slavery was abolished, "but another form of industrial servitude, the wage system, had fallen heir to all of its worst features."[4] The members of the Gold Trust became more and more powerful, and they sought to keep the people jousting with such windmills as the tariff question. The people would have been satisfied with very little.

If at almost any time during the latter part of the Transition Period, the people of this country had been guaranteed just such rations as were provided for soldiers, or even convicts, there would have been no surplus for exportation; and had the whole people been provided with all the clothing that was needed to keep them well-clad, it would have taken the entire product of wool, flax, cotton and leather. But the press of that day, religious as well as secular, was to such a large extent under the control of the Gold Power, that facts such as these were kept away from the masses of the people.[5]

For a long time the people demanded reform legislation. They believed as did the Populists, for "the measures of reform they advocated along political lines were usually of such a nature that had they been enacted into law they would only have prolonged, for a few decades perhaps, the false system which pauperized and degraded the toiling millions."[6] Farmers and laborers sought to increase their own welfare without consideration for the other. Technological unemployment increased, and also strikes. A larger and larger share of profit went to the capitalist. Small merchants were forced to the wall by sharp competition. The large combines could undersell them. The Gold Trust secured domination, but eventually men began to realize that there was no need for such domination. Men organized as consumers, and not as farmers or mechanics or factory workers. Labor

[2] *Ibid.*, p. 257. [3] *Ibid.*, p. 261. [4] *Ibid.*, p. 263.
[5] *Ibid.*, p. 268. [6] *Ibid.*, p. 269.

finally decided "to take charge of the business of exchange . . . and divide the benefits equally among all who united their efforts to establish the largest possible round of exchange between producers and consumers. This was simply the organization of the market for the express purpose of establishing Equity in Distribution, by paying dividends to labor. The people had at last discovered the vital truth upon which the application of the Golden Rule depends, that ORGANIZED CONSUMPTION CONTROLS DISTRIBUTION."[7]

The movement grew rapidly, for the old system was essentially weak. Men organized in small groups and produced for themselves. As men came together, "and utilized the actual values created by their labor as the medium by which exchanges were effected, prices went up as the result of the increase in the currency, and there was no use for money except to pay debts. Under this system, the purchasing power of labor and products was steadily increasing, while the purchasing power of money was decreasing. As long as money was needed to pay debts, products were exchanged for money at the increased price fixed under the labor standard, but when the debts were all paid, the purchasing power of money was gone and poverty had disappeared with it. Every debt had been paid according to contract, and in the payment of these debts the debtors had transferred their poverty to their creditors."[8]

The system is essentially communistic, although private ownership of property is still possible.

All persons may accumulate property which they create by personal labor, if they wish to burden themselves with the care of it. But as there is an abundance in the common stores to supply every want, there is no motive for the private ownership of anything but personal belongings which are ordinarily of no value to anyone else. Members of the community may have anything they need out of the common stock, and intelligent people would not encumber themselves with the care of more than they have a use for. The greed for the accumulation of property which I am informed is so prevalent in the outer world, if manifested here would be taken as an evidence of insanity and would be treated accordingly. It is very difficult for the average Altrurian to realize that people should ever desire to hoard up wealth which it is impossible for them to consume.[9]

Since no one hoards goods, the system of distribution can be managed efficiently. Products are shipped directly from producers to con-

[7] *Ibid.*, p. 279.   [8] *Ibid.*, p. 315.   [9] *Ibid.*, p. 222.

sumer, and nothing is shipped until it is needed. Thus there can never be a glut of the market in one place and scarcity elsewhere.

The price of an article is fixed by the amount of labor expended in its production and distribution. . . . Product pays for product . . . just as it actually does in the outer world, but under cooperation, the elements of interest, profit and rent have been eliminated.[10]

We readily ascertain by statistics, the average number of minutes, hours, and days of labor invested in the production of every commodity which enters into common use. This includes the labor invested in the necessary transportation, superintendence and distribution. Hence in our accounts, the value of products of all kinds are credited and debited as given amounts of labor. This is what in the outer world would be called the price. A given number of hours of labor in one branch of useful service to society is worth just the same number of hours of labor in some other branch, and the exchange is made on that basis. The one primary object of this system of exchange is to secure equal and exact justice to all.[11]

In such an efficiently administered state it is obvious that children would be carefully supervised: "Children are numbered, so we may know how many are to be provided for. When they reach maturity and graduate from school, they are requested to select the names by which they desire to be known. This entitles them to a voice in public affairs and makes them eligible to any public trust. When I gave you a number, the right to food, clothing and education was conferred upon you. When you select names you will be registered as citizens to any public trust for which you may be selected."[12]

Women, too, are treated with respect, for Altruria has just and equitable marriage laws. No religious ceremony is necessary to sanctify a wedding. Marriage is simply a matter of registration. Along with this goes a new attitude toward motherhood. "The mother is always free to select her own conditions. Many prefer these large public homes which are exclusively under the control of women, while others, with different temperaments, prefer greater exclusiveness in their own apartments, but all alike make this period of prospective motherhood, one in which all the environments are calculated to produce the best possible prenatal influences upon the unborn child."[13]

This method of dealing with pregnant women is the sole original contribution of *Nequa*. But that is not surprising. By 1900 reform

[10] *Ibid.*, p. 231.   [11] *Idem.*   [12] *Ibid.*, p. 180.   [13] *Ibid.*, p. 218.

ideas had been so thoroughly discussed that it would have been extremely difficult to inject much new matter into utopia. And *Nequa* was intended primarily to increase the number of subscriptions to *Equity*. It may well have served its purpose, for people with convictions often like to see the same things said over and over.

That Island is even more a political pamphlet than *Nequa*. Even the publishers admit as much when they confess at the beginning: "Our firm is desirous of flooding the country with this work. . . ." It starts out like a run-of-the-mill romance, but it soon bogs down in elaborate discussions of the new transportation and sub-treasury systems. The result is utopian, however, for these things bring eternal prosperity and good will—no utopia can promise much more than that.

The history of *That Island* is supposed to parallel the history of the United States in the last half of the nineteenth century. In *That Island* the corporations were becoming all powerful. "A monied aristocracy was built up by this pernicious monetary system."[14] Liberty became almost unknown, and "the morals of the people too plainly told of the demoralizing effect class distinction and monopoly were making."[15]

But the people were somehow aroused. They became aware of the evils of the credit and banking system, of the stupidity of the protective tariff, of the injustice of the land tax, and of the inefficiency of the railway system. The party of the monopolists and the single gold standard was defeated, and the party of reform began a "new deal." First, there was enacted free coinage of silver with a ten to one ratio with gold. Along with this was established a postal, sub-treasury system which "not only proved cheap, safe, and efficient, but . . . drove usury and accumulative interest out of That Island republic, and annihilated the expensive, degrading credit system altogether, and forced the capitalists to invest their vast fortunes in useful enterprises, instead of interest-bearing paper; and it was not many years until the postal sub-treasury system of That Island became as universally appreciated as the Federal Postal System of the U.S.A. is today."[16]

[14] [Samuel Crocker], *That Island, A Political Romance,* by Theodore Oceanic Islet [pseud.] Oklahoma City, 1892, p. 33.
[15] *Idem.*   [16] *Ibid.,* p. 133.

The protective tariff was abolished because the "very idea of a nation rich in all the essential attributes of nature, demanding protection against less fortunate ones, is the most ridiculous nonsense and clap-trap twaddle that statesmanship can engage in."[17] A graduated land tax was adopted which "consumed the added value to unimproved lands and forced non-resident farm lands into the market."[18] And it became increasingly easy for small land-holders to compete with larger and more efficient producers. The farmer, at any rate, thought this desirable. Finally, the railroads were nationalized. Hours of labor were reduced to eight a day; wages were raised; fares were reduced to one-half cent a mile; freight rates were lowered, and charges were the same for long hauls as for short hauls—but with increased volume and increased efficiency the roads made more money than ever—and their prosperity was reflected in the general prosperity.

At any rate that was the formula which Samuel Crocker and the C. E. Streeter Co. thought would work. It was a formula which appealed to Populists, single taxers, and to depressed and discouraged farmers. The arguments were largely emotional. The farmer was against anything proposed by the opposition—even to the Civil Service Act. That act, they said, would perpetuate government jobs in the hands of the wealthy who could give their children more thorough educations. But one doesn't turn to these political utopias for any sound and reasoned analysis of the facts. The Crockers and the *"Coin"* Harveys and the Grigsbys were pamphleteers fighting for a cause. Inevitably their perspective was bad, and inevitably it seems less accurate to us than it did to their contemporaries. But lost causes come readily to life in their pages—and that is one reason for reading them.

[17] *Ibid.*, p. 124.   [18] *Ibid.*, p. 122.

CHAPTER ELEVEN

THE POLITICIAN CONSIDERS UTOPIA

IGNATIUS DONNELLY was a clever politician, a capable writer, and a utopian only for reasons of expediency. Training in law had led him into reform politics and some influence in Minnesota Republican circles. He was first elected to Congress in 1864, and from then until 1896, when he was disappointed in his hope of becoming the Populist candidate for president, he was active in almost every attempt of the farm groups to enact their reforms. As an elected official he represented not only the Republicans, but also the Farmer's Alliance, the Grangers, the Populists, the Greenbackers, and always himself. Rhetoric rather than consistency was his main stock-in-trade. He changed his mind frequently; his political motivation was usually emotional rather than intellectual. As one of those who were most active in the Populist party, his changing ideas and enthusiasms reflect the political and social ferment of the period. His two utopian novels are shrewdly written political documents, but they show more of his talent for expediency than any literary skill.

His first book, *Atlantis, the Ante-diluvian World,* was a popularization of Plato's notion of a lost continent where civilization developed. *Atlantis* was a success, and in Minnesota, especially, it brought the "Sage of Ninanger" increasing respect. Other volumes of the same sort followed. *Ragnarok: The Age of Fire and Gravel* was an attempt to show that the layers of clay, gravel, and silt on the face of the earth were the result of collision with some great comet. But his great delight was the Bacon-Shakespeare controversy. The main argument of his several volumes on the subject followed the conventional reasoning that since Bacon was the only man of the day sufficiently informed to write the plays, he must have written them. The final proof depended on an ingenious cipher.

Regardless of what he is proving, Donnelly's writing has a convincing air. *Caesar's Column,* 1890, and *The Golden Bottle,* 1892, his two utopian novels, were tremendously popular. *Caesar's Column* sold by the hundreds of thousands of copies; it was widely quoted, and frequently compared with *Looking Backward*, although the only similarity was that the plots of both depended on the injustice of the contemporary economic system. Bellamy's twentieth century people looked back at the inequalities of the late nineteenth century as the absurdity which brought civilization to its senses. Donnelly thought that the Populists' efforts to bring about reform would be the last protest of the underprivileged. He predicted that cycles of depression would continue until all civilization would collapse.

Caesar's Column was begun after a defeat as United States Senator, and he saw in his own failure the failure of all hope for reform. The framework of the story is obvious, but it is surprisingly readable. The plot is worked out by means of letters from Gabriel Welstein, in New York, to his brother in Uganda, Africa. He had come to New York to look for an independent market for his wool, so that he would not lose such a large proportion of his profits to the wool monopoly. Gabriel was a product of a democratic community, and he reacted strongly to the industrial New York of Donnelly's imagination. His letters home emphasized the contrast between what is and what ought to be, the contrast between a plutocracy and a democratic, agrarian economy. Gabriel hates monopoly and soon is involved in the struggle between the "haves and the have-nots." He describes the horrible living conditions of the workers.

Oh! the pitiable scenes, my brother, that I have witnessed! Room after room; the endless succession of the stooped, silent toilers; old, young; men, women, children. And most pitiable of all, the leering, shameless looks of invitation cast upon us by the women, as they saw two well-dressed men pass by them. It was not love, not license, not even lust; it was degradation—willing to exchange everything for a little more bread.

Toil, toil, toil, from early morn until late at night; then home they swarm, tumble into their wretched beds; snatch a few hours of disturbed sleep; battling with vermin, in a polluted atmosphere; and then up again and to work; and so on, and on, in endless, mirthless, hopeless round; until, in a few years, consumed with disease, mere rotten masses of painful wretchedness, they die, and are wheeled off to the great furnace, and their bodies are eaten up by the flames, even as their lives have been eaten up by society.[1]

[1] Ignatius Donnelly, *Caesar's Column*, pp. 45, 46. Page references are to an undated edition published by M. A. Donahue & Co. of Chicago and New York.

The people eat rats and mice, if they can find them. They have no social standards. They are struggling only to keep alive.

Marry! . . . why, they could not afford to pay the fee required by law. And why should they marry? There is no virtue among them. No . . . they had almost gotten down to the conditions of the Australian savages, who, if not prevented by the police, would consummate their animal-like nuptials in the public streets.[2]

And the reason for such horrible conditions was the economy of the late eighties. Donnelly quotes from contemporary magazine articles to show how the present discontent would appear in retrospect. It is a convincing device. He reasons that since nothing will be done about such conditions, there can be only one ultimate result—rebellion. The picture of the Brotherhood of Destruction, the secret society which organized the opposition of the masses, is absurd, but the conception of a tremendous upheaval from below has found some justification in the Russian revolution. The reaction developed slowly but inevitably.

As the domination and arrogance of the ruling class increased, the capacity of the lower classes to resist, within the limits of law and constitution, decreased. . . . The people were walled in by impassable barriers. Nothing was left them but the primal, brute instincts of the animal man, and upon these they fell back, and the Brotherhood of Destruction arose.[3]

Destruction is their only purpose. The masses had been degraded for so long that they were interested only in revenge. Materialism had betrayed these people, and so they would betray civilization. Donnelly does a vivid job of describing the revolution. When the mob gains control, they lose sight of everything but revenge, and gradually they destroy even themselves. Gabriel plays an heroic part in the final debacle, and, with some friends, and the girl whom he has wooed and saved from destruction, he escapes in a balloon to Africa. With most of the old civilization destroyed, they create a utopia on the ruins. Gabriel's conception of the ideal state shows the influence of Populism.

The basis of the proposed Constitution is division of authority, not on the basis of region, but by economic interest. The governing body was to be divided into three branches: producers, employers, and

[2] *Ibid.*, p. 47.   [3] *Ibid.*, p. 98.

a third, smaller group of the intelligentsia who would hold the balance of power when the others disagreed. Treason would be the highest state offense, and going beyond the usual definition, it would include ". . . corrupting the voter or the office holder; or . . . the voter or office holder selling his vote or his services." Education would be universal and compulsory. There would be neither church schools nor private schools. There would be no interest on money. Gold and silver would serve no function as money except in small amounts; and paper money would be issued according to a definite per capita scheme. The state would own "all roads, streets, telegraph or telephone lines, railroads and mines and . . . [possess] exclusive control of the mails and express matter."[4] Town property would be owned only by people actually living on it, and new cities or towns would be established only by the government, on petition. Donnelly remembered his own disastrous experiences of the boom days in Minnesota.

The State was to be the servant not the master of the citizen. "We think that the object of government should be—not cheap goods or cheap men, but happy families."[5]

Caesar's Column was excellent propaganda and gave Donnelly a national reputation. It was widely distributed in the campaign of 1892, for it was one of the most aggressive expressions of the political discontent which characterized the period.

The Golden Bottle, or, The Story of Ephraim Benezet of Kansas, 1892, is even more a campaign document than *Caesar's Column.* Donnelly apologizes for the work in the preface, explaining that it was written hurriedly, during the heat of a political campaign, between political speeches. The book "is the outgrowth of the great political struggle now going on . . . in the United States; and it is intended to explain and defend . . . some of the new ideas put forth by the People's Party; and which concern, I sincerely believe, all the people of the civilized world. I have a hope that the interest of 'The Golden Bottle' may not end with the events which gave it birth."

The book deals with the members of the Benezet family of Butler County, Kansas, who are about to lose their farm. The night before

---

[4] *Ibid.,* pp. 308, 309.   [5] *Ibid.,* p. 314.

they are to be dispossessed, young Ephraim has a marvellous dream, which becomes the story. An old man appears before him, the Pity of God, and shows him how to make gold. It takes him some time to realize what he can do with unlimited wealth. The first experiment is directed at the local bankers. Ephraim offers to lend money to the farmers at two percent interest. There is a terrific demand for money; the bankers think they will be ruined, and they attempt to have him confined as insane. The result of the low rate of interest is rapid prosperity. The farmers discover new hope and new needs.

There was a new fence or a new barn to be built; the men's and women's clothes were worn threadbare, and had to be replaced; articles of furniture were to be bought; they must have a new harness for the team, and something of the luxuries of civilization for the table. . . . The business of the town quadrupled in a month.[6]

Donnelly's purpose, of course, is to demonstrate the practicability of Populist reforms.

He illustrates the need for increased women's rights by the story of Sophie Jenkins, who could not collect the wages she had earned because she would not allow herself to be seduced. With the help of Ephraim's gold she and her friends organize stores so they can sell the articles which they produce. Prices remain the same, but the profits no longer go to a middleman. The girls have more money and they spend more. Donnelly paints a glowing picture of the increasing cycle of prosperity.

Ephraim's realization of the power of gold increases, and along with it a realization of his own power. He appeals to Congress:

Let us get clear of all this nonsense. Let us relegate the worship of gold and silver to the region of witchcraft and spooks, and all the other trash of the under-fed, undeveloped past. Let us establish several propositions:

1. That real money is not a commodity, but a governmental measure of values to commodities.
2. That the government must furnish its people with an adequate supply of this medium of exchange, just as it is in duty bound to furnish them with an adequate supply of postage stamps.
3. That this medium should bear the government stamp and be full legal-tender for all debts public and private; otherwise it is not money, but disqualified rubbish.

[6] Ignatius Donnelly, *The Golden Bottle*, New York and St. Paul, 1892, p. 119.

4. That it should be made of the cheapest and lightest material, with a reasonable degree of durability; and these qualities we find in paper.

5. That it should be so abundant as to enable the community to do business on a cash basis, and not pay interest on the bulk of its transactions.[7]

The logic of this thesis that money is only for convenience and that it should have no value in itself has its effect, but Congressmen will not vote against their friends, and the bankers, speaking through the newspapers, begin an elaborate attack on Ephraim and his proposals. But gold has its power, and he buys all of the protesting periodicals. Disregarding the hostility of the government, Ephraim spends money freely and founds a city. Laid out according to reform standards, the city administration is based on the theory of economic as well as political democracy. There was free power for manufacturers. There was an eight hour day, complete prohibition of liquor, and ideal housing. His city grew tremendously.

Ephraim's reform logic finally wins out. He is elected President of the United States and begins a world-wide campaign:

The new civilization must extend a helping hand to the old. The whole moral influence of this giant republic must be thrown upon the side of the people in their struggles with kingcraft. . . . I do not say we should wage war upon the kingdoms of the Old World . . .; but I do say we should give the people of the Old World to understand, that they are horribly misgoverned; that our sympathies are with them; and that it is better that one-half of one generation should perish in their own heart's blood, if thereby all subsequent generations can be lifted up out of inexpressible misery.[8]

The army which Ephraim directs is all-conquering; the people of the rest of the world understand his purpose. He founds a new Universal Republic, based upon cooperation. Greenback money and a vast program of public works are the basic reforms which set the world machinery again in working order. The land surrounding every large city is cleared and model homes for workingmen are built. Farm land is divided equally. Education becomes universal. In other words, all the peoples of the world have been made prosperous through the application of common sense and greenback currency. Donnelly explains at the end:

[7] *Ibid.*, pp. 129, 130.   [8] *Ibid.*, p. 204.

That dream is an allegory. The Golden Bottle represents the power of government to create its own money. With that power it will do all that you dreamed the Bottle did. It will make money so abundant that the credit system will cease, debts will disappear.[9]

The Golden Bottle was excellent propaganda, although it was not so popular as *Caesar's Column*. The greenback theory was never accepted wholeheartedly by reformers.

These novels mark the high point of Donnelly's influence. At the 1896 Populist convention he was mentioned for the presidential nomination, but William Jennings Bryan and free silver left small place for him. He would not have been a good candidate. He was often right in his theorizing but he was not a sound political thinker. He was an opportunist who did not hesitate to change his point of view. Consistency, however, has never been essential for a utopian novelist.

[9] *Ibid.*, p. 308.

CHAPTER TWELVE

UTOPIA POINTS A MORAL

NOT all utopians were moralists; some were prophets, some were dreamers, and some were simply playing a literary game. Inevitably those who were moralists took themselves most seriously. They insisted too vigorously on the virtues of their own suggestions, and on the futility of the other fellow's. Each of the three men considered in this chapter has a different moral to preach. They have in common, however, a supreme assurance that their prophecies are accurate.

Of these volumes, the two by Albert Chavannes are the most innocuous, the least persuasive. Chavannes was not a good sophist; he was simply a well-meaning man who had come under the spell of the Bellamy Nationalists. He saw all too clearly the abuses which seemed to be crowding in on the generation of the nineties, and he was impatient of them. The solution seemed obvious, and a better world easy to achieve. He determined to arouse the reading public to action. Unfortunately his imagination was as limited as his knowledge of economics.

The first volume, *The Future Commonwealth*, 1892, explains how the increasing power of the monopolists made any true democracy so impossible that a group of socialists determined to settle a new country.

Socioland is an example of socialist wishful thinking. For instance, there are no taxes. "Our Commonwealth carries on business, earns money by legitimate means, and spends it for the benefit of all."[1] "We, the people, thus become a business firm, and hire a certain number of men to manage the work for us."[2] In other words, Chavannes maintains that it is a virtue not to tax, when there is nothing left to tax. The word *taxation* had become a symbol to him, and *no taxation* meant utopia. Socioland is not all utopia, however,

---

[1] Albert Chavannes, *The Future Commonwealth*, New York, 1892, p. 26.
[2] *Ibid.*, p. 44.

in spite of the facts that the public owns the lands, the railroad rates are fair, and the parasite has been eliminated from society. Children are given no chance to grow up slowly and pleasantly; they are apprenticed at an early age and taught the virtues of useful work. And every citizen must do for himself all those menial tasks which everyone can do, and which everyone hates to do. "Having no drones to support, we can accomplish much more, and still be able to considerably reduce the number of hours of labor."[3]

In Brighter Climes, 1895, carries on the story of life in Socioland. In this volume there are some central figures who move from the United States to Socioland, and, inevitably, prosper. The reason for their quick success is Socioland's rational land system. New country is not opened for settlement all at once. Rather, one township is completely settled, and then another—in an orderly fashion. The intention of the founders of the Commonwealth was to equalize the distribution of products, to provide a proper equilibrium between private and public wealth. Their desire to equalize everything carried over into the treatment of the sexes and the ritual of marriage. The marriage contract was defined as a purely civil affair which could be broken at will. Along with this change, the founding fathers wisely decided that there should be no stigma attached to illegitimate births.

If one can accept this much of Socioland, it is easy to accept the rest—free bread, free laundry, no criminal courts or criminals, no advertising, no political parties, and women able to exercise vast power through the acquisition of the vote. Most of these ideas were commonplace in the nineties, but Chavannes carries his missionary spirit too far: He wants to make every impulse useful, he wants the daily papers to carry useful information rather than news. Chavannes meant too well. His utopianism suffers from an excess of virtue.

Edward A. Caswell, too, wrote from the depths of his heart, but everything he wrote contradicted Chavannes. This book *Toil and Self* is a warning and a prophecy. It is not a novel; it is not entertaining; but it does present one of the standard reactions of conservatives to social experiment. The book is supposed to consist of a collection of essays by a Yale Professor of 2400 A.D., essays which explain

[3] *Idem.*

the problem of labor through the ages. To point his moral, he tells of a socialist experiment by an extremely wealthy man: How he built a beautiful city on a Pacific Island, how he selected his immigrants with great care, and how he attempted to direct affairs on a basis of perfect equality. There were no social distinctions: Everyone could choose his own occupation; everyone helped with the menial tasks. Everyone worked; they had to—but not with the same enthusiasm. Lawyers increased. There was an attempt to regulate marriage, but only the weak accepted the decision of the state, and these produced weak, docile children. After the death of the founders, the colony split up into various cults. And the reason, according to Caswell, is that selfishness, not idealism, is the fundamental, motivating force behind all human behavior.

A careful study of all the experiences of the Idealists and Altruistic proves that these theories were specious, weak and untenable, though alluring and picturesque.

Nature has framed the law of selfishness as the one great fundamental necessity, and the only base on which the animal creation and humanity could exist, namely, that every specimen should care primarily for himself, and should primarily devote his entire energy to his self-protection and continuance.[4]

The Professor examines the American labor problem from the same vantage point. He explains how labor took command for a time, in a sort of revolution of the proletariat, and how the revolution inevitably collapsed. He says, in effect, that capitalism is the one efficient system, and that any attempt to achieve communism will have unhappy results.

The most amusing part of the book is the recital of how a scientist discovered a way to control sex, and of how, as a result, so few girls were born that the population began to fall off at an alarming rate. But the book was not meant to be amusing. It is a serious attempt to deal with a situation that seemed immediate and threatening. Caswell was not alone in his predictions of gloom. Most of the reformers, from Edward Everett Hale, Bellamy, and Donnelly, to Thomas Lake Harris, the theo-socialist, prophesied a dark future for the world unless their own suggestions were followed.

[4] [Edward A. Caswell], *Toil and Self*, Chicago and New York, 1900, p. 139.

Hovorre did not become gloomy when he examined the future. Even the increasing monopoly of the day seemed to be for the greater good. According to his pamphlet, *The Miltillionaire,*[5] the earth had become unified through the benevolent despotism of one man, a miltillionaire, who became so wealthy that he was able to force all others to his will. It was a common notion that there would be some such merging of power, that corporations would gradually become larger and more powerful and then consolidate; it was not common for people to expect the results to be good. Reformers were inclined, rather, to look upon the corporation as the most dangerous of their enemies.

The *Miltillionaire* outlines in haphazard fashion the reforms which made this new, completely paternalistic state a success:

1. There are no private homes. Everyone lives in huge, state-owned dormitories.

2. There are no taxes except for the tax on time; that is, everyone must work for the state.

3. Stores are all located outside the city. But stores are simply distribution centers. Goods are supplied free. Money has no function.

4. Cities are circular in form, often with a radius of one hundred miles.

5. There are no private schools and there is no compulsory education. Children learn by asking questions.

6. Both men and women dress in uniform, simple clothing. There is choice only in color.

7. There is no false modesty; men, women, and children bathe together.

8. There is no marriage, and so no divorce. Both men and women can have as many love affairs as they like, provided only that they take care of their children.

9. There is no such thing as formal religion. "For we have learned that True Religion is invisible, and should pervade all of our institutions through our hearts at all times . . . and not ridiculously and hypocritically be relegated to one day in a week, and to one

---

[5] M. Auburre Hovorre, *The Miltillionaire.* This is a paper-bound pamphlet of thirty pages, with no date or publisher given. It was certainly published in the nineties.

particular institution. Pure Religion we know to be Pure Love—which we realize in all our actions, which are invariably deeds of love."[6]

10. Everyone is a vegetarian. There is no hunting or fishing.

11. Cremation is compulsory: "Dead bodies are no longer superstitiously inhumed in the earth to the pollution of the waters of the land."[7]

12. Everyone has an equal share of the world's goods.

The notions about vegetarianism, cremation, simple clothing, marriage, common dormitories, and circular cities appear in one form or another in most of the utopian novels written between 1888 and 1900. *The Miltillionaire* is almost a catalogue of the reforms suggested during these years.

[6] *Ibid.*, p. 12.
[7] *Ibid.*, p. 28.

CHAPTER THIRTEEN

THE CHARLES H. KERR COMPANY AND UTOPIA

THE utopian novels written during the nineties were not, for the most part, brought out by the well established publishing houses. Many were published by the authors, many by the working class press, and many by reform groups. The Charles H. Kerr Co. of Chicago published a good deal of material designed to appeal to reformers and radicals. Most of their publications insist on the necessity of reform. Their utopian novels, particularly, are undisguised political pamphlets. In all of them the message is the same—we can bring about utopia by legal means, if only the people will realize their power.

The first of these novels, *President John Smith,* 1897, is devoted to demonstrating that a better order can be achieved through a peaceful revolution. The cover of the paper bound edition bears this legend: "The right of a citizen of the United States to demand and obtain work at wages sufficient to support himself and family shall never be abridged. It shall be the duty of the government to guarantee employment to all who demand it." F. U. Adams, the author, seems to be a somewhat jaundiced critic:

Not many years ago such an event as the legislative theft of a great franchise was regarded with public horror. A decade ago a national bond steal would have aroused vast indignation. But a nation, like an individual, can become accustomed to almost anything. In view of the complacency with which the American people permit themselves to be deceived, swindled and robbed, and their evident enjoyment of the operation, the author is sometimes of the opinion that he was unduly excited over the events of 1893, and that perhaps general bankruptcy, distress, poverty and national decadence are matters of small consequence.[1]

Today the majority has no rights which a fortified minority is bound to respect. The people of the United States are powerless to enact legislation for the redress of their grievances. Instead of wasting their time in an attempt to pass a free silver bill—which the Supreme Court will promptly declare unconstitutional—they should turn their attention to a crusade,

[1] F. U. Adams, *President John Smith,* Chicago, 1897, p. 7.

which, when successful, will make constitutional any enactment passed by
a majority vote of the free citizens of the United States.[2]

The United States is not a republic. The Republican party is not republican.
The Democratic party is not democratic. Does the Supreme Court represent
the people? Are its members elected or appointed by the people? Are they
responsible to the people? Can the people by any legal process remove or
discipline them when they have trampled under foot some law which
the people have passed after a victorious struggle with their oppressors? No.[3]

The great issue of 1900 will be: "Shall the Constitution of the United States
be so amended or revised that the rights of the Majority shall be Preserved?
Shall the majority rule?"[4]

The novel takes the form of a history of the United States, beginning in the last years of the nineteenth century, and dealing with the
conflict of capital and labor, the rights of the people and the attempt
to enforce those rights, and leading up to the election of 1900, an
election fought on the principle of true representation. Smith should
have won the election, but the votes are not counted accurately and his
opponent is declared the new president. The people rebel; revolution
threatens, and is only avoided by Smith's suggestion that a Constitutional Convention be held for the purpose of changing the basic law.
The delegates are soon elected and the convention approves the
changes proposed by Smith. Some of these proposals seem rational.
It was decided that the President was to be elected by direct vote,
and that he was to take office on January 1; that cabinet members
and certain other public officials should be elected by popular vote;
that on a vote of fifty members of Congress any question pending
should "be submitted to the people for a final decision"; that the
Supreme Court should have only five judges, and that the Court
should have no juridiction over laws passed by the people; that
currency should be "based on the credit of the United States and
redeemable in such products, labor, property, services, assets, or
valuable compensations as shall be . . . at the disposal of the . . .
government";[5] that the government should have the right to take
over any business deemed necessary for the welfare of the people,
the business to be paid for out of profits; that taxes should not be
levied against the "products of labor."

[2] *Ibid.*, pp. 8, 9.   [3] *Ibid.*, p. 9.   [4] *Ibid.*, p. 8.   [5] *Ibid.*, p. 243.

The new constitution is approved by the people, and John Smith is elected President. There is no attempt to solve all the problems at once. Reforms are introduced gradually. And they had to be, for there were many objections which had to be resolved. Foreign powers refused to accept the new money; in return, the United States refused to accept silver as payment for any goods purchased in the country. The stores of silver on hand were used to purchase goods abroad, goods which were sold to the people at cost. The results of this policy were twofold: The great powers were forced to accept the new currency, and the people were enabled to buy goods at low prices. But there was no attempt to make the State completely Socialist:

The government had not extended its scope so as to include all of the forms of industry. . . . The administration confined its attention to the production of actual standard necessities of life and left to private capital the development of the hundreds of specialties which increase with civilization. But in all commodities for which there was a general demand, and in which it had been possible for trusts to assume a monopolistic control by reason of vast resources and good management, the government became an active competitor.[6]

The government insisted on its right to operate distribution outlets whenever it would be for the benefit of the people. Many local concerns were forced out of business, for they "usually found it impossible to long compete against the government shops. It was the policy of the administration to offer such retailers advantageous terms for their stocks of goods on hand, a proposition which was generally accepted."[7]

Democracy was made to work, and it seemed to be utopia. By 1920 the miracle was supposed to have taken place; and, in fact, many of the suggested reforms had actually taken place. The only trouble is that reform and utopia are not synonymous.

At the end of the volume there is a plea to consider the feasibility of forming "a Majority Rule Club in your vicinity." It is also urged that *President John Smith* be used as political fuel. "For ten cents you can add a new name to the ranks of reform."

On the back cover there is this exhortation:

THINK OR STARVE. That is the alternative. Do not longer be deceived by well-worded lies. Read the truth. It will pay you dividends.

---

[6] *Ibid.*, p. 274.　　　　　　　[7] *Ibid.*, p. 275.

The truth turns out to be *The New Time*, "the best reform magazine in the world," edited by B. O. Flowers, who founded the *Arena*, and Frederick U. Adams. *"The New Time* is a fearless advocate of the INITIATIVE and REFERENDUM, Majority Rule, Scientific Government, Monetary Reform, and Physical and Ethical Culture."

This old enthusiasm seems rather pathetic now, particularly the Kerr Company recommendation of other books on Socialism: *The Garden of Eden, U.S.A.,*[8] which tells how "a millionaire established an ideal city in a secluded valley among the North Carolina mountains," and includes a "unique love story"; and *Man or Dollar, Which?,*[9] "a delightful picture of what the world will be when people work to help each other instead of struggling to overcome each other. A unique feature of the book is its story of the universal strike, which proved that the farmers and laborers of the United States acting together are stronger than the money power."

The Co-opolitan[10] develops much the same thesis as *The Garden of Eden, U.S.A.* The book is supposed to be a factual account of the formation in Idaho of a cooperative commonwealth, the brainchild of John Thompson, a man of wealth and intelligence. Thompson had analyzed other cooperative experiments, and was determined to avoid their mistakes. The fundamental thing, he decided, was to develop a new area, where the individuals would have to be dependent upon themselves. Idaho was chosen because it was sparsely populated, because the climate was good and the resources many. A party of some three hundred made the trip with Thompson and established in a fertile valley the city of Co-opolis. Everything went well with the Association. The city grew and gradually became powerful enough to figure as a political force. The Co-opolitans gained control of the state legislature and were able to force the state as a whole to adopt their principles. As the novel ends, other states were beginning to join; first, Washington, and then the Rocky Mountain group. The whole nation seemed almost ready to adopt their principles of cooperation.

The Association succeeded so quickly, it is explained, because everyone does useful work. There are no social parasites, no idlers,

[8] W. H. Bishop, *The Garden of Eden, U.S.A., A Very Possible Story.* Chicago: 1897.
[9] [Anon.], *Man or Dollar, Which?*, Chicago, 1897?
[10] Zebina Forbush, *The Co-opolitan*, Chicago, 1889.

no profiteering middlemen. Figuring on a basis of 3,160,000, which was supposed to be the number of cooperators, it is explained that in a competitive state there would be five thousand lawyers. The Association has only one hundred and fifty. As a result there are 4850 more producers. Instead of six thousand saloon men and bartenders, liquors are handled in regular stores, just as any other commodity. The Association has no place for the eight thousand claim and commission brokers, real estate salesmen, and insurance collectors. There are no personal servants. There are no gamblers, capitalists, or speculators. Commercial men, restaurant men, and hotel keepers all work for the state. And there is no time wasted searching for employment, hunting for customers, or waiting for trade. Labor is not wasted on unproductive activities. Men work hard for the success of the venture because they feel that they have a real stake in society. "Each regarded the idler who 'stole time' as his foe."[11]

There was no private ownership of house and grounds. The State was enabled to take over the property of land-holders by a restricted use of the single-tax plan. A man owns only personal property, which can be willed to his family. But if a man dies his credit is cancelled. He cannot will it to his wife or children. The wife is given a place in the industrial army and his years of service are credited to her. The society makes no provision for the well-to-do.

Idaho's new cities are all laid out on a grandiose scale, according to the Co-opolis plan. "Each one of them covers an area nearly three times as large as that of any competitive city. The streets are all one hundred and fifty feet wide and a park of equal width separating them."[12] There are many parks. "The buildings are all at least fifty feet apart. There is ample sunlight, pure air and space for children to play . . . there are flowers, fountains, artificial lakes and trees in profusion . . . the streets are all paved with asphalt. Most of our buildings are constructed of brick or stone."[13]

The Co-opolitan makes no attempt to outline a complete program for a cooperative existence. There is one fundamental idea: reforms can be achieved in one generation. The logic is simple: cooperation is better than cut-throat competition; thrift is better than wastefulness, in man-power as well as in finance. The difficulties confronting

[11] *Ibid.*, p. 143.   [12] *Ibid.*, p. 165.   [13] *Idem.*

society are not insuperable; they are not inherent in the democratic system; with determination and cooperation the system can be improved without sacrificing the democratic machinery.

This same thesis is repeated in two other books published by the same firm, *The Legal Revolution of 1902,* 1898, and *Letters from New America,* 1900. *Letters from New America,* particularly, amplifies many of the scanty generalizations of *The Co-opolitan.* New America, of course, is utopia, and it is made to seem as though there is every chance of bringing about such a perfect order in the United States. It is not much of a novel, and yet the fiction is developed in some detail—an observer reports on conditions in New America to a Senator in the United States. The Senator wants to learn why New America does not have any conflict between capital and labor. New America proves to be a completely socialized state, with the constitution predicated on three fundamental principles: "First, that every law-abiding and industrious citizen shall be assured of a comfortable living, and of progress according to his merit; second, that the infirm and the aged shall be provided for without the sting of almshouse or pauper pension; third, that no man shall have the power to oppress his neighbor in any economic or industrial way. These three things have been the goal of all our efforts, and who will say today that we are not nearer our goal than any other people upon the earth?"[14] The State says to the workman: "Only efficiency is allowed to enter . . . you must be prepared for your work before you begin it."[15] The State says to the individual: "You shall not use your superior ability for the humiliation of others. . . . You cannot coerce, by wealth or station, the man who is below you in either."[16] The State says to the politician: "Your tenure is based upon efficiency and good behavior. . . . You are a public servant, not the public's king or master."[17]

Based upon these principles, the transition to the new system was gradual. The changes were all constitutional, and were effected over a period of twenty-five years. Individuals were paid for confiscated property, but the newly acquired wealth of the government was behind the currency. Adjustments in economic status were brought

---

[14] Charles Edward Persinger, *Letters from New America,* Chicago, 1900, p. 30.
[15] *Ibid.,* p. 74.   [16] *Idem.*   [17] *Ibid.,* p. 75.

about by a heavy inheritance tax and by a progressive income tax. Our observer is impressed by many things in New America, some trivial and some significant. He is pleased to discover that the railroads are state owned, that everyone is an employee of the government, that hotels are under government control, and there are no fees or tips, that towns are all of moderate size, that they are all served by central sewer systems, that sewage is turned into fertilizer, that garbage is collected daily, that washing is all done in municipal laundries, and that there are no overhead wires. He is impressed, too, by the city planning, which follows much the same formula as in *The Co-opolitan* and *New Era*. The cities are spread out to avoid over-crowding. Public buildings are all in the central, official part of town. The retail and wholesale area is next, and beyond that, separating the business area from the residential, is a continuous and narrow park. In effect, this is the same solution that Edward Everett Hale proposed in *How They Lived in Hampton* and in *Sybaris and Other Homes*.

In *New America* students are supported while they go to school. After they have finished their technical education, they must work for the state. But there is no attempt "to make men equal when Nature failed in that endeavor. We do not seek a dead level, but a country in which a man's progress depends upon himself, and not upon the accident of his birth or the circumstances of his life."[18]

"Railways, steamship lines, factories, mines, business and residence properties, land itself—all belong to and are managed through the people as a whole."[19] Only purely personal property such as clothing and house furnishings is private. Every adult citizen works for the government—women as well as men. "Each married woman is as financially independent of her husband as she was before marriage."[20] She may either continue to work outside the house, or simply receive a wage proportionate to her husband's. Each child, to the number of three, increases the family income. The result is that home life is made more pleasant than it ever was before.

Letters from New America stirs over the material which had been thoroughly prepared by the earlier utopians, Populists, reformers,

[18] *Ibid.*, p. 30.   [19] *Ibid.*, p. 55.   [20] *Ibid.*, p. 52.

material which was about to be seized upon with gusto by the muck-
rackers and dealt with in sensational form. For the moment the book
does a capable job of popularizing.

The Legal Revolution of 1902[21] is more nearly a novel than *Letters
from New America,* and it deals with the more vital problem of how,
by constitutional means, the new order can be achieved. The book
shows the influence of Edward Bellamy. *Equality* is mentioned as "one
of the greatest books ever written. It clearly shows that there can be
no equality until all are equally financially independent by receiving
the same pay. This is ideal and perfect Socialism, and as soon as the
government takes possession of all monopolies, and begins conducting
the business of production and distribution, I predict he [Bellamy]
will have a great following in favor of marching on until that ideal
Socialism is reached. . . ."[22] But Bellamy is not completely sound:
"The picture 'Equality' paints is all right except at the starting
point—the method it has of putting the great scheme into operation."[23] Bellamy simply proposes that the government enter the business of production and distribution, and gradually, "confiscate property by making it worthless."[24] "I say confiscate by law the accumulation of the millionaires, and turn it over to the government for the
benefit of the people who have produced it. Do it outright and
aboveboard, and not by this indirect method of ruining their business.
We don't want these factories and millionaires' concerns closed for
one single day, to deteriorate and depreciate in value, as they certainly would do by Mr. Bellamy's method. . . ."[25] Wellman's solution
is a legal, constitutional revolution, to be effected by means of a constitutional convention. The hero of the story, Mark Mishler, works
out plans to effect such a result. He proposes a convention for the
purpose of dealing with such easily rationalized reforms as the direct
election of senators and the abolition of the electoral college. The
convention is duly called, and these first amendments are quickly
passed. Other amendments are proposed: a graduated income tax, an
inheritance tax, and a provision, whereby "on the petition of one-

[21] [Bert J. Wellman], *The Legal Revolution of 1902,* by a Law Abiding Revolutionist, Chicago, 1898.
[22] *Ibid.,* p. 124.   [23] *Idem.*   [24] *Ibid.,* p. 125.   [25] *Idem.*

tenth of the number of legal voters . . . it shall be the duty of Congress to submit the proposed amendments to a vote of the people, and that any amendment receiving a majority of two-thirds of the votes . . . , or a plain majority in every state . . . shall become a part of the Constitution. . . ."[26] The book devotes a good many pages to this proposal, which was supposed to make the people all powerful. The recall and the referendum still seemed miraculous weapons, and since people expected those devices to be effective it was reasonable enough to assume that the people would know how to use still more power.

The other preliminary reforms of the Conventionists sound like a mixture of the party platforms of the Democrats, the Populists, the Free-Silverites, and the Greenbackers. Amendments provided for the election of all Federal judges and marshals; for the election of postmasters in all towns with a population of more than two hundred; for primary elections; for proportional representation in Congress, to enable minority groups to have representatives; for a uniform system of contracts; for uniform marriage and divorce laws in all the states; for public ownership of telegraph companies and railroads; and for the operation of postal savings banks. In addition, the Conventionists had great faith in the possibilities of monetary manipulation, and so they passed an amendment "providing that neither gold nor silver coin should circulate,"[27] but that it should be kept by the Treasury, and that there should be issued by the Secretary of the Treasury, in favor of the government, "two dollars' worth of certificates for one of gold and silver presented to the Treasury, in addition to the amount issued in favor of the holder of the bullion or coin, thus making three dollars' worth of legal tender certificates to be issued for each one of metal in store, two to belong to the government, and one to the person presenting the bullion. The government certificates were to be paid out only as the government made public improvements of western lands, which another amendment provided should be undertaken at once. . . ."[28] This proposal does not seem remarkable in an age which has demonstrated that currency can be maintained at any given level with little backing it but force

[26] *Ibid.,* p. 57.   [27] *Ibid.,* p. 89.   [28] *Ibid.,* p. 90.

or faith. We would not, however, expect quite the same results as did our law-abiding revolutionist:

The certificates were always on a par with gold and silver, for either could be had for them at any time to settle all foreign balances, and that was all anyone ever wanted either metal for. This so inflated the currency that debts were again easily paid. There was a terrific howl from the bondholders, but it fell on deaf ears, and had utterly failed to longer have any influence.[29]

The final, most revolutionary amendment was designed to make the United States a more truly middle-class democracy.

All real estate, all personal property kept for sale, all moneys, bonds, stocks, notes, or other evidences of indebtedness in excess of a half-million dollars in value, owned by any resident of the United States, or by any non-resident if said property is within the jurisdiction of the United States, shall, on the ratification of this amendment to the Constitution of the United States, become the property of the Government. . . .[30]

Mark Mishler supports his proposal against all attack: "This is not confiscation. It is restoration. That is what I advocate. I champion restoration. Who, may I ask, earned and produced the wealth of the multi-millionaire? He owns railroads. We never saw him shovel any dirt, drive a spike, lay a rail, or even so much as supervise a job from his office or abode. How came he to have a railroad? How long would it take him to build it? Longer than the world has stood."[31] "The millionaires are the drones of society. They produce nothing, yet they eat the heartiest and are the most robust-looking of all our race. We ask the enforcement of the scriptural doctrine: 'If he shall not work, neither shall he eat.' "[32] The amendment was violently opposed. "The representatives of the plutocrats . . . talked of energy, thrift, and enterprise, of push, pluck, and perseverance, as if they had some, or knew what it was. They talked of the 'survival of the fittest,' when if that role had prevailed they would have been dead or in the almshouse. They talked much about the Nation's honor, the public integrity, and maintaining the credit of the country. They talked anarchy, riot, and bloodshed, and [at] the same time continually threatened rebellion themselves."[33]

When it appeared that the proposed amendment must inevitably pass, the wealthy resorted to a desperate expedient. They plotted with

[29] *Ibid.*, p 91.   [30] *Ibid.*, pp. 131, 132.   [31] *Ibid.*, pp. 136, 137.
[32] *Ibid.*, p. 145.   [33] *Ibid.*, p. 152.

the British ruling class, who were ready to cooperate because of their desire to protect their American investments, and Britain shipped troops to Canada and declared war on us. The country was terrified; the plutocrats counted on this terror to defeat the Amendment. Their plan almost worked, but the British were so inadequately prepared for war that they couldn't manage their bluff. The British fleet, which had been sent to harass our Eastern Coast, was captured by stratagem, almost without a shot, and the Army in Canada was forced to surrender because there was no longer any way to get supplies. The captured troops immediately took out first papers, and Canada was on the way to becoming a part of the United States. In the meantime, the traitorous plutocrats had been punished, the amendment had been passed, and the millennium seemed to be at hand.

"There was not a particle of disturbance in the business world"[34] when this transfer of property to the government was effected. Men continued to work at the same jobs, under the same bosses, at the same wages. Stocks and bonds had changed hands, but business continued to operate as before.

The people, the Government, now had that which they had produced, and which had been the means that had enabled the plutocrats to exact from the producing classes one-half of their yearly product, and required them to do double the work they ought to have done to get the plain necessaries of life. With this great leak stopped, should they not enjoy great prosperity? They thought so, and expected it, but of the extent they had no idea. . . . It carried them forward with leaps and bounds from poverty and want to luxury and affluence. It even surpassed their dreams of opulence.[35]

The government "became the owner of department store stocks until it had a controlling interest in hundreds of these institutions in twenty different cities in the United States. This industry, like all the others, was put under one control and management."[36] With the government controlling the great agencies of distribution, it was inevitable that the small retail shopkeeper would be forced out of business. The government simply ran business at cost, "for the benefit of the people and not for profit."[37] "The merchants and middlemen with their families and dependents had constituted over one-third of the whole population. It cost as much to distribute goods after they were made

[34] *Ibid.*, p. 213.
[36] *Ibid.*, p. 229.
[35] *Ibid.*, pp. 214, 215.
[37] *Idem.*

as it did to make them. Here was one-third of all the people engaged in an industry that ten per cent of the number could have easily conducted."[38] But the middleman could not compete with the government. He was forced to earn his bread "either by the sweat of his brow or by the machine he operates."[39]

Gradually the government nationalized agriculture as well as industry. The process was accomplished indirectly, by having the government begin to operate newly irrigated regions. By efficient methods the government was able to undersell all competitors, and as private farms became unprofitable, they were abandoned, and the farmers either moved to the city or went to work on the state farms. Whole counties were operated as a unit, with a tremendous increase in efficiency. The whole project expanded in geometric ratio. As more dams were built, and more areas were irrigated, production became still more efficient, and still more private lands could be taken over.

The book contains several eloquent chapters dealing with the possibilities of irrigation in the West and Middle West, and of how we can increase our wheat crop many times, and also our herds of cattle and sheep, and how we can raise more chickens, and how we can multiply the number of fish in our lakes and streams. "The fish are raised for market now in many lakes and streams, and are fed as regularly as the Government feeds its cattle. The great salmon fisheries of the Columbia are valued as highly and the fish are fed and cared for as well as are the herds on the plains. It is strange that it took the people so long to learn that fish could not be propagated with great success when unfed and made to live, like cannibals, on each other."[40]

The government started on a huge program of public works, for the people had soon produced enough so that they could have all the luxuries that beautify the home and make life pleasant. There was a tremendous increase in the demand for goods, and in the productive capacity of factories. "Yet, with ever-improving methods and machines, a very small per cent of the people are still able to operate the factories."[41]

[38] *Ibid.,* pp. 228, 229.   [39] *Ibid.,* p. 229.
[40] *Ibid.,* p. 307.   [41] *Ibid.,* p. 316.

And there was utopia, achieved "legally and lawfully, without riot or anarchy, but simply by the people asserting their rights and their constitutional authority to change the fundamental and basic laws . . . of their country. The idea of the great common people, the bulwark of the nation, ever having been oppressed seems strange. They were, but they were their own oppressors."[42]

Educate the people, make them see clearly, without colored glasses, and utopia will be more than a dream. This was the doctrine of the Charles H. Kerr Company; this was the dream of the post-Bellamy Socialists; this was the ideal of the late nineties, when Socialism was becoming respectable, when reformers were still optimistic, and before the movement wore itself out in sporadic and vicious muckracking.

[42] *Ibid.*, p. 324.

CHAPTER FOURTEEN

UTOPIA NOW

THE novels published by the Charles H. Kerr Co. weren't the only ones to hope that real reform was just around the corner. A number of other works of fiction insisted that the millennium could be at hand—if man could organize, if honest newspapers could be published, if there could be a new monetary system, if there could be complete prohibition. But none of them realized how tremendous were the "ifs."

One of these novels, *The People's Program*, by Henry L. Everett, insists upon the power of groups organized for reform. Everett protests in the preface that utopian authors "have not given encouragement to the present generation for the achievement of their magnificent plans. They have considered it necessary to allow more than one hundred years for purposes which can be realized almost immediately if the people choose to work in harmony. The author of this story believes in rushing." And the way to speed things up is for literary men and labor unions to work together to increase "the number of their friends and members. The lecture platform and literature pertaining to the labor movement should be everywhere employed to rouse the people to the importance of united action, and to persuade them that they can vastly improve their opportunities and enjoyments in life."[1]

The story explains how easy it would be to mold the social conscience of a generation. The Kings' Daughters in Berlin begin the process. They take measures against dueling, and with their geometric league accomplish their purpose. Streeter, the hero, is impressed. His paper, *The Deutcher Student*, develops rapidly, and so does his love affair. Both prosper. He becomes a political influence, he meets the Emperor, becomes an adopted member of the Hohenzollern family, and urges upon the Emperor the necessity of pushing Bismarck aside, and working for the closer unity of labor and capital.

[1] Henry L. Everett, *The People's Program*, New York, 1892, p. v.

His student reform movement exercises tremendous influence. He moves to the United States and inaugurates a summer rest-encampment, where students study languages, religion, and political and social problems. Along with this he organizes a labor colony in Kansas, modeled after the plan of General Booth of the Salvation Army. The colony becomes a refuge for the unemployed. The older the man, the easier is his job. Hours of work vary, depending upon the age of the individual and the difficulty of the task. Farmers, for example, work eight hours, forest workers, eight hours, construction workers, six hours, store keepers ten hours a day. It is arranged, for the most part, so that a man's work is not the same in both summer and winter. Teachers are one of the few exceptions. They are to teach between the ages of 20 and 30, "and then after studying medicine, should practice until 40. From 40 to 50 they would be occupied with the profession of the law, and after reaching the age of 50 their varied experience would particularly prepare them for the ministry, and the rest of their lives would be devoted to that profession and to literary pursuits."[2]

With these activities Streeter gains such a reputation that he is made Secretary of State. As a result of his influence, this system of variation of labor is made nation-wide. There are difficulties, but mostly these resolve themselves into recalcitrant employers, who are easily persuaded by the threat of competition. The government inaugurates certain reforms, including:

1. Federal ownership of the telegraph.
2. State construction of railroads.
3. Suffrage for women.
4. Free coinage.
5. Taxation of "all private inheritances in estates exceeding $50,000."[3]
6. Pensions for all those over seventy.
7. Sunday closing of all places of business, except drug stores.
8. Investigation of insane asylums and charitable institutions.
9. An attempt to secure peace by granting to Russia, Germany, the United States, and England authority to suppress all warlike actions in their various spheres.

[2] *Ibid.*, p. 169.   [3] *Ibid.*, p. 189.

The result is prosperity and a tremendous religious and educational revival. Men seem to think that they can convert to Christianity the peoples of all the world. Colleges are taken over by the State. French and German become compulsory, but whether the colleges are improved is a matter of debate. And also, of course, it is a matter of debate whether this should be called utopian. In one sense it is. The reforms are definite enough, and the author, at any rate, thinks that his proposed reforms would create a different and utopian world. But the proposals don't seem very revolutionary now. Generally, they are the same as Upton Sinclair's EPIC plan, based on work relief, only Everett provides much more frosting.

Morrison Swift's *A League of Justice* is a forceful pamphlet designed to convince people that inequality, injustice and poverty are inevitable under the capitalistic order, and that socialism, or utopia, is very definitely obtainable. The great stumbling block to socialism is the misery and hardship of the transition period. Swift's solution follows the Robin Hood technique: his collaborators rob the robbers, and give back to the working man a fair share of what he has really earned. The definition of a robber is inclusive:

Any man who takes and uses for himself more than is necessary for his life and health and development, or for the life, health, and development of those dependent on him, while others lack what is necessary for their life, health and development, is a robber![4]

With the vast funds they acquire the leaders establish an honest newspaper, devoted to truth and the honest education of the people. Since the paper contains no advertising and is distributed free, it soon has a tremendous following.

The great lying, gossiping, scandalising, advertising, sycophant, commercial, capital-serving sheets, went about now only as ghosts, through which their bones could be seen. Their absorbers printed no advertisements for pay. . . . Deceitful puffs of quack objects, vegetable, human and mineral, collapsed like a punctured balloon, having no bellows to inflate them. But in the League Journal appeared lists of all the new cooperative establishments, whether factories or stores, and the working people were advised to buy of these only, since their patronage would solidify such industries and compel others to follow their example.[5]

[4] Morrison J. Swift, *A League of Justice*, Boston, 1893, p. 80.
[5] *Ibid.*, p. 21.

Truth is the great leavening agent. The newspaper serves as a prosecutor; it ferrets out the truth and by vast publicity guarantees justice or restitution. The social structure undergoes rapid change. Political parties disappear. Lawyers are forced to perform useful work. Education ceases to be a matter of studying dead languages and dead institutions. Everyone teaches, not just the old "teaching body." "As there was no further use for the school buildings, they were . . . used for educational purposes."[6] There is a new philosophy of religion: "This is the true church; knowledge adapted to life is religion; the enthusiasm to construct a grand, adorable earth is divine love. . . ."[7]

The activities of the League are discovered after fourteen years, but there could be no changing the course of events. There is a terrific hue and cry; thousands are arrested; the leaders give themselves up and are convicted. But then the people rebel; the capitalists, the president, and the judiciary are cowed, and they finally agree to the formation of a new order based on the principles of the League of Justice. In other words, the people have the power to secure utopia for themselves. The only problem is to convince them of that power. Morrison's solution, honest newspapers, is no solution at all, because even pragmatic truth is not obvious. Part of what he says is reasonable enough, but he blunders, as do so many other utopians, in discounting the importance of the "ifs."

George Farnell, a Providence, R.I., journalist, was convinced of the desirability of many of Bellamy's ideas, but he felt that Bellamy had touched much too lightly on the means of transition to that ideal state. It is the means of transition, he thought, not the final organization of society, that should most concern thinkers. He explains his point of view in the preface to *Rev. Josiah Hilton:*

It has always seemed to me that there was a somewhat painful hiatus between the condition of society to-day and the imaginary state of society, as depicted by Edward Bellamy in his "Looking Backward," which hiatus is but very slightly hinted at in his "Equality."

Reverend Josiah Hilton is intended merely as a suggestion of how that gap may be bridged. Perhaps the appearance of this little book will confirm a

---

[6] *Ibid.,* p. 38.
[7] *Ibid.,* p. 40.

critical public in its acceptance for truth of that old and well worn adage, "Fools rush in where angels fear to tread."[8]

There is a story woven into the argument, the story of how Mr. Trevor, an authority on money, convinces the Reverend Josiah Hilton of the wisdom of his views, and of how, together, they prepare to lead a crusade of education. The basis of their argument is that the monetary system is the fundamental cause of the economic dilemma—want in the presence of abundance. This is the old objection of the free silverites and the greenbackers, but the Hiltonites have a new approach. Man's desire for money, runs the argument, is based on fear.

This desire to prepare for future wants was intensified when he (man) found that he could, at little or no cost or trouble to himself, command the services of his fellows; and it was still further intensified when he discovered that he could represent those accumulations for future use in gold and silver, things of considerable comparative value, but of relatively small bulk. It is a very easy step from that point to a state where these thing, (gold and silver), representatives of value themselves, become the only things sought after. . . .[9]

Low wages are a necessary corollary of such a monetary order. Wages, according to Farnell, are never much higher than the requirements of a minimum standard of living. Encouraging thrift, then, is simply encouraging the employer to reduce wages still further. "Wages . . . are but food, clothing and shelter, and the less of food the laborer can get along with, the less of clothing he needs to wear, and the lower the cost of shelter from heat and cold, the less must his wages be."[10]

The solution is a scientific money, based not on a commodity but on labor performed. If the state should want to build a railroad, the system would work in this wise:

The State would first make an estimate of the probable cost. To meet this cost the State might then issue its notes, or promises to redeem, to the extent of that amount. The notes might be valued at and called one dollar each, and the whole million charged against the railroad. These notes would then be paid to the laborers who worked on the road, to the material supply, and to all concerned. The notes would be, so far as these parties were concerned, money, and would be accepted throughout the whole community

[8] George Farnell, *Rev. Josiah Hilton,* Providence, 1898, Preface.
[9] *Ibid.,* p. 54.   [10] *Ibid.,* p. 75.

as current money. In the course of time the railroad is finished and put in operation. Receipts begin to flow into the hands of the State government from that source. After deducting the expenses of running the road, the balance would be applied to taking up, or redeeming, the notes, and when the profits had amounted to a sum equal to the amount of the notes issued, and the notes all redeemed, the State would then receive for the people at large all the rest of the profits of operating the railroad, which could be applied either in a reduction of the transportation rates or to meet the general expenses of the government.[11]

Even the expenses of government could be met by labor notes, notes which would have value simply because they represented labor performed. There would be no need for taxes.

Farnell admits that the change would have to come slowly, that for a time there would have to be two symbols of wealth, labor notes and conventional money. He largely ignores the difficulties in such a situation. And when he comes to dealing with the problem of private ownership of land, he evades the issue, just as Bellamy does, by explaining that we must rely on education.

During the transitional period private ownership in land will continue to exist, perforce, but as that period draws nearer and nearer to a close, the people will have become so fully educated and enlightened,—and these questions are principally questions of education and enlightenment,—interests of the whole people (not to individual interest, as is . . . far too much the case with governments today), that they will see more and more clearly the necessity that the land, too, must be nationalized, that it, too, must come under the control and supervision of the people through their representative.[12]

In the nineties, Brown University, under President Andrews, was considered a hotbed of radical monetary theory. Farnell must have come under that influence. These notions about money based only on labor and faith seem less unreasonable today, even to the conservative, than they must have seemed fifty years ago. Our modern debt structure has proved convincingly the possibilities of a managed currency without any backlog of precious metals.

Morrison Swift and George Farnell approach the lunatic fringe. Perhaps *The League of Justice* should be included in that group, but it is not as absurd as *The Beginning*, a badly written novel praising the virtues of prohibition. The preface has this to say: "Our small

[11] *Ibid.*, pp. 20, 21.
[12] *Ibid.*, p. 83.

debating club was discussing the question as to whether the People's Party's platform, if adopted by the country and put in force and extended as it would have to be, would benefit the great mass of working men, that is, raise the masses." The decision is that it would not—that successful reforms must be more far-reaching than those proposed by the Populists. The solution is education—to save men before they fall rather than afterwards. According to this scheme, the state must educate the child, on the theory that then there is equal opportunity for all. Eventually there would be utopia, complete with centralized laundries, dish washing machines, sample stores, elevated railroads, and well-designed cities. And all this is supposed to be brought about by education and an absence of drunkards.

In the first place they saw that Socialism to be possible, must begin at the bottom and work up, and not at the top and pull down to make all level; and they say, too, that it must be a gradual and natural change, and the people must be educated up to it; but besides there were great immediate benefits. Nearly all the deserving and helpless poor, under the old system, were among married people with large families, where the man was a drunkard.[13]

There is little more to be said about *The Beginning*, except that perhaps the locale of utopia, Chicago, makes the author's insistence upon prohibition more understandable—it does not make it more intelligent.

[13] [Anon.] *The Beginning, a Romance of Chicago as It Might Be*, Chicago, 1893, p. 67.

CHAPTER FIFTEEN

MARS AND UTOPIA

HENRY OLERICH'S *A Cityless and Countryless World*, 1893, is the best of the stories about Mars. According to the fiction, Mars is geologically older than Earth, and so also is its social and industrial system more mature. Martians, then, can discuss Earth's place in the evolutionary scale with some historical exactness and perspective, for Mars had already passed through the same stages.

Mars is a cityless and countryless world. After man had discovered the folly of living in small, primitive units, he began "to locate his large buildings in beautiful parks, at short intervals, in straight lines, on the perimeter of a rectangular community. The large size families and the nearness of the building satisfy his social nature; the arrangement of buildings, in straight lines, gives commercial and mechanical advantages; the large families give him social and domestic advantages which greatly conduce to his health, prosperity and happiness. The form and size of our communities gives us the greatest commercial and agricultural advantage. We all live right on the edge of the agricultural land from which all wealth must be produced either directly or indirectly."[1]

Everyone lives in these large family groups. The smallest dwellings house about a thousand people. There are no small, individual family units; the unit is pretty much the same as in a primitive tribe. And since it is considered desirable for the various members of a family to live in the most perfect freedom with each other, there is no such thing as marriage. The woman chooses her mate with perfect freedom, and also the times when they shall be together and the number of children. Men and women live with each other only so long as they love each other. Since each has his own quarters, there is no economic compulsion one way or the other. No marriage

[1] Henry Olerich, *A Cityless and Countryless World; An Outline of Practical, Co-operative Individualism*, Holstein, Iowa, 1893, p. 238.

ceremony was considered necessary to sanctify a purely physical act. Men and women are chaste simply because they want to be.

One is quick to insist that this whole notion is ridiculous, that marriage, as we know it, is absolutely essential to any sort of ordered existence. But it is easy to find examples of societies in which men and women change mates rather casually without disrupting their social equilibrium. Herman Melville described such a society in *Typee*. There are even suggestions of such radical notions in the current periodicals. John Hyde Preston insists, in the May, 1938, *Harper's*, that collective living is the one way to take the drabness out of married life.

Everyone works, according to his abilities, even the children. All work is respected. It all needs to be done, and there is no thought of demeaning oneself. Since everyone's education, prospects, and attitudes are equal, there can be no looking down on any individual. The hours of work are determined by the demand for labor, but usually two hours a day is enough. Money and labor are almost synonymous, for money simply represents hours of work. All wealth "is produced by productive labor, and a day's, or an hour's, or a minute's productive labor, produces, in an average, so much wealth; and the individual who performs the labor should receive all the money or labor checks, which represent the wealth he has produced."[2] The total labor hours in any community are added, and that much wealth is issued every week. In other words, money, which should represent wealth, does actually represent the exact amount of wealth produced at any given time. When the money returns to the central issuing agency, it is cancelled. There are no taxes, and there is no need for taxes, for the people do the work, and are accredited for it in labor, which is wealth. "Land is not produced by labor, and, therefore, we do not consider land wealth. . . . Of course the improvement made on land is wealth and belongs exclusively to the producers. We recognize the right of owning land only by occupancy and use, not by deed or paper title. . . ."[3]

Officials are not elected by ballot. The best men are chosen for any given task, just as in a family. "Our foreman is leader only just so far as his co-laborers are willing to acknowledge him as such; and when a person of greater ability appears in his branch of industry,

[2] *Ibid.*, p. 172. [3] *Ibid.*, p. 230.

the former leader naturally resigns his position to the superior, because such a resignation is agreeable to the former leader, as well as to his co-laborers. Hence the leader always does the most and best work and receives no more pay than the commonest laborer."[4]

Children are educated by precept, by curiosity, by example—but not in the schoolroom. Parents have a great deal of time to devote to their children, and so they learn rapidly. They are encouraged but not forced to take part in activities. They are, in effect, allowed to do as they wish, according to the best progressive school techniques.

You can easily see that we are all teachers and all pupils at the same time. We study our whole life time and graduate only at death. . . . The teachers, as well as the pupils, perform their manual labor daily; for we believe: That a knowledge of manual labor is the most important education we can receive. That a short, easy day's labor . . . promotes the development of body and mind. That labor must be made so easy, attractive and agreeable that we do it for the pleasure that is in it. . . . That no one should be forced to study or learn what he finds no pleasure in.[5]

Along with these changes in marriage, education, and co-operative living, the Martians were addicted to many of the other practices dear to nineteenth century reformers. They were complete vegetarians, and so, according to Olerich, avoided many diseases. They practiced cremation: there were no funerals, no processions, no monuments. "Our aid and sympathy are always with the living."[6] They were all agnostics, influenced, it would seem, largely by Herbert Spencer. And, of course, they used a number of scientific tricks to simplify living. The streets, for example, were artificially heated, by electricity, in order to simplify the removal of snow.

The transition of Mars from the old to the new order was extremely gradual. The first groups began living together to save work. As the groups gradually became larger and larger and more self-sustaining, they were able to force competitors out of business—but these were often glad to join the more successful cooperatives. This notion that cooperatives would inevitably become all-powerful and transform the state into a socialist order was exceedingly widespread. Both Charles W. Caryl's *New Era*, 1897, and James Casey's *A New Moral World*, 1885, develop the theory in detail.

For the most part, this is another *Looking Backward*, although the

[4] *Ibid.*, p. 243.   [5] *Ibid.*, p. 324.   [6] *Ibid.*, p. 433.

ideas are less convincingly explained. Olerich's most significant point
is that city and country should be fused. He would create, in a sense,
a large number of nearly self-sufficient units, much as he knows in his
native Iowa. But here, again, the idea is better developed in Caryl's
New Era.

Olerich's thinking is half way between an anarchist's and a socialist's. He hates all regimentation, and yet he realizes that a good deal
of it is essential. He writes in the preface:

In this work I shall endeavor to show that social and economic prosperity . . .
can be attained only in a system which recognizes extensive voluntary cooperation as its fundamental principle of production and distribution, and
which concedes to every individual the right to do as he wills, provided he
does not infringe the equal rights of any other person. . . .[7]

This is the sort of book that gives rise to the notion that all utopian
novelists are wide-eyed, irrational reformers. After reading this, one
can sympathize with Stuart Chase's indictment:

They are indefatigable in pointing out the shortcomings of society, but
they are vague as to the precise nature of available substitutes. They seldom define their standards. Yet standards they must have; otherwise it
would be impossible to criticize. They either take it for granted that the
reader shares their inward knowledge, or else, and more probably, the
standards have never been formulated in the critic's conscious processes at
all. They have grown in the back of his mind, darkly.

. . . There is a strange chill about all Utopias; they are inhabited by gods,
not men. . . . The negatives stretch to the horizon, but the positives are
either lacking entirely or, when focused before us, appear cold or a little
absurd.[8]

1893 must have been a good year for stories about Mars, and also
for spiritualistic embroidery. William Simpson's book, *The Man from
Mars,* followed the pattern of *A Cityless and Countryless World,* but
the reforms are more imaginative and also less soundly developed.
The hero of the story is a hermit who studies wild life, the stars, and
the foibles of civilization. One evening while he is studying Mars
he suddenly collapses, and, in a stupor, sees before him a handsome
and spiritual Martian who casts no shadow. But even though he
is an intangible and spiritual being, he is able to give the hermit a

[7] *Ibid.,* p. 6.
[8] Stuart Chase, "A Very Private Utopia," *The Nation,* 126:559.

long lecture on what is wrong with Earth, from the vantage point of a civilization many centuries more advanced. He reflects upon Earth in the same manner that we adopt when we reflect upon the middle ages. "In your present state, you appear to us as a world of discord, confusion, strife. While we were long ago resolved into a single, homogeneous people, you are still divided into nations and countries unridden yet of the barbarious pride of conflict."[9] He goes on to explain the basis of Mars' placid civilization:

We acknowledge as the foundation of all material progress that the honest accumulation of wealth should be the privilege of all; and that the rights of property should be protected, and the enjoyment of it secured to everyone. Yet with these principles firmly and successfully carried out in our government, we have, for many centuries, considered it necessary to support and sustain the interests of the labor class by special legislative action. You have pursued a directly opposite course.[10]

In our philosophy we recognize only two honest ways of accumulating wealth. One is the saving of wages, and the other the profits on capital; and our legislation has been chiefly directed to make the chances of acquiring wealth by these two methods as easy as possible.[11]

In other words, the simplest way to make labor recognize property rights is to give labor some property. "Landlordism, as it exists with you, is unknown amongst us."[12] If the profits from land increase, so do the taxes. In return, the state provides free water, light, and heat. Taxation on Earth, he says, is ridiculous. The "ground rents alone now consume every ten years the whole cost of all buildings and contents. In other words, every vestige of the accumulated labor of your city goes into the pockets of its landlords every ten years."[13] Simpson had certainly studied the ideas of Henry George.

New cities on Mars are planned. The government erects the public buildings in the center, and then the surrounding private buildings must all be passed on by a board of architects to insure that they conform in style and material. "Our city grows in solid expansion. There are no straggling suburbs."[14]

All forms of labor are respected. "We produce more wealth than you in a given time because, with a few exceptions, all are engaged

[9] William Simpson, *The Man from Mars,* San Francisco, 1893, p. 29.
[10] *Ibid.,* p. 67.　　　　[11] *Ibid.,* p. 69.　　　　[12] *Ibid.,* p. 75.
[13] *Ibid.,* p. 81.　　　　[14] *Ibid.,* p. 107.

in the business of production. By this increased productiveness every consumer is richer. He is able by a smaller amount of labor to procure a greater number of the objects of desire."[15] "We hold it to be a demoralizing evil that wealth should be obtained without industry."[16] Although all labor is equally respected, it is not all equally well paid. Manual labor is paid on a basis of skill, strength and agility, and professional men are paid according to talent, intelligence and capability. If it were only possible to determine who has the most ability, or intelligence, or capability, the idea might be reasonable— but not even Superman would pretend to make such judgments.

Strong bodies are respected; weakness is scorned. Everyone must pass periodic medical exams; and unless his physical record is good, no one is allowed to marry. In some respects, then, the ideas sound modern, particularly in the discussions of architecture which insist upon free use of glass in construction. In such other respects as the insistence upon the necessity of cremation, and the possibilities of the airplane, Simpson is simply following the conventional Bellamy pattern. But conventional or not, this is one of the utopian novels that was widely read. The spiritualistic trim and pseudo-mystical web-spinning, however, might well have been more appealing than the utopian framework.

[15] *Ibid.*, p. 109.
[16] *Ibid.*, p. 136.

CHAPTER SIXTEEN

THE UTILITARIAN CONSIDERS UTOPIA

NOT all of the men who made plans for a better world were left-wing reformers, and not all were wishful thinkers. John Bachelder, Alexander Craig, and Alvarado Fuller were very definitely right-wing in their thinking, more devoted to utilitarianism than to idealism. In their novels the state becomes efficient, paternalistic, and dull. If *utopia* is synonymous with the efficient state, then here is utopia—but not the sort to dream about.

John Bachelder was a successful inventer, a successful manufacturer, and an extremely unlucky business man. Becoming interested in the sewing machine at an early date, "he bought a small machine-shop, retired from business, and devoted his time to mastering the machinist's trade." Eventually he "developed the continuous feed, the vertical needle, and the horizontal table, all features of the modern sewing machine."[1] But he was forced to sell his patents before they became valuable, and so missed several million dollars. If this wasn't enough to make him susceptible to socialist doctrine, he had two unlucky experiences as a manufacturer: the first venture was forced under by the post Civil War depression, the second by the panic of 1877-78. After this second failure he became interested in literary matters, and with the publication of *Looking Backward* started to write a sequel which might deal more accurately with scientific detail. The result is a pleasant novel, *A.D. 2050*, which is loaded down with sound scientific and mechanical observation. His reflections on the capitalistic system, however, are influenced more by his own bad luck than by any careful study of Edward Bellamy.

According to Bachelder's story, the people of Long Island and New York had quickly become dissatisfied with the "plausible rhetoric and universal panaceas" of Bellamy's world, and had broken away, to form a new state, Atlantis, and to govern themselves in keeping with the principles of a modified capitalism. The secret of

[1] Article on Bachelder in the *Dictionary of American Biography*.

their independent existence was their knowledge of electricity, which they were able to use as a weapon, both in peace and war. This whole system demands that power and authority be centralized. Only six men are allowed to know the secrets of their electrical skill. Officers serve terms of ten years. They are elected, but only those can vote who have certain property qualification. The administrators gave the people only so many rights and privileges as seemed consistent with the greater good. Thus, there were no patents; there was limitation of income; there was no jury system—on the theory that boards of commissioners and judges could most accurately determine matters of truth and justice. On the other hand, the citizen had to do those things which were for his own good. Light, heat, and water were provided free. The citizen was born in a state hospital, raised in state nurseries, and all his life treated by state-paid doctors. He was given no chance to waste his money on patent medicines. He was not allowed to remain happily illiterate. He must be trained and conditioned by the educational factory, for the one aim of the state was to produce useful, not happy, citizens. "All our legislation is intended to aid and elevate, to check monopoly and abolish caste."[2]

Since their own citizens were so thoroughly virtuous, it was thought necessary to be completely cold-blooded in dealing with other countries. Atlantis needed no import taxes to protect its own efficient industries, and so it insisted on free trade with all other countries. And there was no immigration permitted. "It was necessary to exclude the ignorant and degraded masses of other nations to improve and elevate our own people. No intelligent or humane government of people invite infectious diseases. As an economic question it is simply one of trade, with demand and supply as the arbiter. Our advantages have been gained in a moral and properly legitimate way, and it would be the height of folly to throw the corn to the swine and subsist on the husks ourselves."[3] In modern terminology, then, Atlantians were Machiavellian isolationists.

Eventually, the rest of the country realized the emptiness of communism, that it had become established only when the contending forces had exhausted themselves, and that its longtime result was

[2] [John Bachelder], *A.D. 2050*, San Francisco, 1890, p. 51.
[3] *Ibid.*, p. 46.

"a dearth of intellect and energy." Only after the people had realized this, could there be any restoration to prosperity. This model was the system of Atlantis—"the leading and guiding star of the world."

During the confused transition period, when the old United States was adopting Atlantian principles, the country was attacked by the Chinese—but the greater speed, power, and technical skill of the Atlantians enabled them to overwhelm the enemy fleet. After this, all of the countries of the world gradually became republics, with Atlantis as the mother and protector.

The merits of the Atlantian system are not completely obvious to the casual reader—unless it be that their system encouraged such discoveries as the scientific transformation of sewage into fertilizer, and the development of "fabrina," a nylonish substitute for silk. But these don't seem to be enough to change this country of useful endeavor and strait-laced morality into utopia.

Ionia is not the remote, isolated country that Alexander Craig makes it out to be. *Ionia* is the lineal descendant of Plato's *Republic* and Bacon's *New Atlantis,* with certain such fresh characteristics as temples of music instead of churches, and efficient, machine-minded administrators who are concerned only with the practical.

Ionia, which is lost in the Himalyas, much as is Shangri-La, was originally settled by Greeks who had been forced out of their homeland by Alexander. The government was first republican, then monarchical, and finally again republican. The government has a single legislative body, the senate, which is elected by the representatives of the people. Every man has a vote, which he casts annually for the representative of his district. These magistrates elect the senators, who serve for three years, one third of their number being renewed each year. Each legislator is paid a moderate salary, a salary not sufficient to form an inducement to aspire to office. On the other hand, any man who refuses to accept an office is subject to a heavy fine.

Duty is more important to the Ionian than liberty:

The western nations are given to making a panacea of liberty and worshipping it as a panacea for all political ills, whereas it is merely a negative quality after all, and means no more than the absence of despotism. . . . with us duty comes first and liberty afterwards, and as the good of the individual can only be obtained through the well being of the whole community, we insist that each member of it must sacrifice just as much of his liberty and his personal advantages as the present and future good of society requires.[4]

Acting on this principle, then, the Ionians solved the Jewish problem simply by denying Jews the right to marry. In such fashion, of course, all the problems in the world could be solved by refusing to allow anyone to bear children.

The secret of Ionia's wise men and fair women is supposed to be four basic laws:

1. The Land Law, which gives title of all land to the state, and so prevents the formation of a landed aristocracy.

2. The Law of Inheritance, which provides that inheritance shall only be in the direct line, that no one shall ever inherit more than one hundred thousand pounds, and that all over that amount shall go to the state.

3. The Criminal Law, which deprives all criminals of "the power of procreation," on the theory that the criminal class must then gradually disappear.

4. The Marriage Law, which limits the privilege to those who are well and strong and can prove that they will be able to support a family. Large families are discouraged, simply because it is considered desirable to keep the population constant.

All labor is respectable. There are servants, but they are treated as members of the family. Craig does not allow himself to wonder if the servants themselves would be enthusiastic about such a relationship.

In other respects, too, the state encourages the communal spirit. People live together in huge apartment houses. Busses are free, and so are heat, water, and light. In spite of such governmental benevolence, taxes are light because they are properly distributed, on a sort of single tax principle. The government owns the land; the city leases it from the government, and the individual, in turn, leases it from the city at a fair price. Thus, any increase in the value of land is enjoyed by the people and does not go into the pockets of speculators.

Perhaps the most striking example of Ionian rationalizing is this attitude towards advertising:

[4] Alexander Craig, *Ionia, Land of Wise Men and Fair Women*, Chicago, 1898, p. 216.

Our people do not believe in bargains, but are willing to pay a good price for a good article. We thus save the immense sums which go to support your far too numerous newspapers, as well as the money which is spent in disfiguring your streets and public conveyances.[5]

Some of Craig's dream is conceivable, but it leaves the reader with a good many doubts. Would the Ionian's marriage program work; would their criminal class continue to flourish; and the average citizen continue to search out bargains in every activity of life? A paternalistic government can create efficiency; it can make the people economize; it can make them rationalize their economies, but it cannot make them enjoy the process.

Ionia is not the sort of utopia that provides fuel for pleasant dreams. The utopian should not always have to think about the greater good. We all have too many idiosyncrasies and we take too much pleasure in making our own mistakes.

Craig would certainly have approved of Alvarado Fuller's *A.D.2000*, 1890, for here, too, is an insistence upon increased centralization and less democratic nonsense. Both think of their efficient, highly mechanized states as democratic, but they leave only a shell of democratic procedure. It would be quite easy to call Fuller's program dictatorship. Even an out-and-out fascist is likely to rationalize his views and believe that he is concerned with the greater good. The hero of the novel, Junius Colby, dissatisfied with life as an impecunious Lieutenant, arranges to be entombed for one hundred years, to be awakened, finally, by an ingenious device manipulated by the changing force of magnetic north. The pseudo-scientific hocus-pocus is remarkably well worked out. Junius comes to life again in 2000 A.D., and, in due course, is adopted by the President, who turns out to be the great-grandson of one of Junius's former army friends. And yet he is unhappy, for he cannot forget the girl he loved a hundred years before. But there is a miracle; a letter is found which explains that his fiancée had also been entombed. She is found; Junius falls in love with her, little realizing who she really is; they marry, and Junius has a new interest in political and philosophical problems.

The key to this better world is four-fold: A milder climate, a more efficient judiciary, more equitable taxation, and a strict central

[5] *Ibid.*, p. 139.

control over profits and wages. The improved climate, secured by damming and controlling the Gulf Stream, is not the least rational of these proposals for securing a better world. For instance, Fuller wants to supplant the jury system with the court martial system, to put justice in the hands of trained jurists, who must enforce definite penalties, and from whose decisions there is no appeal except to higher courts—and then only on condition that if the lower court is sustained, the penalty be doubled. There are no taxes except on tobacco and liquors. Thus the people were to be denied even their petty vices. The government operates on the revenue from state ownership of railroads, telegraph, and post-office, and on all profits of more than twenty per cent, which are confiscated. Fuller admits that the result would be to keep wages high. He forgets that in such case the government would collect little in surplus profits.

Most utopian novels have ingenuity, idealism, sweetness, or a naive style to recommend them. *A.D.2000* is interesting for only two reasons: the pseudo-scientific stage setting is elaborate, although neither as elaborate nor as amusing as that contained in any issue of *Popular Mechanics*, and, along with *A.D. 2050* and *Ionia*, the book illustrates the fact that the political philosophy of some of those who fancied themselves utopians was extremely reactionary.

CHAPTER SEVENTEEN

THE UTOPIA OF ESCAPE

OCCASIONALLY a man writes simply to tell a story, without pointing a moral, and without shaking an admonitory finger. It is the fashion to speak of such writing as "escape literature." In the nineties, the utopian framework was extremely popular; utopias were in the air and seemed to present an opportunity for a writer who was searching for the key to public taste. W. N. Harben, a Georgian, was looking around for fresh subject matter. He had learned to write by studying the Leather-stocking tales, and he had absorbed one lesson—that plot is more important than characterization. His first novel, *White Marie,* dealt with the tragedy of slavery, and although he disclaimed any intent to preach, Southerners regarded him as a traitor. With such warning he tucked his social conscience away and devoted himself to adventure stories, "to stories of detectives, of far-wandering balloons, and of literary life in New York."[1]

The Land of the Changing Sun, 1894, is one of his apprentice novels. The story shows imagination and vigor; it has some rousing action and a pleasant enough love story. Two aeronauts land on a deserted island, but they are almost immediately captured by the crew of a submarine which noses out of a lake. As captives they are delivered, by way of the lake, to a vast internal kingdom, lighted by an artificial, electric sun. Shipwrecked sailors had stayed on the island originally because there were large deposits of gold and silver. Later, discovering the wide-spreading caves and the salubrious air in them, they had migrated within the earth and set up a new order of government. The kingdom is not utopia—except that the citizens are magnificent physical specimens. But this is achieved by a drastic policy. The infirm or "tainted" are isolated, behind a great wall, and left to starve. One of the aeronauts is so weak that he is left to die in the wasteland of the "tainted." He escapes, however, along with an Alphan, and discovers that the sea has broken into the earth. If it reaches the

---

[1] Article on Harben in the *Dictionary of American Biography.*

internal fires there will be a tremendous explosion. The catastrophe is postponed but preparations are made to abandon the kingdom, return to the outside world, and start a new government.

As utopian novels go, this is extremely readable. The ideas are not those of the reform movement, and there is no shred of social significance apart from the expressed belief in a better public health program.

Generation after generation we improve mentally and physically. We are the only people who have ever attempted to thoroughly study the science of living. Your medical men may be numbered by the millions; your remedies for your ills change daily; what you say is good for the health today is tomorrow believed to be poison; today you try to make blood to give you strength, and half a century ago you believed in taking it from the weakest of your patients. With all this fuss over health, you will think nothing of allowing the son of a man who died of a loathesome hereditary disease to marry a woman whose family has never had a taint of blood. Here no such thing is thought of. To begin with, no person who is not thoroughly sound can remain with us. Every heart beat is heard by our medical men and every vein is transparent. You see evidences of the benefit of our system in the men and women around you.[2]

Although we are likely to sympathize with Harben's conception of the greater good, the terms on which he secures this perfect race seem much too severe. And it is the terms which are important, for all reforms must be based essentially on compromise.

Albert Adams Merrill carried his literary bluff much farther than Harben. He made a great pretense of having written a serious study of economics and politics, but his only real concern was to tell a good story. He succeeded in doing that, and he also succeeded in providing good utopian stage sets. *The Great Awakening,* 1899, follows the most popular of the utopian plots—the hero comes to life in another century, only this time he had really died. There had been some slight mistake about the transmigration of souls, and he awoke in the twenty-second century to find himself in another man's full grown body, but with his old, adjusted and conditioned nineteenth century mind. He learns about the new era from a professor, in the best Bellamy technique, and eventually he learns enough about the transition from the nineteenth century system to become a teacher of Mediaeval history.

[2] W. N. Harben, *The Land of the Changing Sun,* New York, 1894, p. 66.

As an historian, he looked back at the nineteenth century as "the Age of Degeneration, because men had degenerated from producing to controlling wealth."[3] Henry George was reckoned as the only intelligent economist of that day, simply because he understood that with progress came inevitable poverty. "His medicine for the disease was a single tax on land." Had his prescription been followed, social degeneration might well have been postponed indefinitely. The single tax "would have stopped land speculation,"[4] and would have kept the poor from becoming the victims of all speculation.

Conditions had continued to become worse, each depression more severe, and each recovery leaving more unemployed. In the year 2021 there was a violent upheaval; the old capitalistic structure was discarded. What money there was in circulation was divided equally, but at the same time the basis of money was changed so that it represented real wealth. Four fundamental laws were promulgated:

1. "Stability of government is necessary to the greatest production of wealth.

2. "A condition in which industry is absolutely free from all government interference is necessary for the greatest production of wealth.

3. "Private ownership of any necessity tends to diminish the production of wealth in proportion as that ownership becomes a monopoly.

4. "Equal distribution of wealth is necessary for the greatest production of wealth."[5]

It is impossible for the reader to determine where private ownership ends and state capitalism begins. He is simply assured that the system works and that the problem of taxation, for instance, had been solved by having the government deduct expenses before the surplus from the national income was distributed. But along with this vague rationalizing are some very specific suggestions. Merrill proposes electric pumps for hydrants, an increased use of steel and glass in construction, an increased use of pneumatic tires, and roads made of asphalt. He suggests airplanes as effective weapons in police work. He also considers them as weapons of war, but decides that since their

[3] Albert Adams Merrill, *The Great Awakening*, Boston, 1899, p. 35.
[4] *Ibid.*, p. 135.   [5] *Ibid.*, pp. 206, 207.

striking power would be so terrific, neither side would be willing to risk the consequences of war. Along with all the other utopians, he wants to change our clothing, to do away with silly fashions and to attempt with every garment "to get the greatest beauty compatible with usefulness."[6] Merrill recognizes that our marriage system is not perfect. His solution is birth control, so administered "that the birth of children is regulated regardless of the gratification of passion," and designed to keep the population static. He almost succeeds in making his idea sound reasonable.

If we will believe the preface, there is a very definite moral contained in *The Great Awakening:* "Progress depends upon two things: first the accumulation, and then the diffusion, of knowledge; and these should go hand in hand to attain the best results. Skepticism leads to investigation, and investigation leads to the accumulation of knowledge. To believe is to remain stationary, to doubt is to progress. Let every man, then, investigate for himself, adopt systems, not because they are old, but because they are good, not because they exist, but because they should exist. Let every man think for himself and express his thoughts freely. This is the philosophy of the twenty-second century, and its goal is happiness and plenty."

Merrill proposes a worthy moral, but this is not a book that is read to increase one's skepticism, or to make one think more clearly. It is not good Henry George; it is not even very good Bellamy; but, like *The Land of the Changing Sun,* it is a pleasant, rather lively escape novel.

[6] *Ibid.,* p. 139.

CHAPTER EIGHTEEN

COOPERATION—THE NEW WAY TO GOD AND UTOPIA

ECONOMIC problems were becoming more and more obvious in the nineties, and an increasing number of Americans were seeking reassurance in revealed religion. Americans had drifted away from the stern philosophy of earlier days; life had become easier, and so had religious observances. But when the world seemed to offer little hope of fulfilling earthly ambitions, more men turned again to God. God and utopia became almost synonymous.

Bradford Peck, Charles Caryl, and Milan C. Edson are very different in background and thinking, yet all three of them have an almost mystical faith in cooperation. With them, the word itself came to have almost a religious significance.

Bradford Peck is not a much better thinker than the others, but he is, at least, less rhetorical. He was the owner of the largest department store in Lewiston, Maine; he was a man who had made a great success of his own affairs, and who, suddenly, had no tolerance for the economic chaos which was troubling the country. He wanted to reform the world, and since he had never heard Carlyle's comment on the lady who tired of her reforming efforts and decided to accept the world as she found it: "By God! she'd better!"—he went ahead. Like Caryl of the *New Era* he thought that his proposals were eminently practical. He was a business man, he reasoned, so any enterprise of his must be, at once, businesslike and successful. First a city, then a state, then any group of states, and finally the whole world could be run on the basis of a super Sears Roebuck or Montgomery Ward organization. The trouble with the world, he thought, was lack of cooperation. That was no new idea: farmers, Populists, Knights of Labor, and theosophists had been saying the same thing, but their attempts at cooperatives always started out on too small a scale. Peck wanted to start on a grand scale. He realized that the one essential was plenty of capital. With capital the enterprise could have a broad enough base so that the members would not have to trade or work outside the organization. Translated into modern terms, his idea is production for use. Upton Sinclair had the same idea in his EPIC program, and so, too, during the depression, did the Commonwealth Federation in Washington State.

According to the preface, Peck had already made a small start on the project in his home town of Lewiston. He wrote *The World a Department Store,* 1900, to popularize his ideas and to arouse thinking people to the abuses which were everywhere. It is not a good novel; it is a very bad novel, even for a department store owner. He steals from Bellamy the idea of having a man awake in a new world—this time, after sleeping sickness. His hero, Mr. Brantford, goes to sleep in 1900 and awakes in 1925, to find his family gone and a new city, a new life, and a new ideal of the meaning of life. Peck follows Bellamy, again, in assigning Mr. Brantford an important place in the community as an interpreter of the old world of twenty-five years before. What had become of the other middle-aged people who would have lived through the era one never learns. There is included the love story of Mr. Brantford and Miss Brown, and, for good measure, the relation of how two other young couples get married. Everything in the new order has to be explained to Mr. Brantford, and he retaliates with a good deal of moralizing. That is the worst part of the book. Peck was a devout Christian, and the book is loaded down with his own analysis of Christian virtue. The sinfulness of nineteenth century habits is emphasized: Men drank liquor, they wasted themselves and their bodies in saloons; they smoked tobacco and destroyed the vigor of their strength; they even, on occasion, allowed themselves to be tempted by wicked women.

Peck admits that his system is not fully worked out, but he does hope that the "Cooperative Association of America, in a feasible way, may evolve by continued growth from its . . . small beginning in the city of Lewiston, Maine."[1] It is not intended, he explains, "as a literary effort, but as a work from one business man to others who know the cares of business life, and written so a youth could understand it."[2]

The novel visualizes a world already reformed, and explains in detail how the change was accomplished:

[1] Bradford Peck, *The World a Department Store,* Boston, 1900, Preface.
[2] *Idem.*

We commenced by first acquiring capital from the sale of shares, established a treasury department, and then, came the gradual development of other departments, until we operated directly every industrial branch from the farm to the loom. Our treasury department was a most important feature from the start, money being essential for the carrying out of our plan, purchasing as we did vast amounts of real estate. Labor was utilized by the changing over and rebuilding of vast sections of our cities, towns, and villages, as well as by laying out numerous farms, which were put upon an entirely different basis, enabling them to be worked in a thoroughly systematic, practical, and businesslike manner. Roads in the farming sections were all macadamized and put into such condition as would in every way facilitate the handling and shipping of the farm products.[3]

A vast army of people were thus given employment in all branches of work. This required at the outset immense sums of money. As our organization developed and the different branches of our enterprise grew by continually acquiring property, we extended our trust life into different parts of New England, thus spreading until every section of our country became associated with our organization; and to such a degree did our organization extend that it has now the control of the national as well as the state elections, our membership being sufficient to bring about this result.[4]

We came in contact with fierce competition from rival business enterprises. This was to be expected, as many of these outside competitors looked upon cooperation as a scheme to rob humanity of their individuality. The fight commenced with price-cutting, but the battle was of comparatively short duration. One of the strictest laws of our organization was that no member under any condition should patronize any outside enterprise.[5]

As concerns were forced out of business, they were taken into the Association, which gradually became all-powerful. At the same time the Association was forcing changes in the operation of civic affairs.

In our medical department every member of our Association is examined periodically by a physician, and should he find any member showing the slightest symptom of disease or nervousness, the patient is immediately given a vacation, often times going away for a trip into another section of the country.

Our streets and highways are under the charge of a board of engineers. The construction of buildings is under the charge of both boards of architects and engineers. The general affairs are governed by the executive board through the voice of the people. Members cannot occupy prominent positions unless they show that they are truly fitted for such positions.[6]

Newspapers, magazines, and books are all printed at a special

[3] *Ibid.*, p. 72.   [4] *Ibid.*, pp. 72, 73.
[5] *Ibid.*, p. 73.   [6] *Ibid.*, pp. 70, 71.

depot. And none of them carries advertisements of any sort—not even patent medicines. Men and women have come to depend, instead, upon the Association-paid doctors. And the citizens want to keep in the best possible physical condition because, then, they can work more efficiently. It is easy for them to lead regular lives because they have been properly conditioned.

From the commencement of the life of the . . . Association . . . people of all classes began to reform their manner of living, and as they became members and co-workers, admitted that the condition of life, with all its foul influences of dishonesty permeating every form of human existence, at that time caused them to imitate what their predecessors did. Lawyers, in the framing of laws, so constructed them that when law books were opened for reference it required other associates to determine the real meaning of such laws. We have discarded from the Association every law book . . . in vogue.[7]

Peck insists always that he is a business man and that the "Cooperative Association is organized on business principles,"[8] but he insists too much; he is, essentially, a preacher. His enthusiasm carries him away: "Let us join the new twentieth-century movement of cooperation, uniting under one organization, or people's trust, throwing aside individual creeds, and recognizing the one standard, advanced in the simple teachings of Jesus Christ, that great commandment, 'Thou shalt love the Lord thy God with all thy heart,' by practicing in every-day life truth and love for our neighbor."[9]

Peck's book suggests the continuing influences of Bellamy, and also an increasing interest in religious motivation. *The World a Department Store* glorifies the same brand of evangelical Christianity as *In His Steps*, and both of them stem from the same strong faith that influenced John Eliot.

Like Peck, Charles W. Caryl thought of himself as a business man. His *New Era* was an attempt to outline plans for the formation of a cooperative community. Caryl imagined that his proposals were realistic in the extreme, simply because he was basing the whole project on man's selfish, acquisitive instinct, rather than on any hope that man was essentially good. The fallacy underlying his conception was the result of planning on too grandiose a scale. His diagram for a model city is reasonable enough in layout—it resembles in many ways the proposals of Frank Lloyd Wright. The city is designed in a circle, with public buildings, including an elaborate crematorium, in the center, and radiating out with the houses of the members, beginning with generals and ending with privates. Outside the homes of the privates would be a factory circle. And then, beyond that, the gardens which would supply the city. An outline map of the city is enclosed, as well as an elaborate prospectus. Taste has changed in the last forty years, and, on the basis of the sketch, one is grateful that no such cities were built.

His suggestions as to the necessity of changing the basis of our currency are reasonable enough, provided that one remembers that his home was in a silver producing state, and that the Federal Reserve Act had not been passed. Caryl was simply remembering the free silver controversy which was debated so violently in the campaign of 1896.

The book is half novel, half play, and historical characters are introduced in an effort to give realism. There are remarks by such strangely contrasting figures as Tolstoy, General Booth, Emma Goldman, Mary Ellen Lease, B. O. Flowers, Bellamy, and Eugene Debs. The story suffers, however, because they speak only in platform utterances. The whole volume is terribly dull.

The plan begins with helping the miners. Mr. Sutta, the hero, intends to purchase a number of mines, to give a portion of the stock to the miners so that they will work more conscientiously, and then to turn over all capital profits to the New Era Union for the development of a model city. The whole project is to be incorporated for ten million dollars, in paid-up, ten dollar shares. After the mine gets under way, all the workers will be supposed to become full members of the community, the fee to be equal to the pay of three hundred working days.

In order to succeed, the mines would have to pay very large dividends. But that was part of the plan: "As soon as possible the New Era Union can secure promising gold mines and put its members at work producing as large an amount of gold as possible. Also a coal mining department, for mining coal on a large scale. Also a building department, to build homes, factories and public buildings.

Also all kinds of factories to produce everything needed by the members."[10]

If a community were once self-sustaining, the members would find that they enjoyed an increasing material prosperity. But during the period in which they weren't self-sustaining, they would have to exist on bare necessities. Everything beyond this essential minimum would have to be reinvested in capital goods—just as have been the profits of Russia's increasing industrial efficiency. It would be impossible to convince men that utopia, or even a cooperative society, on such terms, was desirable. The only possible way to get men to "cooperate" would be by force—just as Russia has done.

According to the system, workers would be divided into seven different classifications, with wages ranging from two dollars a day to twenty-five dollars a day.

To enable the New Era Union to maintain this system of compensation, regardless of the wages paid by competitive companies, the members will be paid in checks that must be redeemed by the New Era Union for everything needed by the member, any surplus not required for immediate use to be invested in the bonds payable in gold, that is really equivalent to the members being paid in full in gold, except that the checks require that each member purchase the supplies produced by other members on the same basis of compensation.[11]

Free coinage of silver, it is insisted, would simplify the beginnings of cooperatives and model cities. Since Colorado is full of silver, free coinage would make it unnecessary for miners to find their capital in the East. If free silver is impossible, it is proposed that the state should issue script and so keep the money in the West.

The initiative and referendum are suggested as the weapons which make it impossible for plutocracy to prevent the formation of New Model Cities. "The thinking, intelligent people would see at once that the initiative and referendum is the only way to prevent their office holders selling them out."[12]

There is a constant reiteration of the notion that if reform doesn't come, there will be revolution. Eugene Debs is supposed to say: "The people are ripe for a great change. All they lack is direction and

[10] Charles W. Caryl, *New Era*, Denver [about 1897], p. 10.
[11] *Idem.*   [12] *Ibid.*, p. 58.

leadership."[13] The New Era Union was prepared to offer the leadership. And it offered not only a fully developed plan, but also some inspirational poetry. The poem *Wait* reads as follows:

Even now the moaning of the storm is in the distance heard,
Even now the tranquil firmament with thunder clouds is blurred.
They're swelling big and bigger still, and yet you sit and smile,
Secure behind your money bags for yet a little while.
Soon, soon the awful storm will burst upon you like a flood;
The gutters of your crowded streets will overflow with blood.[14]

It is unfortunate that Caryl's writing was not as ingenious as his scheme. Had the book been well expressed, it might have sold, and then his scheme for turning the profits over to the New Era Union might have given the Union enough money to get out a second edition full of advertising, sold at high prices. And then—but there is no use going on. The whole thing smacks of Yankee ingenuity; it isn't absurd, but it is full of unnecessary complications—like one of Milt Goldberg's cartoon inventions.

Milan Edson's *Solaris Farm*, 1900, is a love story, set in an aura of spiritualism, and showing the influence of Jefferson, Bellamy, and Henry George. Edson quite frankly admits his political prejudices:

Strong in my conviction that all civilizations are false which do not civilize the lowest units of any social order, I have written Solaris Farm as my contribution towards the improvement of agriculturalists as a class, of the race as a whole; towards the establishment of a truer civilization, organized for the purpose of securing the same degree of progress for the lowest orders of humanity, which have been or can be attained by the highest. In any social or political fabric, wide differences of wealth, of education, of refinement in its subdivisions are dangerous; which, when once established, will surely destroy all progress, all vitality, by slowly eating away the social, industrial and political life of the nation.[15]

The solution, as Edson sees it, is for the farmers to organize, to work together. They can compete against any monopoly "by coming together everywhere in force; by pooling their issues; by helping themselves; by organizing cooperative farms . . ., armed with schools in which skilled workmen may be taught to successfully carry on profitable allied manufacturing industries. Monopolistic farms cannot then successfully compete."[16]

---

[13] *Ibid.*, p. 159.   [14] *Ibid.*, p. 77.
[15] Milan C. Edson, *Solaris Farm*, Washington, 1900, Preface.   [16] *Ibid.*, p. 206.

According to Edson, the farmers should find it easy to help themselves. They do in his story. His people learn "that the true purpose of work, is not to make and hoard money . . .; that money is not a necessity; that it is only the means to an end. They have learned that confidence in each other . . . largely takes the place of money."[17] They learn these lessons by means of a cooperative farm, a farm devoted to sensible forestry, sensible soil control, and sensible living. This first farm must inevitably succeed, and so inevitably must other "Solaris Farms" be established in other districts. Gradually they would force out competition, until the whole country would be one vast cooperative. In the process "each co-operative farm, will become a new center of permanent wealth; a new center of social progress; of organized labor; of distribution and exchange. These new centers, by again bringing together the food and the consumer, will save millions for themselves, which under the competitive system were thrown away in freights and commissions."[18] Scientific agriculture and careful planning would guarantee the success of the experiments. The members would study methods of breeding, methods of drying and canning vegetables, methods of growing extra-fancy fruits and vegetables. Along with this scientific planning, some manufacturing side-line would take up the work-hours of slack periods and provide extra income; the manufacture of bricks, pottery and aluminum is suggested.

Up to this point the suggestions are reasonably sound—but they have been directed more at proving the possibilities of co-operative farming than in demonstrating the necessity or inevitability of any set of reforms. There is, however, a representative collection of reforms included. No political pamphlet or utopia could be written, in that age, at least, without such a list. The Solaris Farmers believe in cremation; they believe in paper script to take the place of money; they believe in model cities with "beautiful" public buildings; they believe that housework should be done cooperatively; they believe that men and women should retire, with an adequate income, at fifty; they believe that education can be made a game, and that children can be taught to think the acquisition of facts more entertaining than hop-scotch.

[17] *Ibid.*, p. 285.   [18] *Ibid.*, p. 393.

Solaris Farm falls very definitely into the usual pattern of political utopias. Edson is more directly concerned with the farmers than other writers—just as Charles Caryl was more concerned with the Colorado miners—and for that reason his imagination is more limited. Our own imagination is not limited, when we consider the farm, simply because we have had dinned into our ears for so long the basic principles of scientific farming and erosion control. But Edson was ahead of his time, and what seemed utopian to him seems perfectly obvious to us.

None of these volumes has any great interest now, but that is because the word *cooperation* has lost its magic, semi-religious significance. These volumes are full of an optimism which we can no longer understand. Today we are inclined to be somewhat cynical about such an optimistic, enthusiastic faith; we are much more conscious of the failures than the successes.

CHAPTER NINETEEN

TWO CALIFORNIANS

THOMAS LAKE HARRIS and Joaquin Miller were both literary poseurs and, on occasion, mystics. Both were in the California tradition. Then as now California attracted dreamers and crackpots, social planners, misfits, extreme extroverts and individualists. Both men wrote utopian novels which it is a kindness to classify as simply queer.

Joaquin Miller was, at least, a skilled writer, and his novel, *The Building of the City Beautiful*, 1893, is far better than Harris's effort, *The New Republic*. When *The City Beautiful* was first published, B. O. Flowers reviewed it in *The Arena* as a serious and revolutionary piece of social criticism. Actually, there are few ideas in the little volume, and those few are by no means revolutionary, but Joaquin Miller was probably taking himself seriously when he wrote it. At any rate, he must have been pleased to find someone else exaggerating the importance of his work, a job he so often had done for himself.

Joaquin Miller advertised himself as the poet of the Sierras. His poetic reputation has fluctuated. Some critics have praised him highly; others have dismissed him as a brash plagiarist and liar. He liked to think of himself as the Byron of the West, but he usually overplayed the role. Individualism was more than a matter of faith with him—it was also an act. *The Building of the City Beautiful* shows his taste for the exotic. The language is self-conscious and somewhat Biblical; the heroine is a sort of Old Testament prophetess; the ideals of the city are based on the Sermon on the Mount, and aimed at establishing individual freedom above all else.

The volume does not add anything to the store of utopian thinking. Indirectly, at least, *Looking Backward* was the chief source, though Miller need not have read *Looking Backward* to have been influenced. During the early nineties the Theosophist Society of Oakland was extremely active in disseminating Bellamy's ideas, and it is unlikely that Miller could have been ignorant either of the book or its thesis.

Some of Miller's own experiences went into his account. In 1886 he purchased some land overlooking San Francisco Bay and set about building "The Hights," his home for many years. He hoped to have there, living with him, kindred souls, of a poetic nature; he wanted a refuge against the city and a place where he could play the role of poet and frontiersman. *The Building of the City Beautiful* is partly personal experience, partly mystical nonsense, and partly a reflection of contemporary utopian thinking.

His city was in the American Southwest, built on the ruins of an ancient Toltec city. Miller is extremely vague about every phase of his city planning, but the main feature seems to be communal ownership. Everyone is a full partner in the city's growth. There are no special privileges for the influential:

The curse of all society is the granting of special privileges which are the survival of the divine right of force and fraud. I determined that my city should exist for the granting and preserving of equal rights. I determined that there should be no privileges granted to the few. We have no monopoly laws; we have no patent rights, or copy-rights, even.[1]

Miller had certainly heard of *Progress and Poverty*.

There are two ways, he says, to eliminate privilege: ". . . extend the same favors to all or withhold them from the few. . . . We believe in the latter method. . . . With us, possession is dependent upon personal toil or the free gift of friendship."[2]

In common with the society of *Looking Backward,* everyone works, and there is no social discrimination about the type of work. He uses a variation of Bellamy's method of providing volunteers for all necessary jobs. The harder and more unpleasant the work, the greater the reward. "It was marvellous how soon invention turned itself in the direction of making heavy tasks light, and changing or abolishing whole industries."[3]

Everyone was a worker, and ordinarily two hours a day were enough to support a man. It is only when there are parasites, he explains, that some men need to work excessively long hours.

[1] Joaquin Miller, *The Building of the City Beautiful*, Trenton, N.J., 1905, p. 170.
[2] *Ibid.*, p. 188.   [3] *Ibid.*, p. 189.

There was no money. One of the citizens had discovered how to produce gold, and the leaders of the city intended to change the methods of international business.

I tell you that commerce, free and open interchange between men and nations, will only begin when honor is made a basis instead of base metal—when this mighty nation of the United States shall say to the nations of the earth. . . . Here is my honor, my promise to pay; I have done with shifting and varying values that wreck and impoverish and make miserable my people. . . .[4]

Miller is carefully vague about the details of finance; he does not explain how commodities or credits could be exchanged. There would be no wealthy men, although some, of course, would have more than others.

The State does not equalize possessions, but it equalizes opportunities; and there are no wide differences in possessions such as the outside world shows.[5]

Miller eliminates politics from his city by having the government administered by those who live the longest. The only election, he explains, is the election of nature. Everyone who reaches the age of seventy becomes a Senator; the oldest members of the Senate comprise the Council, and the oldest of these is the President.

Although the city is in the desert, irrigation, he says, will make plants grow twelve months in the year, and that is important to his society of vegetarians. Better still, the desert sands can be the chief ingredient of their universal building material, glass. His insistence on the virtue of glass sounds contemporary: "We make glass houses, railway ties, railway tracks, and railway cars, as you can see here, out of the sand."[6]

The most unusual quality of this slight novel is the semi-religious framework, and his reluctance to be specific and matter-of-fact about his dream world. It was probably lack of interest in the details rather than modesty which so limited his planning. The plot is tenuous and the story halting. The best that can be said for it is that it reflects Miller's individualism. A more direct appraisal might refer to the same individualism as nonsense.

Thomas Lake Harris was successively Baptist, Universalist, Spiritu-

---

[4] *Ibid.*, p. 178. [5] *Ibid.*, p. 178. [6] *Ibid.*, p. 148.

alist, "Independent Christian," and utopian experimenter. His two experiments in practical communism were undertaken to carry out his religious principle of "The Use," of which the distinctive practices were "open breathing," a kind of respiration by which the Divine Breath was supposed to enter directly into the body, and a system of "celibate marriage," whereby each individual was left free to live in spiritual union with his heavenly counterpart.

His book, *The New Republic*, 1891, is a strange mixture of theology and economic determinism. A great deal of his jargon is incomprehensible, but his book adds up to a severe indictment of the capitalistic system. "200,000 men," he writes, "are the legal owners of more than half of all the properties and resources of this nation of more than 60,000,000. . . . Capitalized Egoism, by the law and spirit of its nature, can never stop in its inroad whilst any value remains to be possessed that it has not already appropriated, unless meanwhile it is mastered and abolished. Yet this is the Power which Social Nationalism has to meet."[7]

He praises the work of Laurence Gronlund, Lassalle, and Edward Bellamy, and he visualizes the imminent collapse of the social structure. But the work of the Bellamys and Gronlunds is not enough, he insists, to effect a decent reformation. There must be a "centric and concentric nucleation." The workers must find themselves and then each other. Eventually they can effect a new kind of cooperation, and the evolutionary process will bring about a new era of cooperation and good will. "Paradise is in the air; the atmosphere of our social hope is impregnated by diffused elysium."[8]

Since the church can be of no help and since capital will never voluntarily relinquish its grasp, workingmen must organize. "The stronghold of Plutocratic Egoism is in the egoised Church, which proffers to its adherents an egoised and private salvation."[9] Harris feels that there is hope in the increasing self-consciousness of labor: "The hereditary bondsmen of toil, having comparatively none of the false knowledge to unlearn, are proving themselves wise in the culture that includes all cultures, the ethics of Sociology."[10] Such an

[7] Thomas Lake Harris, *The New Republic*, Santa Rosa, 1891, pp. 16, 17.
[8] *Ibid.*, p. 54.   [9] *Ibid.*, p. 51.   [10] *Ibid.*, p. 34.

awareness can play a significant role, he believes, but he is afraid that their energy will be dissipated by fruitless bickering.

The New Republic is directed to the "Workers in Social Humanity, Nationalist Clubs, Socialistic and Labor Unions and kindred Societies; in the hope that contact of mind with mind and heart with heart may serve for mutual encouragement and advance of action in the common cause."[11] Perhaps some of these may have read *The New Republic,* but the book could not have had much influence. Its interest lies in suggesting how widespread the radical movement had become by 1891, and how varied was the group which supported Bellamy's Nationalism. Harris's analysis of the problem is typical. He talks about cooperation and the necessity and inevitability of evolutionary change. He says that the workers must rely on themselves. But he doesn't offer any real suggestions. He admires Karl Marx, but he is not willing to accept the implications of his economic determinism. He is rather like Edward Everett Hale; he wants to do something, but he contents himself with easy generalizations about cooperation. He is more skilled in sermons than in economics.

[11] *Ibid.,* Dedication.

CHAPTER TWENTY

SHELDON AND HOWELLS—CHRISTIAN DREAMERS

MOST of the attempts at practical communism in America have had a religious basis. And all of the most successful experimenters—from the Rappites and Zoarites to the Perfectionists, the New Zionists, and the followers of Father Divine—have been motivated by a strong spirit of Christian martyrdom. John Eliot proposed a theocratic utopia with some slight hope, at least, of living to see such a community. The Labadists, the Ephratans and the Mormons set off into the back country and worked out their lives to suit themselves. But after the Civil War it was no longer so easy to find land suitable for experiment. And men were less fanatically devoted to religious principle; perhaps fanaticism diminishes as prosperity increases. The country didn't stay prosperous. There were hard times in the seventies, eighties and nineties. The increasingly large numbers of immigrants made certain that there would always be a depressed class to work for minimum wages. These fresh immigrants were not articulate, but by the nineties they had found a number of champions. Some of these champions worked with the Populists; others followed the example of Edward Bellamy and attempted to launch a Nationalist movement. Some few, and among them Charles Sheldon, went back to the traditional American solution, religious reform.

The novel which sets forth this solution, *In His Steps*, was originally written for Sunday School children in Topeka, and published in 1896 in a Chicago religious weekly, *The Advance*. The book has had an amazing success. Perhaps part of the reason for this success has been the fact that the publishers neglected to file two copies of the magazine when applying for a copyright. As a result the book was in the public domain, and publisher after publisher printed editions. According to *The Publishers' Weekly*, some twenty-four million copies have been sold; in the United States, at least, it has had a larger circulation than any other book except the Bible.[1] It has been trans-

[1] Edward A. Weeks, "The Best Sellers Since 1875," *The Publishers' Weekly,* 125:1504.

lated into twenty-seven foreign languages, including Arabic and Japanese.[2]

It is difficult to account for such incredible sales. There must be more of an explanation than the large number of cheap editions. Perhaps its success is due to its naive expression of faith. Perhaps it expresses a hope which is inherent in all people. Or perhaps its uncritical evaluation of human problems, designed for Sunday School consumption, is perfectly adjusted to the intellectual requirements of most of the reading world.

In His Steps tells of the spiritual awakening of a minister, Henry Maxwell, who is shocked out of his pleasant acceptance of Christianity by the appearance in Church one Sunday of a tramp who comes forward after the service and asks what the Church can possibly offer to the destitute:

"There are a good many others like me. I'm not complaining, am I? Just stating facts. But I was wondering as I sat there under the gallery, if what you call following Jesus is the same thing as what He taught. What did He mean when He said: 'Follow me!' The minister said . . . that it is necessary for the disciple of Jesus to follow His steps, and he said the steps are 'obedience, faith, love and imitation.' But I did not hear him tell you just what he meant that to mean, especially the last step. What do you Christians mean by following the steps of Jesus?

"I've tramped through this city for three days trying to find a job; and in all that time I've not had a word of sympathy or comfort except from your minister here, who said he was sorry for me and hoped I would find a job somewhere. I suppose it is because you get so imposed on by the professional tramp that you have lost your interest in any other sort."[3]

"I heard some people singing at a church prayer meeting the other night,

'All for Jesus, all for Jesus,
All my being's ransomed powers,
All my thoughts, and all my doings,
All my days, and all my hours,'

and I kept wondering as I sat on the steps outside just what they meant by it. It seems to me there's an awful lot of trouble in the world that somehow wouldn't exist if all the people who sing such songs went and lived them out. I suppose I don't understand. But what would Jesus do? Is that what

[2] Charles M. Sheldon, "The Ethics of Some Publishers," *The Christian Century,* 50:120.
[3] Charles M. Sheldon, *In His Steps,* pp. 8, 9. References are to the Grosset and Dunlap edition [c. 1935].

you mean by following His steps? It seems to me sometimes as if the people in the big churches had good clothes and nice houses to live in, and money to spend for luxuries, and could go away on summer vacations and all that, while the people outside the churches, thousands of them, I mean, die in tenements, and walk the streets for jobs, and never have a piano or a picture in the house, and grow up in misery and drunkenness and sin."[4]

After this indictment of professing Christians, the man collapses and dies, but the minister has been shocked into some real thinking about the meaning of Christianity. He proposes that his congregation join him in a determined effort to follow Jesus.

> Our motto will be, 'What would Jesus do?' Our aim will be to act just as He would if He was in our places, regardless of immediate results. In other words, we propose to follow Jesus' steps as closely and as literally as we believe He taught His disciples to do. And those who volunteer to do this will pledge themselves for an entire year, beginning with today, so to act.[5]

Most of the congregation join in the plan. Immediately there are complications. They discover that each must interpret the meaning of the pledge for himself. That is extremely hard on some consciences. A few treat the promise as of no real meaning, but others undertake the most difficult tasks. Edward Norman, editor of the *Raymond Daily News*, found himself in a particularly difficult position. He decided, almost immediately, that his paper shouldn't carry reports of boxing matches. He knew that many people were more interested in the sports page than in the rest of the paper, but he saw no reason to cater to their taste. He decided that he would have to do without advertisements for tobacco, liquor, and patent medicines. This was bad enough, but worse was his decision to do without the Sunday edition. He felt that people could better occupy themselves with spiritual problems than with reading the Sunday paper. And when he decided to be completely honest in politics, to be concerned only with truth, and to determine the desirability of any project from a non-partisan point of view, that was the final blow. Subscriptions were cancelled by the hundreds, for most people didn't want to read a paper unless it bolstered their own particular set of prejudices. The paper would have been bankrupt had it not been for the wealth of Virginia Page, another of those who were making an effort to follow Jesus. The paper was subsidized and

[4] *Ibid.*, p. 10. [5] *Ibid.*, pp. 15, 16.

was able to keep going, in spite of the fact that it attacked false advertising, the ruling politicians, and the hypocrisy of many professing Christians.

Milton Wright, the merchant, reorganizes his department store, and although he loses money for a time, finds relations with his employees and the public so much improved that he begins to feel that Christianity is not completely inconsistent with sound business practice. The moral in these cases would seem to be that God will find a way.

Alexander Powers, the Superintendent of the Railroad Yards, is not so lucky. When he discovers that the railroad is breaking the law by giving rebates to favored customers, he turns his evidence over to the prosecutor and starts looking for another job. He finds work as a telegraph operator, but the public and his own family can not understand his motives and think he is simply crazy.

Rachel Winslow and Virginia Page are well brought up young ladies, but they become very much concerned about life in the slums, and they devote themselves to a campaign to remove both the spiritual and material causes of social degradation. They fight the saloons, they help in evangelical services, and they try to rescue a prostitute from the consequences of her sin. They have some success, but the effect on the slum dwellers is not so striking as the effect on the girls themselves. Life has much more meaning for them. They are far happier than they were when they busied themselves only with society.

The Reverend Henry Maxwell finds more and more responsibilities. He feels that he and his fellow church members should take an active part in local politics, and try to get control away from the gamblers and the cheap politicians. And he insists that it is the duty of church members to be positively concerned about the unfortunates of the city. It is not enough to salve the conscience by contributing to charities. He begins to wonder how those who own tenements can properly hold up their heads in church and call themselves Christians.

The movement spreads beyond the little town of Raymond. A Chicago minister is aroused. He tells his Bishop what has happened, and together they found a Settlement House in Chicago's most desolate area. The project succeeds from the beginning, and with that success comes a realization of how superficial had been their earlier Christianity.

Utopia hasn't been achieved at the end of the book, and only a very few men have been strong enough to make an effort to follow "in His steps." Henry Maxwell realizes that the path he has determined upon is long and difficult. He realizes that men will persecute him, and that he will be held up to ridicule. He realizes that many men are not willing to face the truth of Christianity because the faith demands too much. But he also realizes that Christianity provides a solution for man's economic and social ills. Much has been accomplished, he knows, and much more can be accomplished. He realizes that it is futile to expect miracles over night, but that as men continue to work in this new spirit of self sacrifice, their influence and the influence of the experiment will become increasingly more powerful. By such means, he believes that Christendom can be regenerated.

Only a utopian could dream of Christendom regenerated. Most people are willing to forget that Jesus himself was pretty much of a utopian. A community run according to the Sermon on the Mount, in which every member seriously attempted to follow "in His steps," would certainly be utopia.

W. D. Howells was a Christian dreamer, too, but he was also a prosperous Bostonian. His two utopian novels, *A Traveler from Altruria*, 1895, and *Through the Eye of the Needle*, 1907, are expressions of gentlemanly wishful thinking. There is a certain amount of social satire in his novels, but it is all so leisurely and good natured that it doesn't carry conviction. He does occasionally make an effort to reconcile his Christian faith with the world about him—but he can only compromise. His whole way of life made it impossible for him to be a sharp observer of political and economic conditions. The Boston of Beacon Street and a polite literary tradition molded his thinking. He was occasionally shocked by the brutalities of the industrial system. He did not like injustice in any form, and he began to feel that the Socialists had some reason for their attacks on capitalism. Howells always meant well, and he felt that he should deal with social problems in his novels. These social-conscience novels are not his best; his "mind was driven by his will into regions where it never felt at home."[6]

A Traveler from Altruria is supposed to be a realistic criticism of

[6] Van Wyck Brooks, *New England: Indian Summer*, New York, 1940, p. 391.

American economics from the point of view of a member of a perfect society. Altruria is a newly discovered continent which has long possessed Christian doctrine, and which, in economic and social structure, is some hundreds of years ahead of the rest of the world. Mr. Homos, one of the first Altrurians to visit the United States, wants to discover how our civilization functions. He visits Mr. Twelvemough, a purveyor of superficial romances, who undertakes to interpret for him the complexities of our existence. Homos has taken seriously the statements about equality in the Declaration of Independence. He looks for a real equality, a real democracy, and in looking for that equality and democracy he gives his host some difficult moments. Homos won't let the waitress carry heavy loads for him, and he wants to help the porter shine shoes. In this Howells suggests that he was himself more troubled by such petty irrationalities than by the fundamental problems of the day.

Twelvemough tells Mr. Homos that Americans esteem work, and that there is no class structure, but, as he is questioned, he has to confess that Americans do not esteem work for itself, and that there is a very definite class consciousness. A banker tries to explain:

I don't know . . . how the notion of our social equality originated, but I think it has been fostered mainly by the expectation of foreigners, who argued it from our political equality. As a matter of fact, it never existed, except in our poorest and most primitive communities, in the pioneer days of the West and among the gold-hunters of California. It was not dreamed of in our colonial society, either in Virginia or Pennsylvania or New York or Massachusetts; and the fathers of the republic, who were mostly slave-holders, were practically as stiff-necked aristocrats as any people of their day. We have not a political aristocracy, that is all; but there is as absolute a division between the orders of men, and as little love, in this country as in any country of the globe. The severance of the man who works for his living with his hands from the man who does not work for his living with his hands is so complete, and apparently so final, that nobody even imagines else, not even in fiction.[7]

Mr. Homos feels ill at ease with Twelvemough; he cannot understand his complacent admission that humans are utterly selfish, and that their ultimate ambition is to get something for nothing. It is only when he meets Mrs. Camp, Reuben, and Lizzie that he feels at ease. These people know the meaning of work; they have social con-

---

[7] W. D. Howells, *A Traveler from Altruria*, pp. 44, 45. Page references are to the Harper's edition of 1908.

sciences, and some perception, at least, of the changing social structure. It is such men and women who have to work, and, working, to think, who can profit from the lessons of Altrurian history. He delivers a lecture on Altruria to an audience of working men and women. He starts out by explaining that Altruria had gone through a long period in which the monopolies kept getting bigger and bigger, absorbing more and more power, until finally all power except the vote was in their hands. Monopoly absorbed monopoly until there was only one left.

The Accumulation had advanced so smoothly, so lightly, in all its steps to the supreme power, and had at last so thoroughly quelled the uprisings of the proletariat, that it forgot one thing; it forgot the despised and neglected suffrage. The ballot, because it had been so easy to annul its effect, had been left in the people's hands; and when, at last, the leaders of the proletariat ceased to counsel strikes, or any form of resistance to the Accumulation that could be tormented into the likeness of insurrection against the government, and began to urge them to attack it in the political way, the deluge that swept the Accumulation out of existence came trickling and creeping over the land. It appeared first in the country, a spring from the ground; then it gathered head in the villages; then it swelled to a torrent in the cities. I cannot stay to trace its course; but suddenly, one day, when the Accumulation's abuse of a certain power became too gross, it was voted out of that power. You will perhaps be interested to know that it was with the telegraphs that the rebellion against the Accumulation began, and the government was forced, by the overwhelming majority which the proletariat sent to our parliament, to assume a function which the Accumulation had impudently usurped. Then the transportation of smaller and more perishable wares . . . was legislated a function of the postoffice. . . . Then all transportation was taken into the hands of the political government, which had always been accused of great corruption in its administration, but which showed itself immaculately pure compared with the Accumulation. The common ownership of mines necessarily followed, with an allotment of lands to any one who wished to live by tilling the land; but not a foot of the land was remitted to private hands for the purpose of selfish pleasure or the exclusion of any other from the landscape. As all business had been gathered into the grasp of the Accumulation, and the manufacture of everything they used and the production of everything that they ate was in the control of the Accumulation, its transfer to the government was the work of a single clause in the statute.[8]

Once the people regain what the monopolies had usurped, the state becomes socialist. There is no money in the new Altruria; everyone works, and, in return, everyone gets what he needs, just as in a big

[8] *Ibid.,* pp. 184, 185.

family. Mills and shops are beautiful as well as useful. Machines have become servants, not masters. "Our life is so simple and our needs are so few that the hand-work of the primitive toilers could easily supply our wants; but machinery works so much more thoroughly and beautifully that we have in great measure retained it."[9] Altrurians don't ever loaf or shirk; rather they are cheerful and willing workers. "In Altruria *there is no hurry,* for no one wishes to outstrip another, or in any wise surpass him. We are assured of enough, and are forbidden any and every sort of superfluity."[10]

Altruria is supposed to be an example of what happens when people practice the Christianity they profess. "We love the realities," Mr. Homos explains, "and for this reason we look at the life of a man rather than his profession for proof that he is a religious man."[11] Life is so pleasant and well adjusted that Altrurians have no fear of death. They feel that since life has been a heaven on earth, there can be no reason to fear either heaven or death.

Equality and plenty eliminated all crime of property. "Where there was no want, men no longer bartered their souls, or women their bodies, for the means to keep themselves alive. The vices vanished with the crimes, and the diseases almost as largely disappeared. People were no longer sickened by sloth and surfeit, or deformed and depleted by overwork and famine."[12]

Mr. Homos' final message to his audience was that they should not try to go to Altruria, but, rather, that they should bring Altruria to themselves. The working people approved his ideas; the well-to-do thought he was a quack. The present-day reader is quick to agree that Howells-Homos is pretty much of a quack—that he touches glibly or not at all on the serious problems which should confront any utopian.

Through the Eye of the Needle is a continuation of *A Traveler from Altruria.* The first half of the novel consists of a series of letters from Homos to an Altrurian friend, letters which deal again with the contradiction between American theory and practice, with our plutocratic attitude towards servants, with the fact that servants are really slaves, though "they cannot be beaten, or bought and sold except by the week or month, and for the price which they fix them-

[9] *Ibid.,* p. 200. [13] *Ibid.,* p. 201.
[11] *Ibid.,* p. 204. [12] *Ibid.,* p. 208.

selves,"[13] and with the isolation and snobbishness of apartment-house life. Howells is more concerned with such things than with the underlying social, political and economic problems. The second half of the novel tells how Mr. Homos took back to Altruria an American bride, and how she reacted to the life. Her clothes, which she had thought so fine, are put in a museum, and she is finally convinced that their free-flowing, semi-Grecian garb is more comfortable and more beautiful. She doesn't even mind wearing the same clothes indefinitely. Fashions remain constant, for "you get things only when you need them, not when other people think you do."[14]

Everyone works, partly because it is necessary to work to eat, and partly because *"work* is the ideal." Altrurians don't even believe in labor-saving devices. If they used machinery very much, there might not be enough menial tasks to go around, and that would upset the basic Altrurian philosophy; and also, one suspects, the ideas which Howells absorbed from William Morris's *News from Nowhere.*

The yacht of a wealthy American, Mr. Thrall, is wrecked on the coast, but instead of being treated well because he was wealthy, he was treated severely because he was presumptuous. According to the Altrurian point of view, he was no better than a pauper, for he had only money. He was made to work before he was given food. His wife protested violently at the necessity of having to do something useful, but eventually she found satisfaction in working with others: "Don't you think it is beautiful here, to see people living for each other instead of living on each other, and the whole nation like one family, and the country a paradise?"[15]

Howells' one intelligent suggestion has to do with the desirability of spreading out the population in small villages, and avoiding any increase in the city population. Here he was probably influenced by Edward Everett Hale, and also by his own rather idyllic conception of the New England village economy.

Through the Eye of the Needle is a poor novel and worse social

[13] W. D. Howells, *Through the Eye of the Needle,* p. 34. Page references are to the Harper's edition of 1907.
[14] *Ibid.,* p. 181.
[15] *Ibid.,* p. 231.

criticism. He overlooks many essential points. There is no adequate substitute for money. He does not explain how the technical details of his society are arranged and the system of distribution is worked out. He says that the citizens have cards, but that explains nothing. He does not explain how work is allotted, but rather assumes that such a simple matter could be arranged voluntarily. He says that his society functions under a modified handicraft system, but under such a system he gives his people every advantage that they could have with a machine economy.

Howells demonstrates, really, that the society novelist cannot easily manufacture novels out of the material of the political economist. Howells reveals himself as a successful man who can afford to have delicate sensibilities and feel sorry for the poor. He is a socialist of a sort, but he is too well bred to take his doctrines seriously. He seems to imply always that we shouldn't worry if conditions are bad, that they will have to get much worse before they get better, just as in Altruria. Education will show us eventually how to effect changes in the system. In the meantime there is nothing to do but remain cheerful and confident—and contribute to worthy charities.

CHAPTER TWENTY-ONE

DREAMS OF TWO DECADES

ALMOST all of our American utopians have been concerned with reconstruction, with plotting the features of a better world. Few of them have been cautious, careful planners. They have not been afraid of innovation or of complete change. They have not been afraid to say that the American system was decaying. They have not been afraid to propose a socialistic, communistic, or even totalitarian solution. None of our institutions has been held sacred—the family, the church, the state have all been attacked. With every attack, however, there have been suggestions for improvement. It is surprising how often these suggestions have been acted upon. Whether these utopian novels are denouncing an institution, or praising some reform enthusiastically, they are always intensely, almost mystically serious of purpose. They are never light-hearted or casual. Reform was a serious business. The fate of their country, and the world was at stake; reformers did not intend to fail from lack of zeal.

All of us have dreams which center upon a carefree life. It is natural that some of these novels should make utopia simply a place of escape. E. E. Hale and W. D. Howells were primarily escapists, although they did have some sound ideas. And so were the men who wrote *The Land of the Changing Sun* and *The Great Awakening*. Their books were in the same literary tradition as Samuel Butler's *Erewhon* and William Morris's *News from Nowhere*.

It would be futile to pay any great attention to the literary sources which molded these various novels, for the literary sources are much less important than the economic, political, and social views of the authors, which were developed by the political pressure of the moment. The reflections of Plato, Sir Thomas More, Bacon, Campanella, Cabet and Samuel Butler have inevitably had some influence, but, for the most part, the influence has been thoroughly diluted. Most of the ideas in these novels came from contemporary sources. Many of them were simply "in the air." And they were "in the air" for a variety of reasons. The explanation is three-fold: Economic unrest, resulting from the Civil War, the close of the frontier, and an unbalanced economy; social unrest, resulting from a new and critical evaluation of the meaning of democracy; and the American communistic tradition. The experiments of the Labadists, Kelpians, Ephratans, Rappites, Zoarites, Shakers, Amanites, Mormons, Owenites, and Fourierites had a tremendous influence on men's thinking. Such experiments had continued over several generations, and it was obvious to the dullest that they did not all fail as economic ventures.

When they dissolved, it was because some individual or individuals among them grew avaricious and disrupted the organization, or because the young people resented the discipline and restriction necessary to that way of life. They did not fail because they were communistic. The reverse was the case. They succeeded in building up more prosperous groups than those founded by the individualistic, "devil-take-the-hindmost" settlers, and many of their communities were shining examples of efficiency, thrift, and sound economic planning.

Their communism was that of peasants, small tradesmen, and artisans. . . . It was definitely lacking in the incentive necessary to the social and economic progress of industrial civilization.

[It] . . . was based upon religious idealism instead of economic reform.[1]

It was obvious, usually, that the reason for the success of these colonies was religious enthusiasm and fanaticism. Utopian dreamers could realize that, but they could also insist that a properly directed economic enthusiasm would have as much influence—that since man was primarily selfish, he ought to respond to economic stimuli at least as well as to spiritual stimuli. He ought to, perhaps, but he doesn't. That is one reason, at least, why these utopian dreams have taken shape only as badly written novels.

Idealists are likely to vary widely in their concepts of a better order, but the remarkable thing about these utopians is that so many of them agree on essentials. Of the forty volumes here considered which were written between 1883 and 1900, twenty-seven of them propose a modified capitalistic state, and five more propose a completely paternalistic, almost totalitarian state. Four describe a communistic state, but of these, three were satiric, and the fourth, *Nequa*,

[1] V. F. Calverton, *Where Angels Dared to Tread*, New York [1941], p. 172.

did not admit that the system described was communism. None of them actually recommended anarchism, but a few so simplify governmental processes that the dream becomes, essentially, philosophical anarchism. The dreams of totalitarian efficiency were written in opposition to Edward Bellamy. He was considered a dangerous radical, and so there was a tendency to praise those theories to which he was opposed. So, too, the three satires which portray a communistic state purport to be describing the evils of socialism. It was convenient to exaggerate such socialistic concepts as a classless society, equality of work and reward, and behavior motivated by a faith in the greater good. The twenty-seven socialistic novels vary in every respect except one—and that is their common faith that if men would only work together, with good will, there would be more than enough for all.

In sixteen of these same forty books it was predicted that the change to a better world would come very slowly, as a result of education. It is surprising, perhaps, that more of these reformers didn't adopt this socialistic faith in education, this belief that while a complete change would come slowly, it was still inevitable. Many of them, however, were as optimistic about the future as they were pessimistic about the present. Seventeen thought that reform could come immediately. A few thought that the increasing number of monopolies would inevitably make the state socialistic. The novelists whose work was published by the Kerr Company of Chicago relied on a legal revolution, simply because they had a deep faith in man's native intelligence. Two of the novels maintained that socialism could come only as the result of revolution, and six of them insisted that socialism would inevitably bring revolution. In other words, there was even less agreement about the path to the better world than about what it should be. That should be obvious, however, for past experience is very little help in predicting the future.

Since so many of these men assume that socialism will come gradually, as the result of education, it is interesting to examine their hopes for a new educational system. Most of those who wrote in the Bellamy tradition ignored the problem, feeling, probably, that his treatment of the subject had been adequate. For the rest, six insisted upon state controlled education, from the cradle to the grave. They explained that the trouble with the nineteenth century system was the uncertainty about purpose. Educators didn't know whether they were training students to seek truth, to think clearly, to understand the Bible, or to be God-fearing members of society. These utopians had no doubts about the proper purpose of education. Students should be conditioned and trained, from the very beginning, to be good, honest, conscientious, obedient citizens of the state. Four of them thought that education, through the college level, should be compulsory for all; the others were willing to let those without ability start productive labor at an earlier age. Two of them insisted on studying only practical subjects, and along with this a system of apprenticeships. They would waste no time on dead languages. Three of them carried this insistence on the practical one step farther by having no formal education at all. Children could learn, it was maintained, simply by asking questions, and everyone could serve as a teacher.

Some of the reformers made education much too simple a business. In *Young West,* for instance, the whole process was made easy by hypnotism. But regardless of how they simplified, almost all of their attempts at educational reform were in the same direction as what we are now pleased to call "modern" or "progressive" education.

These utopias were usually peopled by modest, peaceful, quietly religious citizens. Religion was not just a matter of observance; it was also an essential part of life. In the late nineties, the utopian novels showed a quickening interest in a sort of mystical, evangelical religion. God became both the inspiration and the guide to utopia. The best example of this new spirituality is *In His Steps,* but it is obvious in at least five of the other novels.

Along with this new religious enthusiasm, and partly, perhaps, as a result, went an occasional rationalizing of religion into a matter of ethics and sociology. Two of the books insisted that formal religious observance was completely unnecessary. There is this passage in *The Miltillionaire:*

. . . True Religion is invisible, and should prevade all of our institutions through our hearts at all times . . . and not ridiculously and hypocritically be relegated to one day in a week, and to one particular institution. Pure Religion we know to be Pure Love—which we realize in all our actions. . . .[2]

---

[2] Hovorre, *op. cit.,* p. 12.

It was inevitable that many utopians should have concerned themselves with women's right. And any consideration of women's rights immediately resolved itself into a consideration of the marriage law. One of the books insisted on a prolonged period of courtship, for the purpose of protecting th individual against himself. Another insisted on a rigidly controlled system of marriage for the protection of the state—to insure that all the offspring would be strong and properly cared for. Five other books made marriage and divorce simply a matter of registration, on the theory that marriage, more than anything else, produced constraint and bitterness between the sexes. It was reasoned that if men and women were equal before the law and could leave each other at will, then they would live together in perfect bliss. These were completely serious suggestions.

Many other reforms were proposed regularly. Model housing appeared in almost modern form. And so did suggestions for a simplified tax system. There were proposals for everything from a single tax on land to a single tax on time. Henry George had a tremendous influence in the eighties and nineties, and the cumulative effect of *Progress and Poverty* has probably been greater than that of any other American volume on economics. There were plans for better eating, to be achieved either by pellets or vegetarianism; there were plans for better streets, better clothing, better stores, better fertilization, better irrigation and crop control, and not only a better, but an absolute control of the weather. And, of course, there were a few utopians who put their whole faith in a revised financial system. Americans have been self-conscious about money since the days of Jackson's first attack on the United States Bank. For a time the Greenbackers thought they had found an easy formula for prosperity. Later, free silver, fanned by "Coin" Harvey's pamphleteering and Bryan's oratory, completed the job of giving the amateur economists confidence in monetary nostrums.

The intellectual range represented by the proposals is amazing. Some were intelligent and well developed, others were ingenious, and still others were simply crack-brained. The political range veers from the extreme left to the extreme right. These utopians weren't always clear thinkers, but they did make an effort to understand their world, and to re-examine it in terms of the new economics. And although they wrote fiction, some of the ideas which they suggested have had a continuing influence on American history.

During the eighties and nineties our economic structure came of age, and acquired the conflicts and problems of a mature economy. Along with the economic transition from a less complicated world went an intellectual transition—from the world of Emerson to the world of Dreiser. "Emerson was the apotheosis of two centuries of decentralization that . . . found its inevitable expression in the exaltation of the individual, free and excellent, the child of a beneficent order; whereas Dreiser was the first spokesman of a later America once more falling within the shadow of the pessimism that springs from every centralized society. . . ."[3] Considered in this light, these utopians have a literary significance apart from their influence as propagandists of a new order. They show one result of the changing environment. They mark one phase of the literary and intellectual transition between Emerson and Dreiser, between transcendentalism and muckraking, between the rebellion of the individualist and the rebellion of the man with a social conscience. The ferment which the utopians helped to stir up determined the intellectual and literary attitudes of the next generation of writers, the generation not only of Dreiser, but also of Stephen Crane, Frank Norris, Upton Sinclair, Lincoln Steffens and Edith Wharton.

The publishers of the late nineteenth century gave their readers a good deal of safe and innocuous "moral pap," as Louisa May Alcott described her own work. And since they were interested in profits, and there was scant protection for foreign copyrights, there were also a great many popular editions of the English novelists—of Dickens, Conan Doyle, Stevenson, Kipling and Wilkie Collins. Although Americans read these editions enthusiastically, they kept their interest in contemporary social problems. During the eighties and nineties there was a constant supply of straightforward radicalism. The utopians and reformers and Populists were all extremely vocal. They shouted and preached reform at every opportunity. What they

[3] V. L. Parrington, *The Beginnings of Critical Realism in America*, New York, 1930, p. 319.

wrote was not "polite" literature, and it was seldom taken seriously by contemporary critics. Lost causes are so easily forgotten that it is difficult even now to take seriously these men who did so much ranting and raving. But they were taken seriously by their contemporaries who bought books, and they left their mark on our literature.

CHAPTER TWENTY-TWO

MUCKRAKERS—AND PRACTICAL UTOPIANS

THE election of McKinley marked the end of the popular enthusiasm for reform. The millennium no longer seemed right around
the corner; political cure-alls and nostrums did not have the same
universal appeal.

The reformers closed up shop politically, but they continued to
take stock of the corrupt practices which they found about them. In
this they were helped by a small group of journalists, the muckrakers,
who realized that the more sensational their material, the more certain
their audience. These men were not motivated entirely by a desire
for reform. When asked about the origins of the movement, Lincoln
Steffens replied, "I was not the original muckraker; the prophets of
the Old Testament were ahead of me, and—to make a big jump in
time—so were the writers, editors and reporters . . . of the 1890's
who were finding fault with 'things as they are' in the pre-muckraking
period. But . . . I did not intend to be a muckraker."[1] The label came
from Theodore Roosevelt, who "picked the name out of Bunyan's
Pilgrim's Progress and pinned it on us."[2] Regardless of their motives
in stirring up scandal, *McClure's, Collier's, Cosmopolitan,* and *Everybody's* gave their findings a large audience. Their articles were carefully documented and thoroughly libelous, and they soon filtered down
into the public consciousness. They started with the conviction that
corrupt practices existed, and usually discovered that there was more
rather than less than they had expected.

Steffens explains in his *Autobiography* that he was always surprised
to find out what pleasant and agreeable fellows he had singled out as
the chief villains. He almost felt that he had missed his calling, that
he should have been a political boss, for he had a sneaking sympathy
with the rationalizing which made the public fair game. His final
conclusion was that it was not the bad men who were responsible for

---

[1] Joseph Lincoln Steffens, *The Autobiography of Lincoln Steffens,* New York,
[c1931], p. 357. [2] *Ibid.*

graft and political spoils, but rather that it was the fault of thoroughly respectable and personally honest citizens who wanted special privileges for their own projects. The desire for such privileges guaranteed the existence of the boss, for he was always able to deliver—if he got his price. He usually did, and the result was a political system which could not function honestly.

The findings of the muckrakers were taken seriously. The public showed an increasing appetite for the detail of corruption in business and government. Polite fiction began to contain passages which indicated that not even high society was pure and incorruptible. Pollyanna had gone out of style—heroes and heroines understood the economic facts of life. The characters in David Graham Phillips' novels, for example, become increasingly aware of the corruption of business, and talk a good deal about the social responsibility of the wealthy. Blacklock, the hero of *The Deluge,* 1905, is an expert at the bucket shop technique, and explains at great length how easy it is to manipulate stocks, to pay unearned dividends and leave the owners of securities with pieces of nicely engraved paper representing depreciated values. Phillips is a capable observer, but he is not a critic. There were a great many similar novelists who were concerned with the abuses of wealth and the problems of the poor, but who had nothing more effectual to suggest than the formation of missions and settlement houses, and the instruction of the poor in such useful arts as budgeting and cooking.

Somewhat farther to the left were the novels of those men who were critics as well as observers. There had been a good many such novels since *The Gilded Age* was published in 1873, and the strictures became somewhat sharper as the knowledge of business methods increased. *The Autocrats,* 1901, by Charles K. Lush, shows how business men can use bribery and blackmail. William H. Smith's *The Promoters,* 1904, is a satire on contemporary ethics. Upton Sinclair's *The Money Changers,* 1908, and *The Metropolis,* 1908, attempt to show how dangerous can be the influence of the banker, and how easily he can manipulate stocks and create panics for his own profit.

This interest in corruption is not exclusively the concern of the lesser novelists. Frank Norris's *The Octopus,* 1901, and *The Pit,* 1903; Robert Herrick's *The Memoirs of an American Citizen,* 1905;

and Theodore Dreiser's *The Financier,* 1912, and *The Titan,* 1914, are detailed accounts of the results of business initiative and the desire for power. Their characters practice the techniques of contemporary business and are adept at everything from watering stock to buying representatives. Norris is more of a story teller than is Dreiser, who is concerned with ethics, and tries to make his money-changer, Frank Cowperwood, into a villian. Cowperwood is skilled at every corrupt business practice, but he is such an engaging fellow, and does such a reasonable job of rationalizing his practices, that it is easy to accept him at his own estimate, as an honest and reasonable business man. Robert Herrick shows a greater concern for ethical matters in *The Memoirs of an American Citizen.* Van Harrington, the meat packer, is a success because he has mastered the practices of business. At the end he wonders how valuable his success with dollars has been, and tries to forget himself in his new duties as Senator. Herrick obviously sympathizes with Harrington. His vices are those of an American citizen—and so they have to be rationalized.

The Jungle, 1906, shows no such easy sympathy with the practices of business men. It is the story of Chicago's packing industry and of the tragic difficulties which confront so many immigrants. The story is heavily pessimistic; the life of every character is a tragedy. It is not really surprising that it was refused by five publishers. Eventually the first edition was published by Sinclair himself.

The book received more publicity than any novel for a long time. Readers were interested in what they ate; they were fascinated by the material which dealt with the lack of sanitation in the packing industry. The passages which told about spoiled and infected meat and filthy conditions made up only eight pages in *The Jungle,* but that was enough to give the public something to remember. Sinclair complained that he had been made a celebrity "not because the public cared anything about the workers, but simply because the public did not want to eat tubercular beef."[3] Actually, Sinclair was extremely lucky to have such an audience. *The Jungle* was printed at an opportune moment. It served as a spectacular climax to the work of the muckrakers, and to the work which had already been done in the

[3] Quoted in Mark Sullivan's *America Finding Herself,* Vol. II of *Our Times,* New York, 1927, p. 480.

cause of pure food and drug legislation. And it made Sinclair, an unknown young Socialist, a literary personage whose future work would be given immediate attention.

Utopianism had stopped for breath in the early years of the twentieth century. After the disillusioning years under McKinley, the aggressive enthusiasm of Theodore Roosevelt had a great appeal. The muckrakers presented an immediate challenge to progressives, liberals, and reformers, of all shades of opinion. The muckrakers pointed out so many chances for political reform that they made the framework of the government seem thoroughly good. All that was necessary was to shake off the encrustations of privilege which had grown up since the days of the founding fathers. The faults in our government may have been more obvious than ever before, but the remedies were also obvious. The muckrakers presented a challenge, and they made utopia seem closer to home than it had ever been.

A sketch of *Portland, Oregon: A. D. 1999*[4] was published in 1913. Unlike his immediate predecessors, who busied themselves with describing the future, Jeff W. Hayes, the author, has little to say about matters of government or economics. He assumes that the Progressives had been successful, and that the good of socialism had been incorporated into politics. Although blind, he was the editor of the *American Telegrapher*, and had a talent for describing mechanical details. The Portland of his imagination was lighted from a single source over the center of town, and, in dry spells, watered by a series of sprinklers suspended thousands of feet in the air by balloons. Compressed air had become an important source of power, and concrete had taken the place of wood in construction.

Portland had become a larger industrial center than New York, the result of the Alaska trade and the stimulus of the Panama Canal. But in spite of such growth the city had become pleasanter than ever before. Since transportation was all by air, there was no need for hard-surfaced streets, and they had been torn up and replaced by grass and roses.

This pamphlet still has a good deal of interest to anyone familiar with the city. Mr. Hayes had the knack of being specific; the buildings,

[4] Jeff W. Hayes, *Portland, Oregon: A.D. 1999*, Portland, 1913. A separate printing, also in 1913, was called *Paradise on Earth*.

names and institutions which he mentions are still to be found, and it is interesting to reflect on the extent to which his imagination has been vindicated.

The most interesting of these pre-war utopians who came under the influence of the muckrakers is Edward M. House—the same House who was later to be President Wilson's friend and confidant. His novel, *Philip Dru: Administrator,* 1912, reflects his sure knowledge of politics, and presents a practical and precise program for making the United States utopian.

Edward M. House, Texas Colonel and friend of the great, had the means and the ability to gratify an interest in politics. He first became skilled in Texas politics; he worked behind the scenes and served an apprenticeship as guide and advisor to several successive governors. He was not so much interested in recognition or office as in knowledge and power. According to his biographer, "He studied the political art from its lowest common denominator to the top, using the state of Texas as his laboratory. He studied the organization of the precinct, the voting district, the county, the city, with its peculiar problems. . . . He met and probed every politician, important and unimportant, who came his way."[5] Mr. House once said of himself that his ambition was "so great that it has never seemed worth while to strive to satisfy it."[6]

In 1910, when he was ready to enter national politics, he became enthusiastic about Woodrow Wilson's increasing influence, and also his "amenability to advice."[7] House wrote of their relationship: "We knew each other for congenial souls at the very beginning."[8] "I cannot tell you how pleased I was with him. He seemed too good to be true. I could hardly believe it would be possible to elect him. You know, in politics you can almost never elect the best man—he has done something, said something, or has something about him, which prevents his success. You have to take the next best man or perhaps the next to the next best man. And he seemed to have a good chance of success."[9]

House soon became active in the Wilson campaign headquarters,

---

[5] Arthur D. Howden Smith, *Mr. House of Texas,* New York, 1940, p. 25.
[6] Matthew Josephson, *The President Makers,* New York, 1940, p. 385.
[7] Smith, *op. cit.,* p. 52.   [8] *Ibid.,* p. 42.   [9] *Ibid.,* p. 43.

for he loved politics and was thoroughly familiar with all the Machiavellian niceties of the business. D. F. Houston, who was later Secretary of Agriculture under Wilson, commented upon House's activities in 1911: "He has a vision. . . . I should like to make him Dictator for a while. . . ."[10]

In the next year, 1912, House wrote and published anonymously his one novel, *Philip Dru: Administrator,* which outlined an ideal program of reform for a dictator, or administrator. It was written during a convalescence, in the "odd moments of thirty days." The ideas are much more remarkable than the style. On first publication it excited comment "out of proportion to its sales—comment that was as often skeptical as friendly. As soon as the new Administration gave voice to the character of the legislation it wished enacted, this comment redoubled."[11] The author had not succeeded in preserving his anonymity.

The outline of the story is similar to two of the novels published by the Kerr Company some dozen years earlier, *President John Smith* and *The Legal Revolution of 1902.* House pictured, as had these novels, a corrupt government which had become more centralized and ruthless as it had become, also, more efficient. The government was dominated by two men—Selwyn, the boss, a composite portrait of Nelson Aldrich and Mark Hanna, and Thor, the financier, modeled after J. (Jupiter) Pierpont Morgan. Eventually a revolutionary group emerged and took control by force. Philip Dru, soldier and dreamer, becomes the administrator of the government during an interim period while a new government is being organized.

The first step in reorganization is a new tax structure, worked out according to the lessons of Henry George. Improved property was to be taxed at a low rate; unimproved property at a very high rate. This was supposed to keep the wealthy from piling up unearned increment, and would "open up land for cultivation now lying idle, provide homes for more people, cheapen the cost of living to all, and make possible better schools, better roads, and a better opportunity for the successful co-operative marketing of products."[12]

[10] D. F. Houston, *Eight Years with Wilson's Cabinet,* Garden City, 1926, Vol. I, pp. 21, 48.

[11] Smith, *op. cit.,* p. 49.

[12] [Edward M. House], *Philip Dru: Administrator,* New York, 1912, pp. 178, 179.

In addition there was to be an income tax—$\frac{1}{2}$ of 1 per cent on the first thousand, and increasing to a maximum of seventy per cent on incomes of ten million or more. In 1912 the income tax no longer served as a bogey to frighten the thrifty. A few years earlier, when the income tax law of 1894 was being considered by the Supreme Court, Joseph Choate had "warned the judges that it was 'now or never'; that the 'communist march' must be stopped; that property demanded immediate and unconditional security in its rights."[13] The final acceptance of the income tax amendment in 1913 marked the cumulative influence of the reform group—populist and utopian, progressive and muckraker.

Perhaps Philip Dru's most radical proposal was a Federal Incorporation Act which would make corporations share with the government and states a percentage of their earnings. This plan would place government and labor representatives on the board of every corporation. Both the government and labor would share in the profits. Labor would be given "a certain percentage of the earnings . . . after a reasonable per cent upon the capital had been earned. In turn, it was to be obligatory upon them not to strike, but to submit all grievances to arbitration. The law was to stipulate that if the business prospered, wages should be high; if times were dull, they should be reduced."[14]

All public utilities were to be taken over entirely, and the books of any company were to be open to the public. There is no mention of the ingenious book-keeping such legislation would bring about. The telephone and telegraph companies were to be absorbed by the postal department. This phase of the program, at least, goes back to the Nationalist organization which was spawned on the ideas of *Looking Backward*.

The new constitutions proposed for the national government and the separate states showed a knowledge of practical politics, and were designed to simplify and standardize the administration of government. The executive was required to outline his program to the House (as did Mr. Wilson), for that body, along with the

[13] Charles A. and Mary R. Beard, *The Rise of American Civilization*, New York, 1927, Vol. II, p. 335.
[14] House, *op. cit.*, p. 183.

President and his Cabinet, had the sole power to initiate legislation. The President and the Cabinet would be allowed to frame their own legislative proposals, and these would not be "referred to committees, but are to be considered by the House as a whole, and their consideration shall have preference over measures introduced by other members."[15] This would eliminate some of the futile bickering between House and Senate and the frequently inadequate compromises.

Other reforms included new regulations for the control of holding companies, similar in spirit to the Securities and Exchange Commission; a new tariff law, abolishing protection; a new and aggressive interpretation of the Monroe Doctrine which would justify policing our neighbors; a new banking law which would destroy "the credit trust" and provide a "flexible currency bottomed largely on commercial assets"; loans on easy terms to farmers; and regulations which would eliminate loan sharks, and provide money at reasonable rates.

The similarities between Wilson's program and the Philip Dru-House program soon attracted attention. In his cabinet notes for November 1, 1918, Franklin K. Lane, Secretary of the Interior, commented: "But he [Wilson] likes the idea of personal party-leadership —Cabinet responsibility is still in his mind. Colonel House's book, *Philip Dru*, favors this, and all that book has said should be, comes about slowly, even woman suffrage. And yet they say that House has no power."[16] Although House was always reluctant to discuss the novel, he did acknowledge "that while he had revised his opinions as to some measures he recommended, he continued to consider most of them as expressing his political and ethical faith."[17] Speaking for himself, Mr. Smith, his biographer, says, "I know of no novel, including the works of H. G. Wells, which so deeply and positively influenced the trends of contemporary life. I always believed, personally, that Mr. House was a bit thunderstruck by the extent of the reforms he inspired, and came to believe that it would be better not to tinker too broadly with the foundations of the Republic."[18]

Some of the ideas expressed in *Philip Dru* have come to life in the

---

[15] *Ibid.*, p. 241.
[16] A. W. Lane, and L. H. Wall, editors, *The Letters of Franklin K. Lane*, Boston, 1922, p. 297.   [17] Smith, *op. cit.*, p. 50.   [18] *Idem.*

New Deal. It would be foolish to assume that the novel was largely responsible. It was not. The ideas had been slowly evolved during many years. But one can find, if one will look, many similarities between the programs of Franklin Roosevelt and Philip Dru-House. As far back as 1912, House had been for "adequate wages," compulsory recognition of unions, old age pensions, laborer's insurance laws, and government administered loan societies. He had wanted the Constitution brought up-to-date, and the Supreme Court reformed, and its power limited to the extent that the judges "could no longer pass upon the constitutionality of laws, their function being merely to decide . . . what the law was."[19]

According to Mr. Smith, again, even "the phrases conceived by Mr. House echo in the speeches and 'fireside talks' of the man who studied politics under him for more than twenty-two years. Others, it is true, words and ideas, were transmuted by Mr. Wilson into his sonorous prose."[20]

There is no reason to assume that this novel had any direct influence by itself; but Mr. House, who revealed himself in the novel, had a remarkable influence. He was a thoroughly enigmatic personality—aloof, shrewd, calculating, powerful. The novel indicates the extent to which his ideals were watered down by the demands of politics. And it serves to illustrate some of the sources of the "New Freedom" and the "New Deal." Few reformers have had more power than Mr. House—and no other American utopia has come so close to being brought to life.

[19] House, *op. cit.*, p. 168.   [20] Smith, *op. cit.*, p. 370.

CHAPTER TWENTY-THREE

THE PREOCCUPIED TWENTIES

THE American people thought of the first world war as a crusade. They accepted the slogans, and they believed them for a time: they believed that they were fighting for a better world, for a world of peace and cooperation—for a real and immediate utopia. Idealism soon turned to disillusion. *The People of the Ruins,* 1920,[1] predicts the inevitable decay of all civilization. Men have been worn out by a succession of wars; they have finally achieved peace, but only as the result of exhaustion. They no longer dream of utopia, nor hope for luxuries; they simply want to live out their lives in quiet apathy. Poverty has become the rule. There is no such thing as idealism; disillusion and weariness have become the chief characteristics of this ruined world.

The cynicism shown in this novel was common during the twenties. After Harding came to the presidency, "Internationalism," or any thought of a better world, was brushed aside in favor of more urgent matters. Utopia was old-fashioned and naive; there was a new, hard-boiled, post-war world; men wanted to make money and be amused, or excited, or thrilled. These were the days of Mah Jong and cross-word puzzles and Dr. Coué, of a new interest in sex, in Freud, and the freedom of the libido. Flappers and free love were more appealing than ideas dealing with economics or some intangible future. Literary folk busied themselves with the concerns of the present. They were self-conscious about leading a full life; they cared more about self-expression than they did about self-respect. The so-called "intellectuals" liked to think of themselves as bohemians. In the metropolitan centers they gathered in restaurants and enjoyed what they thought was fine talk, high living, and intellectual freedom. Many of their ideas came from H. L. Mencken, the brightest of the bright young men. He and his *American Mercury* set the tone of rebellion against respectability and sentimentality, against Babbitts

[1] Edward Shanks, *The People of the Ruins,* New York, 1920.

and Rotarians, and against what Mencken liked to call the "bilge of idealism." Mencken was, in fact, an iconoclast who had regard neither for silence nor consistency. His influence was all-pervasive, and it was not an influence to make men more likely to accept uncritically any sort of utopian prophet.

The decade produced a quantity of first rate fiction: *Babbitt, Arrowsmith,* and *Main Street; An American Tragedy; A Farewell to Arms; Death Comes for the Archbishop; U.S.A.;* and Eugene O'Neill's full length psychological thriller, *Strange Interlude.* But the taste of the great mass of readers was not keyed to the intellectual. They preferred Bernarr McFadden's *True Story,* which set a new record in rapid growth, and by 1926 was selling two million copies. The publishers of the new and lush sex-adventure magazines provided stories with appealing titles which gave them a news-stand advantage over the older magazines. Publishers became as conscious of the censor and of how far they could go as was the newly appointed Mr. Hays of the movies.

In 1928 *The Nation* ran a series of articles in which various critics and writers described the world they would like to live in. Most of their essays spoke of the futility of discussing an ideal society. Edna Ferber ruled out of her world "any editors so unimaginative as to request writers to do articles on the subject of Utopia."[2] H. L. Mencken rationalized the assignment: "Do I limn Utopia? Well, why not? Utopia, like virtue, is shot through with relativity. To a man in jail, I dare say, the radio is a boon."[3] Sinclair Lewis was, at least, specific about what he did not want.

I can imagine nothing more horrible than a world in which every one beamed like a Y.M.C.A. secretary, insisted on helping all the brethren who damn well wanted to be left alone, and conversed with mellifluous omniscience about Keats, the quantum theory, S. Parkes Cadman, four-wheel brakes, S.A., and Chateau Yquem. For imperfect humanity it would be intolerable. It would be like sitting through eternity listening to the Archangel Michael recording your every foolishness, while the Dominions beside the throne sang regularly every seven seconds, like energetic but slightly humorless crows, "Hallelujah."

[2] Edna Ferber, "A Few Things Altered or Abolished," *The Nation:* May 30, 1928 (126:609).

[3] H. L. Mencken, "What Is This Talk About Utopia?" *The Nation:* June 13, 1928 (126:662).

I'm awfully sorry, but I do not believe that mankind will ever be ideally perfect. I am convinced that in the year of our Lord 19935 there will still be old women who peer out between curtains in the hope of discovering titillating improprieties; there will still be people who serve, and people who give orders; there will still be radical *Nations* and conservative *Saturday Evening Posts,* for both of which reasonable people will give equal thanks.[4]

With so many popular and spicy magazines on the news-stands, and with the intellectual set enjoying the role of iconoclast, it is not surprising that there was no time for utopianism. Our idealism had been pretty well dissipated. It was not until after 1929, when we all knew the meaning of depression, that men began to dream again of a golden age, and wonder about a cure for neglected economic problems.

[4] Sinclair Lewis, "Mr. Lorimer and Me," *The Nation:* July 25, 1928 (127:81).

CHAPTER TWENTY-FOUR

THE DEPRESSION YEARS

Part I. The Prophets: Dr. Townsend, Huey Long, Upton Sinclair

THE depression years of the thirties brought forth a good deal of undiluted utopian thinking—almost as much as in the nineties. A number of economic panaceas were formulated, and some of them were helped along to public recognition by fictionalized accounts of what reform should mean. And all too frequently reform meant some way to satisfy what has occasionally seemed to be a national ambition, getting something for nothing. In the nineties this showed itself in the demand for cheap money; for free silver and inflation. In the thirties there was the Townsend plan, with its faith in the magic of printing-press money; the Share the Wealth plan of Huey Long, and Upton Sinclair's Epic Plan. These programs were utopian, for they pointed to a promised land. The unhappy thirities made men self-conscious about economic problems, and the world crisis. Men were stubborn in their reasoning about the causes and the cure of a depression; social planning was more frequently discussed than baseball or liquor laws. More than ever before, the radio became a political force; the uneducated listened with increasing attention to the various formulas for recovery. In the public consciousness it was always the simple solutions, depending on paper money, and backed by a catch phrase, which had the greatest appeal.

These formulas represented the contemporary American dream—greener pastures, manna from heaven, and something for nothing. "Always we have progressed in two directions simultaneously, building a massive materialism which outdid anything on the face of the earth, and projecting castles in the air, like a great confession to heaven that our material life was not sound. In the heart of nearly all unweaned Americans lies the waiting Utopian, aching to believe in the New Jerusalem, certain that there must be just one wise answer to all the problems of economics and politics if only it could be found."[1]

Dr. Townsend, Huey Long, and Upton Sinclair had few of the same ideals, but their rise to political influence depended on the same things: The promise of greener pastures and a cure for the depression—and, probably most important, extremely able publicity.

Dr. Townsend was a country practitioner turned social planner, a humanitarian and not an economist. He had seen a great deal of human wretchedness, and he believed implicitly that there must be a solution. He thought he had found that solution, and millions of Americans agreed with him. They approved of his humanity and they wanted to believe, as he did, that there were economic short-cuts which would solve all problems and make every one happy. In effect, he was a utopian dreamer, who saw in his dream world what he could not find in reality.

The Townsend plan was actually two plans—one to help the aged and the indigent; the other to increase business activity and solve unemployment. The two programs have usually been considered together, but the economic analysis of the second has been clouded by the sentimental appeal of helping the old folks. They would be treated generously. All unemployed men and women over sixty would be paid two hundred dollars a month, on their promise to spend the money within thirty days. He reasoned that so much money in circulation would create an enormous demand for goods, which would increase employment and guarantee continuing prosperity. This was the Revolving Pension Plan. Originally the pensions were to be financed by a ten per cent sales tax, but the more appealing transaction tax of two per cent was quietly substituted. What this would be, the Townsendites would not explain. The tax had one major virtue—it sounded simple—and one major vice, which was usually ignored, that it would be a tax on the consumer rather than on wealth. As the amount of money in circulation increased, the consumer would get less and less for his money. The result would be inflation, and pensions which would quickly diminish in value. The Townsendites believed that they were tapping new and idle sources of wealth, but

[1] Raymond Gram Swing, *Forerunners of American Fascism*, New York, 1935, p. 122.

they were not creating wealth at all, only redistributing it. The plan would simply subtract from the total number of those who produce wealth. There would be more money to spend, and less to buy.

But the Townsendites believed in their formula, and they were not easily discouraged. Dr. Townsend has had millions of aggressive supporters who have campaigned on the basis of their slogan, "Support the Townsend Plan, and then let it support you!" In 1946, as well as in 1935, Congressmen have found it expedient to introduce bills based on the plan.

Huey Long was a dangerous influence, and he was dangerous in proportion to his intelligence. An arrogant, unscrupulous liar, he cared little for consistency. He had a loud voice, he was persuasive, and he would promise anything. Huey became the dictator of Louisiana because he promised the world to his followers, and because he had the shrewdness to back up those promises with obvious good works. He built new roads; he took the very poor from the tax rolls; he spent vast sums on education; he talked about helping illiterates; he forced the reduction of power rates; and he posed, always, as the friend of the little man, and the foe of the utilities. He also increased enormously the indebtedness of the state, but debts are not as obvious as roads and schools. It was the few promises fulfilled which made him powerful—and also a menace.

Huey Long's national influence depended on his Share the Wealth program, which would "limit poverty by providing that every deserving family shall share in the wealth of America for not less than one-third of the average wealth, thereby to possess not less than $5,000 free of debt."[2] In addition, he promised a system of pensions, and a tax structure which would reduce the great fortunes "to such a few million dollars as will allow the balance of the American people to share in the wealth and profits of the land."[3] This was not all. He would limit the hours of work, and the workers would be given their fair share in the conveniences and luxuries of life.

As a politician Huey had three great talents apart from his intelligence—a loud voice, great skill at invective, and shrewdness as a pamphleteer. The best example of his pamphleteering skill is his fictionalized account of what he would do *when* he was elected

---

[2] Quoted in Swing, *op. cit.*, p. 99.   [3] *Idem.*

President. Modesty was not one of his virtues. He probably did expect to become President. And if he had not been shot by one of his many enemies, he would, at least, have made his fellow Senators even more aware of the power of his voice and of the multitude of his promises.

His book, *My First Days in the White House,* is pretty poor fiction. First of all, he imagined himself the newly elected President, faced with the pleasant tasks of appointing his cabinet and solving the problems of the nation. Solutions come quickly, for he had a facile imagination which was never troubled by abstraction or over-simplification. He was seldom specific. And there was no reason why he should be, for he had learned one political lesson well—that people will believe anything if they hear it repeated often enough.

The book consists of a listing of promises, unsubstantiated and alluring. All of them had a familiar ring. He would:

1. Put in motion a ten billion dollar reclamation project to control floods and make fertile the dust bowl,

2. Reform all education, and send every boy and girl to college, [There is no explanation of method except that teachers should be paid more.]

3. Modernize the penal system, and

4. Provide adequate medical attention for the whole country. He gives the Mayo brothers the job:

Your new patients are to be 130,000,000 people, living in the United States and called Americans. I would like to have you prescribe for them the preventive measures and curative, medicinal treatment which they need. I would like you to help men in stamping out a number of diseases that take a terrific toll of human life and human effort from the American people every year. I intend to have the federal government provide the facilities and equipment which you will need to carry out this work.[4]

This would be only a beginning, for the federal laboratories would be expanded and their work extended "to include every known disease for which there is not a known cause or a satisfactory cure or preventive."[5]

His last two proposals did not have the same universal appeal,

[4] Huey Pierce Long, *My First Days in the White House,* Harrisburg, 1935, pp. 60, 61.
[5] *Ibid.,* p. 61.

but they were directed at organized and aggressive pressure groups whose political support he needed. He would:

5. Enact the Coughlin banking bill, which would put the federal banking system under the control of elected officials, and, finally,

6. Enact, as the capstone of his program, his Share the Wealth plan, which would make every man a king, and, more important, a capitalist.

My First Days in the White House was published in the fall of 1935, shortly after Long had been shot. Senator Huey Long might have become a martyr, but he had almost as many enemies as friends—and then the machine he had put together so carefully fell apart when treasury agents asked too many questions about the income of his friends. It was not long until Huey and his Share the Wealth plan became a joke, but it might have been otherwise. Some of the predictions of Sinclair Lewis's *It Can't Happen Here* might have happened here. When hard times come again there may well be other Huey Longs who have an equal talent for formulating promises and laying out a design for utopia.

Upton Sinclair had far less influence than Dr. Townsend and Huey Long. Sinclair's followers were numbered in thousands; theirs in millions. Dr. Townsend had a social conscience, Huey Long had brains, and Upton Sinclair had both, but that was not enough. The combination was not as effective in building up a following as either of the others.

In 1934 he undertook his most ambitious political project, campaigning for governor of California on the democratic ticket. The first step in his program was the publication of a sixty-four page pamphlet, *I, Governor of California, and How I Ended Poverty*. On the front cover is this boxed message:

This is not just a pamphlet.
This is the beginning of a Crusade.
A Two-Year Plan to make over a State.
To capture the Democratic primaries
and use an old party for a new job.
The EPIC plan:
(E)nd (P)overty (I)n (C)alifornia!

His plan seemed to be politically practical: it was the most reasonable of the proposals with mass appeal; it seemed to offer a workable and inexpensive solution—and, for a time, many conservative Californians were interested. Other Californians were terrified, for they remembered some of his novels and the fact that he had called himself a Socialist.

Sinclair believed in production for use. The EPIC plan proposed to abolish relief and put men back to work. Sinclair maintained that there was no such thing as overproduction, only mal-distribution. Keep people working, he said, and there will be no poverty.

This could be done, he hoped, by two legislative acts giving the state authority to establish

1. State land colonies, whereby the unemployed may become self-sustaining, [and]

2. To acquire factories and production plants whereby the unemployed may produce the basic necessities required for themselves and for the land colonies, and to operate these factories and house and feed and care for the workers. . . . The industries will include laundries, bakeries, canneries, clothing and shoe factories, cement-plants, brick-yards, lumber-yards, thus constituting a complete industrial system. . . .

Script was to be issued to simplify the distribution of supplies within the system.

In addition to these basic proposals, Sinclair recommended a number of other specific reforms which he thought would make the land plan more feasible, and which would, also, have a mass appeal:

1. The abolition of the sales tax.

2. Passage of a state income tax law beginning with incomes of five thousand dollars.

3. An increase in the state inheritance tax.

4. Increased taxes on public utility corporations.

5. The elimination of taxes on all homes with an assessed valuation of less than three thousand dollars.

6. A state tax of ten per cent on all unimproved lands. [This goes back to Henry George's feeling that all wealth has its origin in increasing land values. Sinclair wanted to make it impossible to hold land for an increase in price. With this proposal land would quickly revert to the state, and there would be plenty available for the use of the unemployed.]

7. A liberal pension plan starting at fifty dollars a month.

This program was particularly effective in appealing for the votes of those groups which offered some specific for the curing of all human problems. Sinclair was supported by the Theosophists from Ojai, by the Rosicrucians from San Jose, and by some advocates of the Townsend Plan, the Rust taxation plan, and the Synchro-Tax. The main part of the election book is an account of the difficulties Sinclair expected to face in his campaign. He listed a great many, but he did not quite do justice to the organizations which actually did fight him. In the last few pages he visualized victory:

One by one the land colonies became self-supporting. After the first year they began paying off their bonds out of their sales of produce.

The opposition to EPIC began to collapse. . . . The reason was the success of the colonies in planting crops, and the success of the factories in turning out goods. The California farmers knew how to farm, the workers knew how to work, and the managers knew how to manage. It became evident that there was going to be a publicly owned productive unit of enormous dimensions in the State. It also became evident that the workers in the State-owned industries liked the idea. . . . The problem of the business cycle had been solved. Those who needed goods had the means to buy, therefore production and consumption balanced. . . .

Another reason for the dying away of opposition was that the opposers did not have so much money to spend. The graduated taxes were taking a large part of the wealth of the unproductive classes. The profit-takers were losing their customers, and they saw co-operation booming, and realized that the old system was doomed. . . .

The people lost their fear of the State, for they discovered that it had become a new thing. It was no longer the incarnation of selfishness, an instrument of repression of exploiting classes. It became the people themselves, doing what they wanted done with no one to prevent them. The sole question became, what was the most convenient and practical way to get a particular job done.[6]

Sinclair waged an aggressive campaign. He defeated George Creel in the primaries, and came very close to defeating the Republican candidate, Governor Merriam. The final vote was: Merriam, 1,138,000; Sinclair, 879,000.

After the election Sinclair published an account of his adventure,

[6] Upton Sinclair, *I, Governor of California, and How I Ended Poverty*, Los Angeles, n.d., pp. 59, 60, 61.

I, Candidate for Governor; and How I Got Licked. The main reason, he explained, for his defeat, was the ruthlessness of the opposition, and the tremendous amount of money spent on publicity. Sinclair's own appeal had been directed at the uneducated; by spending more money, the Republicans had made an even better appeal to the same group.

The Epic program did not promise quite as much as the Townsend Plan or Share the Wealth, but it was none the less utopian. Sinclair overlooked some difficulties and minimized others. He had to convince his following. And he was enough of an optimist himself to have few doubts about the wisdom of his formula, although he had a great many doubts about his ability to defeat Governor Merriam. Had he won, it would have been interesting to watch how much he would have had to limit his promises when he was confronted by the immediate problems of the executive, and the completely different program of the New Deal.

Part II. Technocracy and the Promise of Abundance

In 1932 and 1933 Americans became conscious of a new word, "technocracy." They didn't know what it meant, exactly, and they were not going to learn, but their interest brought about the publication of a great many books and magazine articles which tried to tell them. The word was first used to refer to the activities of a group of men who were interested in the results of the rapid mechanization of industry. By shrewd publicity their activities aroused this great enthusiasm and attained the dignity of a movement.

There was very little new in "technocracy" except the word itself and the respect it was accorded. Howard Scott, the organizer of the original group, became a prophet. Few of his predictions were new; they came, rather, from such well-known sources as Adam Smith, Thorstein Veblen, Karl Marx, and Irving Fisher. But the sources of his ideology did not matter—few of his readers knew the difference, and, anyway, they were anxious to believe the new gospel, and had no desire to quibble about its origins. Before long the meaning of "technocracy" had been expanded to include both a threat and a promise—a threat of technological unemployment, and a promise of greater abundance than ever before.

This willingess to accept the promise of plenty, this faith in the fruits of the machine, is typical of the American dream. For a hundred years and more we have beguiled ourselves with visions of a utopia which was a sort of mechanical heaven, where the goods coming off the conveyor belts were always bigger and better and more functional. The Technocrats capitalized on this faith with their romantic and frequently exaggerated promises. Their influence was soon dissipated, however; and their chief prophet, Howard Scott, was forgotten. The public turned its ear to the more alluring promises of the rabble-rousers, to the Father Coughlins and Huey Longs, whose proposals were enlivened with thoughts of easy money.

The Technocrats, nevertheless, left their mark on us. They left us with a greater enthusiasm for the new—with a taste for magazines called *The New Science* and *Facts of the Future*. And they left us with the so-called funny books and their men of tomorrow: Flash Gordon, Superman, Captain Marvel, the Phantom, Captain America, Bullet man, and Prince Valiant. These heroes live in a strange new world—where men must struggle with the force of new machines, and the mysteries of the atomic age. There is no looking back in these comic strips; they are all concerned as was H. G. Wells, with "the shape of things to come." The future they predict is made more complicated rather than more simple by the new scientific developments. Such things are a matter of taste; today the new and the different seems to attract us more than the charms of a simple life.

The Technocrats had taken over from Thorstein Veblen a supreme faith in the engineer—not only as a production man, but also as an expert on human relations. And always they emphasized the fruits of a new system rather than the difficulties which would complicate its beginnings. They seemed to expect the politicians and industrialists to step aside, acknowledge their own incompetence, and invite the engineers to take charge. [That is one of the virtues of utopia—the changes are effected so easily.] This same weakness is evident in *Prohibiting Poverty*[7] and *The New Industrial Dawn*.[8] Both authors take joy in prophecy, and both think they are prescribing the means of attaining that prophecy. The first of these was originally published

[7] Prestonia Mann Martin, *Prohibiting Poverty*, New York, 1932.
[8] A. T. Churchill, *The New Industrial Dawn*, Seattle, 1939.

by the Rollins Press in Florida, but then was distributed by Farrar and Rinehart, in the expectation of a nation-wide sale. Thirteen editions were published in the next seven years, and Mrs. Martin attained the dignity of being commended by Mrs. Roosevelt.

Her scheme required the use of an industrial labor force which showed the influence of Bellamy, as well as the Stuart Chase-Technocratic groups, who assume that more efficient methods of production have so simplified the problem of existence that all that is required is a more direct system of distribution. Mrs. Martin reasoned that better distribution depended on a thorough reorganization of society, a reorganization which could be accomplished by state-directed labor groups. Everyone would join such a group at the age of eighteen and serve for a period of eight years. Their labor would produce all the basic necessities of life—food, clothing, and shelter. Once an individual had served his time, he would be eligible for these necessities for the rest of his life. His time would be his own, and he could, if he chose, engage in private business, and enjoy the profits of capitalism. As an entrepreneur he would be free to deal in luxury goods, and to supply any sort of personal service. In other words, her solution was supposed to give citizens the security of socialism, and also the profits which might come with personal initiative.

The eight year tenure in the labor army was fixed upon as necessary to maintain twelve million workers, whose labor would be required to produce the basic necessities. Her figures, with which she is generous, are based on computations of Stuart Chase's New York Labor Bureau. The difference between her eight years and Bellamy's twenty-four years of service is largely the difference between computing the necessities of life and everything. The balance between luxuries and necessities is constantly shifting. Those who consider themselves little better than paupers today might well have been considered prosperous, in terms of possessions, only a few decades ago.

Mrs. Martin says nothing of the difficulties involved in setting up such a program, and of how those people of more than twenty-six would be treated during its first years. She insists always on its major virtue—that it would prohibit poverty. It would, of course, according to her definition, but it might also create more new problems than those it solved. These are ignored in favor of listing certain secondary advantages:

1. Women would be more independent than ever before.

2. The energy and strength of young people would be used, rather than wasted. Schools would teach every child a trade. Those with special aptitudes would have plenty of time to continue their education after graduation from the labor service.

3. It would do away with our enormously expensive system of pensions.

Mrs. Martin indulges in a great many footnotes to bolster her reasoning. Chief among her experts is Henry Ford, but he is not cited as a utopian. His remarks are not surprising:

> What the world is waiting for is a social and economic Blueprint.... The day's work lies at the foundation of the world.... Every man who eats and wears clothes and enjoys creature comforts does so at the cost of someone's labor. He ought to yield an adequate return of useful service for what he receives.[9]

Mrs. Martin's plan might possibly satisfy men in Mr. Ford's position. Men supplied with the necessities of life would probably not be so aggressive about an adequate wage. And a nation without poor might conceivably get along with less regulation of the business groups Mr. Ford represented.

The New Industrial Dawn is similar to Mrs. Martin's volume, except that it is admittedly fiction, and admittedly based on the plot of *Looking Backward*. The new world order is seen through the eyes of a banker who had slipped into a drunken stupor in 1929 and somehow recovered after the millennium. The change to the new era had come about by evolution, not force, but its beginnings were in the thirties, when a President had been elected on a "Platform of Plenty," which had as its fundamental thesis that poverty can be eliminated by keeping everyone working. On a given day the government took over, and from that time on everyone worked, and everyone received the same wage, ten dollars a day. There was no inflation, for everyone was a producer as well as a consumer. And best of all, it is explained, this is not socialism or democracy either, but a "Meritority," democratically administered.

[9] Martin, *op. cit.*, pp. 4, 14.

The plan is simple enough in outline (keep everyone working, and divide the results of an expanded production), but the execution would not be simple. The story is documented with a great many statistics, but they do not make the economics any more convincing than do the author's predictions about the world of tomorrow: A society without thieves; a more strong and healthy population as a result of careful government supervision of foods; free food, clothing, and lodging; and a super control of eugenics which would allow "the size, weight and physique of our people" to be "regulated by law."

Prohibiting Poverty is more carefully reasoned than *A New Industrial Dawn,* but both are cut from the same pattern. Both are in the tradition of the eighteen nineties when every city boasted amateur economists planning detailed utopias. These two are a little more reasonable and a good deal less ingenious than Dr. Townsend's program. Both realize, at least, that the consumption of goods must, in the final analysis, depend on production. In the thirties, however, it was those who sent their voices out over the air waves who were given the attention of the people—and of those whose job it was to enact the people's pleasure into law.

Part III. Escape to Shangri-La: Lost Horizon and Islandia

Lost Horizon is a novel of escape born of the depression. In 1933, when the book was first published, economic forces seemed to be as destructive and hopeless as the menace of atomic energy does now.

Shangri-La, the lamasery lost beyond the horizon, is a dream world calculated to appeal to a depressed, disillusioned, and pessimistic generation. *Lost Horizon* offers a temporary escape from the real to the ideal—from a world concerned with the essential problem of existence, to an intellectual oasis hidden away from the immediacy of every-day life.

There are no panaceas in *Lost Horizon,* because there are no economic problems in the Valley of the Blue Moon. Food and clothing are raised by the natives; luxuries are imported. Foreign exchange is easy, for the valley is provided with a gold mine.

Shangri-La is as distant in spirit as in miles from civilizing and corrupting influences. The Christian monks who inhabit the monastery and rule the valley have mastered the secret of long life. That in itself might have had no appeal to the readers of the mid-thirties if it had not been for the fact that the monks devote their extra years to contemplation and the pursuit of wisdom. Nothing is of immediate importance to them—least of all hard work, of virtue for its own sake. Their most persistent belief is moderation in all things. According to Father Perrault, founder of the monastery,

We inculcate the virtue of avoiding excess of all kinds—even including . . . excess of virtue itself. We rule with moderate strictness, and in return we are satisfied with moderate obedience. And . . . our people are moderately sober, moderately chaste, and moderately honest.[10]

Shangri-La depended for justification on the wisdom and ideal of Father Perrault, who had been troubled by the realization that all the loveliest things in the world were transient and perishable. In the world outside his valley

he saw the nations strengthening, not in wisdom, but in vulgar passions and the will to destroy; he saw their machine power multiplying until a single-weaponed man might have matched a whole army of the Grand Monarque.

But that was not all. He foresaw a time when men, exultant in the technique of homicide, would rage so hotly over the world that every precious thing would be in danger, every book and picture and harmony, every treasure garnered through two millenniums, the small, the delicate, the defenseless—all would be lost. . . .[11]

The purpose of Shangri-La was to preserve the culture and wisdom of the past.

"Here we shall stay with our books and our music and our meditations, conserving the frail elegancies of a dying age, and seeking such wisdom as men will need when their passions are all spent. We have a heritage to cherish and bequeath. Let us take what pleasure we may until that time comes."

"And then?"

"Then, my son, when the strong have devoured each other, the Christian ethic may at last be fulfilled, and the meek shall inherit the earth."[12]

This dream, then, envisioned a new world arising from the ruins

[10] James Hilton, *Lost Horizon*, Page references are to the Pocket Book Edition, p.

[11] *Ibid.*, pp. 149, 150.   [12] *Ibid.*, pp. 150, 151.

of the old, a world which would again appreciate the lost treasures of art and learning. Shangri-La was to be the repository for the wisdom and learning of the old world.

The dream of the early thirties was also of a new world, a world of plenty and leisure, of wisdom and justice. Shangri-La was a made-to-order utopia whose success was inevitable because it promised a better world.

Lost Horizon was first published in the spring of 1933, but its sale depended largely on the recognition given Mr. Hilton's pleasant but trivial *Good Bye Mr. Chips,* which was published in the fall of 1934. *Lost Horizon* was "discovered" by certain of the popular critics. Mr. Woollcott, for example, called it "one of the most enthralling tales spun in our time." At the end of October, 1934, *Lost Horizon* was on the *New York Herald Tribune's* list of best sellers. It stayed there until the middle of August, 1935—in terms of sales the most successful utopia since *In His Steps.* And both were successful for the same reason; they were thoroughly in tune with the thinking and emotional reactions of their generations.

The success of the Hollywood version of the novel made it seem more nearly American than British. Since it expressed so aptly the mood of a generation, it is convenient to forget that Mr. Hilton deals almost exclusively with British situations and types.

Just as Shangri-La served as an escape from the depression, so Austin Wright's *Islandia*[13] helped its readers forget the first year of the second world war. Most utopian novels are so short that the details of everyday life are left to the imagination of the reader. Not so with *Islandia.* It deals lucidly and endlessly (1013 pages) with the life and social relationships of the people.

Islandia is not a new land, eager to be exploited, but the most distant part of the Karain continent, whose people have long believed in the virtues of isolation and the simple life. So long as the world powers had other areas to exploit, Islandians managed to live their own life. Their civilization was older than ours, and they had a carefully rationalized and consistent philosophy of life. Since their economy had been relatively static for several hundred years, they

[13] Austin Tappan Wright, *Islandia,* New York, 1942.

were not yet convinced that the benefits of an industrial revolution were adequate recompense for the dislocations which it would cause. They felt that their agrarian economy gave them a sense of personal security and a happiness which they would not have had in the more industrialized and competitive civilization of Europe and America.

As the story unfolds the Islandians are preoccupied with a political crisis. One faction feels that the country must be opened to foreign trade—that the transition will be made peacefully or by force, and that trade and foreign investments will stimulate every phase of the country's economy. The opposition group cannot see the difference between "modernizing" and plundering; they cannot see the wisdom of allowing foreigners to profit from the oil and coal and mineral wealth of Islandia.

The story is told by John Lang, a young Harvard graduate who has been sent to Islandia as Consul, with instructions to help his fellow Americans find ways to do business. He is not a success as a Consul, for he comes to agree with those Islandians who want to continue the policy of rigid exclusion. By the time the political conflict had come to a head, he had been replaced as an official, and was free to analyze and report events from his own point of view. Eventually the exclusionists win, but he had served their cause so enthusiastically that he is invited to remain and become a citizen. He returns, instead, to the United States, and discovers that his native land has lost its charm. He sees his fellow countrymen as hurried and unhappy men whose way of life made neuroses as inevitable as the unremitting lust for money. He had acquired an Islandian facility at rationalizing which led him back to that country and a life as a gentleman farmer and writer.

Leonard Bacon wrote in the introduction to the book that Austin Wright had "some judgmatical streak in him that clearly separated him from the run of the mine faculty member. What he said always was established on some rock of intelligence. . . . His Utopia was neither worse nor better than things as they are. It was different and thus afforded a yardstick, a measure, a standard of comparison. The premises are different, but Reason holds his wonted place." For example, he analyzes at length, in terms of John Lang's three love affairs, the principles which determine our concepts of morality and marriage. The Islandians are self-conscious and outspoken about sex; and they make constant distinctions between various kinds of physical desire and friendship. The reader almost suspects that this absorption in personal relationships may be one reason for their way of life. Their days would not allow time for the concerns of business in a competitive society.

Islandia is the most carefully written and literary of American utopian novels. Austin Wright was a Professor of Law at the University of California and the University of Pennsylvania. *Islandia* was a hobby and was written slowly, over a period of years, as an elaboration of a dream world which had absorbed and amused him as a child. It is not a utopia for a generation that demands excitement, and new machines. The appeal is the same as in Shangri-La—security, leisure, and the meditative life. In 1942 most Americans were so completely occupied with the war that they had no time for a long, discursive novel dealing with ideas. Had it been published at the end of World War II rather than at the beginning, the sale might have been far greater.

CHAPTER TWENTY-FIVE

ANOTHER WAR AND MORE DREAMS

Part I. *Granville Hicks*

DURING the thirties Granville Hicks was the literary editor of
the *New Masses* and an influential left wing critic. His work
was the most scholarly and accurate published by the American
Communists. Shortly after Stalin and Hitler came to temporary
terms, he resigned from the party and did a good deal of public rationalizing about his motives. The Communists were not as idealistic
as he had expected, and they did not agree with his conviction that
the freedom of the individual was of fundamental importance.

In 1940 Hicks wrote a utopian novel, *The First to Awaken,* which
acquires additional meaning from his own uncertainty about the
proper basis of government. Unlike most utopians he provides no
set formula for the good life. There is, however, a good deal of
comment about the diversity of men's ambitions and a realization
that the satisfaction of material wants is only the first step to utopia.

The plot is similar to *Looking Backward.* The hero had become so
disillusioned by the inequalities of 1940 that he deliberately sub-
jected himself to a medical experiment which allowed him to sleep
for one hundred years. The society of 2040 had evolved rapidly, but
most of the changes were the result of plans first set in motion by the
New Deal. Since the changes all seem reasonable and people have
learned to respect the privacy of the individual, adjustments are easy.
The principles of government are familiar, but his guide, a modernized Dr. Leete, does a good deal of explaining:

"As you have already seen, we get medical attention free, transportation
free, telephone—and also telegraph and postal—service free. These are
services provided the useful citizen by the community. All this is a logical
extension of practices in your day. It was an easy step from uniform postage
rates to free postage, from the general distribution of water to the general
distribution of light."

"This didn't happen all at once. It began with the nationalization of the
basic industries . . . and . . . the development of large scale, cooperative

enterprises. But for a long time the various services, though they were
provided by the government . . . were paid for by the individual. Gradually,
however, one service after another fell into the category of social supply. So
today some seventy or eighty percent of a man's wants are taken care of
without any money transaction."

"But isn't this wasteful?" I interrupted. . . .

"Why, yes, it's somewhat wasteful. But look at it the way it works out.
I dare say that when you were growing up your family was careful to put
out every light that wasn't actually in use. Isn't that so? Well, in later
years people stopped watching the lights so carefully. This was chiefly because, even under capitalism, electricity had become so much cheaper that
one light more or less didn't make a great deal of difference. Now it's true
that, if electricity is supplied free, people aren't going to run around turning
off lights, but it's also true that the cost is not too excessive. And the
waste is actually much less than the cost of bookkeeping that's involved
in measuring each individual's consumption and charging him for it."[1]

Everyone who did any useful work was a member of a cooperative.
The cooperative supplied the individual's fundamental needs, but
over and above that he was given an income, which varied in relation to his job. "The most dangerous and arduous and unattractive
types of work had an A rating. . . . Most factory work, transportation,
and the more monotonous types of services had a B rating. Work
that could be supposed to bring its own satisfaction—teaching, medicine, managing, planning, and the like—had a C rating. The D
category included not only students but also other kinds of privileged
individuals."[2]

The first consequence of this completed New Deal had been an
acceleration of the growth of cities. The engineers surpassed themselves in devising ways to crowd more and more people into smaller
and smaller areas. They created a technological era in which efficiency and regimentation were ends in themselves. But eventually
production became so easy that everyone had enough, and there was
no incentive to work for more. The desire for great cities disappeared;
population gradually spread out in smaller communities.

With this choice of the town instead of the city, went the choice,
also, of diversified production in every area. Efficiency was no longer

[1] Granville Hicks and Richard M. Bennett, *The First to Awaken*, New York, 1940,
pp. 66, 67.   [2] *Ibid.*, p. 69.

the only consideration; it might have been more efficient for each area to specialize, but such efficiency was at the sacrifice of the individual, and so was not considered.

The scientific marvels of 2040 are familiar to anyone who has read recent advertisements. Scientists took full advantage of new materials—they built Dymaxion houses of steel and glass and plastics; they cleaned them with an air conditioning machine which sucked up every particle of dust; they drove their cars along beamed highways; they kept track of the time on twenty-four hour clocks, and the years on a thirteen month calendar.

Men and women worked only four hours a day. The rest of the time was their own, for play, study, or hobbies. They had more personal freedom than ever before, and there were fewer rules to govern conduct. Men had learned that happiness could not be analyzed and pre-determined, and that the good life was not the same for everyone.

At the end of the novel one of the characters summarized for himself, and for Hicks, the results of this new way of life:

Today we are beginning to be strong enough to face our limitations. We know that ours is a species just sufficiently adapted to the world in which it finds itself to permit survival. The world was not molded to our heart's desires. . . .

A very wise man of the nineteenth century said that, once man was freed of bondage to his belly, once it became relatively easy to take care of his physical needs, civilization could begin. How true that is you know better than I. But remember that it is merely a start that has been made. History is ahead of us, not behind. Thousands upon thousands of years were spent in the building of a foundation, and, now that it is finished, we must realize that it is a foundation and nothing more. No one feels more acutely than I how good it is that we are reaching out to new ideals, but new ideals bring new possibilities of failure. The struggle is never over.[3]

In 1942 Hicks wrote another novel, *Only One Storm,* which serves as a supplement to *The First to Awaken.* Here he makes the point that since the future is so uncertain the sensible course for a wise man is to concern himself with the present. His chief character comments: "It would be wonderful if you could work out a plan for the democratic control of the whole machinery of pro-

[3] *Ibid.,* pp. 343, 344.

duction and distribution, but if you can't, . . . it's a good idea to see that the six hundred people of Pendleton are as well governed as possible."[4]

It seems to be apparent from these two novels that Mr. Hicks is too much an idealist to be satisfied with the pragmatism of the communists. After all, the Marxian prediction of a class struggle does not simplify the task of the man who dreams of utopia.

Part II. *Franz Werfel*

Star of the Unborn is the last book of a strangely cosmopolitan, Czechoslovakian-Jewish refugee, Franz Werfel, whose books have all been written in German, and yet have, on occasion, earned the dignity of becoming best sellers in the United States. After his flight from Europe he settled in Hollywood, an experience calculated to make anyone self-conscious about our customs and ideals.

Star of the Unborn is more American than European in point of view, and it is also contemporary—for it reflects the confused motivation of our day, the search for intellectual justification, and the feeling which so many have that we are on the last lap of human progress, that our discoveries of atomic power hold within themselves the key to self-annihilation. If the book may be classified as American only by careful definition, so also it is utopian only by definition. The publishers call it a travel book, but the only travels are those of a distraught mind into the future.

There are no material wants in Werfel's world. Food and the other necessities of life are produced by a small group of trained laborers. Astro-mental men and women are parasitic, and no longer do any useful work. The machine had become so efficient that it was no longer necessary for everyone to be a producer. In terms of the desires of past generations, utopia had already been achieved. The economics of life had been thoroughly simplified. There are no political, social, or technological problems. There is no poverty, no disease, and no excitement. Existing had become so simple that "not-existing" seemed equally pleasant. No one used blunt verbal symbols such as "death." The term "retrogression" had acquired such an

---

[4] Granville Hicks, *Only One Storm*, New York, 1942, p. 331.

agreeable connotation that the very existence of Astro-mental society was threatened.

Their cities are built below ground, a reminder of the destructiveness effected by the final, and conclusive astro-mental war. The houses are none the less luxurious for being below ground. There is no individuality in design—everything had been standardized—and yet there is no dissatisfaction; men's ingenuity seems to have been exhausted at an earlier period. Men no longer wondered at some of these earlier accomplishments. The mathematical-mental method of traveling, for example, had become a commonplace. This was a device based on a "fundamentally simple insight into the relativity of all moving points in the cosmos. . . . In short, when we travel, we do not move toward our objective, but we move our objective toward us."[5]

This distant world of the future is described by a world traveler, a residual spark of life from the twentieth century. He has come to be completely out of sympathy with his hosts, and he tries to explain his point of view:

The world without economics is a paradise. But what's the use when man isn't paradisiac? He is the content which he pours into every form. And so all forms are immaterial in the end, since they always enclose the unvarying measure of human insufficiency. I don't know whether the caveman was happier than the denizen of a New York skyscraper around the year 1930, and whether the latter was happier than my host . . . in his subterranean house full of fancy light effects, dynamic wallpaper, family recipes prepared by a stellar process, and many other miracles. I only know that a skyscraper or a cottage around 1930 was infinitely more comfortable and more pleasant than the limestone cave of the troglodyte, and that the meanest homestead in Panopolis is incomparably more civilized than a millionaire's villa of my lifetime, not to mention the cloud-shrouded office-sierras and commerce-canyons of Manhattan. Man has succeeded in making great improvements; no one but a stupid ignoramus can deny that. There's only one thing that he has not been able to improve, and that is himself!

The world without economics . . . stands higher than the world with economics, or rather, it is more highly developed, in the same way, for example, as an electric hotel kitchen is more highly developed than the open fire at which the savage roasted his hunk of buffalo meat. . . . But it doesn't follow at all that the more highly developed food tastes better.

[5] Franz V. Werfel, *Star of the Unborn*, New York, 1946, p. 22.

. . . Every gain is based on a loss and vice versa. I hope that . . . the world without economics will be maintained. It's a better world, even though man isn't any better in it. But even if man hasn't become any better morally, still he has become esthetically more beautiful. He's not only become more beautiful, but also more intuitive, and to make up for it, on the debit side, less emotional and colder. If man was formerly guiltily innocent, he is now innocently guilty. . . .⁶

That speech pretty well summarizes the intellectual content of *Star of the Unborn.* The world-traveler had been unable to adjust himself to the future. He had retained a faith in life; he still believed that the individual should want to live, and that progress cannot be an illusion. Werfel has much in common with his world traveler. He had lived too long and seen too much to be an optimist, but he did not want to admit that his faith in his fellow men was unjustified. He does, however, seem to be aware that "progress" is an illusive concept, and that we should stop reassuring ourselves with familiar assumptions about the future. That habit has been an essential ingredient of the American dream. It remains to be seen whether we can develop some equally satisfying "faith for living." This last book of Werfel's shows only skepticism.

Part III. Conclusion

Americans have always had a faith in the new, and yet they have consistently flavored their dreams with a dash of skepticism. From the very beginning this has been true. Sir Thomas More was as skeptical as any other man about the promises he outlined in *Utopia.* When he wrote it, he was playing with an idea. In some measure, perhaps, he was an idealist, but this was a day when idealism had not been overworked. The England of 1516 was miserably insecure and corrupt, and the common man had no hope and few dreams beyond the Christian promise of a life after death.

Somehow Sir Thomas More's notions became fused with men's hopes for a better world in this life as well as in the next. Men came to anticipate a generous and friendly new world rather than a lavish Heaven. Eventually this faith was enunciated by philosophical and social thinkers who talked a good deal about natural rights, and very little about respect for any authority. This doctrine of natural

⁶ *Ibid.,* pp. 636, 637.

rights has had an influence on the whole course of our economic and political development. It has served as justification for those who have exploited a virgin country, and it has been the chief argument of those who have tried to equalize all men before the law. Its most recent application has been the appeal of Roosevelt and Churchill to the "Four Freedoms"—a statement which we recognize as an ideal but acknowledge with skepticism.

Even our most roseate dreams have been partially tempered with skepticism. During the American Revolution, Benjamin Franklin could write to an English friend, Joseph Priestley, in this fashion:

It is impossible to imagine the heights to which may be carried, in a thousand years, the power of mind over matter. We may perhaps learn to deprive large masses of their gravity and give them absolute levity, for the sake of easy transport. Agriculture may diminish its labor and double its produce; all diseases may by sure means be prevented or cured, not excepting that of old age, and our lives lengthened at pleasure even beyond the antediluvian standard. O that moral science were in a fair way of improvement, that men would cease to be wolves to one another, and that human beings would at length learn what they now improperly call humanity.[7]

This letter shows a skepticism, mixed with a belief in the promises of science, which makes one think of the uncertainty in the mind of Werfel's world traveler. He was sure that a world without economics was good—if only human nature could be relied upon.

Franklin's optimism is also characteristically American. Among the utopian novelists this has been apparent in an insistence that man is fundamentally good, that his selfish instincts are usually subordinated, and that somehow or other, by some sort of Emersonian compensation, any given economic or political development may be rationalized into a blessing. But even utopians have seldom been so enthusiastic that they have forgotten their "if's." Most of our utopian dreams have been on a contingency basis. It is not surprising, then, that our present hopes for a better world should be clouded with reservations.

During most of the war, we did not look ahead. As a people, we were so preoccupied with the war that we had no enthusiasm for any dreaming—except of peace.

[7] Charles A. and Mary R. Beard, *op. cit.,* Vol. I., pp. 455, 456.

Skepticism has reappeared inevitably. We have wanted peace so intensely that now we are afraid that we cannot keep it. Our skepticism comes partly from fear—and partly from a sense of insecurity. The weapons which brought us victory provide us with no guarantees about the future. We must have faith in a world which has yet to show that it can work together. Such a faith is in our American tradition.

DYSTOPIAS AND UTOPIAS—A POSTSCRIPT

U TOPIANS were as plentiful as social critics in the nineteenth century. The inequities of their own day, the poverty and the injustice they saw everywhere around them, gave them incentive to look for the ideal. As they looked at the world in which they lived, these men of imagination and of social conscience found it easy to draft specific blueprints for the ideal state.

By the mid-twentieth century we seem almost to have achieved utopia—at least in terms of wages, food, labor-saving devices, and through the extension of social welfare legislation. The contemporary United States, whatever its failings, may seem surprisingly utopian by comparison with the past, or by comparison with what can be found elsewhere. In spite of our achievements, however, we continue to have grave doubts about the promises of politicians and utopians; we are inclined to be cynical about ideal societies and human perfectability. Skepticism seems to be a normal reaction to this age of anxiety, for the frustrations and uncertainties of the cold war are ever with us.

Inevitably there have been dystopian novels in the post war years. Just as utopians feel that dramatizing the ideal will have an effect on our social development, so the dystopians feel that some admonitory finger-shaking may shatter illusions or make us face up to some of the impossible alternatives that seem to lie ahead. Some of these men are simply pessimists who visualize the most distressing resolution of our problems. But whether they are social critics or jeremiahs, their work has had a dramatic impact on our imaginations, and has left its mark on the literary course of the nineteen-fifties and sixties.

Two of the novels, *One*[1] and *Fahrenheit 451*[2], are in the tradition of *1984*. Both assume states which insist upon total conformity, and both

[1] David Karp, *One*, New York, 1953.
[2] Ray Bradbury, *Fahrenheit 451*, New York, 1953.

deal with individuals who cannot or will not conform to the pattern of the ruling elite.

David Karp's *One* is an unpretentious, deadly-serious account of the "benevolent state" whose ultimate concern is the happiness of its citizens. And happiness, the state insists, comes only from conformity. To secure the cooperation of the citizens, the state relies upon an elaborate system of spies who must always be alert for heresy. These spies reveal as much about themselves as about others. One of them, the chief character of the novel, is revealed as an unconscious heretic, and individualist guilty of intellectual pride, and so a serious threat to the status-quo. Once his heresies have been analyzed, the psychiatric persuaders take over, and, systematically, by drugs, threats, brutality, he is reduced "to a cipher—from one to nothing." He emerges from the treatment an utterly different person, a reasonably content, thoroughly harmless individual. But he remains an individual, reluctant to lose his own sense of identity, and so must be destroyed.

One is a remarkably effective novel. Perhaps its most terrifying quality is the thoroughly normal existence that its citizens seem to live —ignorant of and indifferent to the price that must be paid for the apparent benevolence of the state.

In Ray Bradbury's *Fahrenheit 451,* state conformity is largely self-generated. People have what they want—constant entertainment, sports for everyone, group activities for everyone, and three and four-wall television sets. Fun has become a way of life. Thinking has gone out of style; no one has time to think. Books have stopped selling, but the people, sure of their own taste, "let the comic book survive. And the three-dimensional sex magazines, of course."[3]

In this busily other-directed world, the firemen have become the guardians of social morality—their function is to destroy books. On the fireman's helmet is the number 451, "the temperature at which book paper catches fire and burns." The purpose is to protect men's peace of mind, to guarantee that they will not think, will not ask questions, and will not concern themselves with the relevant. The rationalization for all this is simplicity itself:

If you don't want a man unhappy politically, don't give him two sides to a question to worry him; give him one. Better yet, give him none. Let him forget there is such a thing as war. If the government is inefficient, top-heavy, and tax-mad, better it be all those than that people worry over it. . . . Give the people contests. . . . Cram them full of noncombustible data, chock them so damned full of 'facts' they feel stuffed, but absolutely 'brilliant' with information. Then they'll feel they're thinking, they'll get a sense of motion without moving. And they'll be happy, because facts of that sort don't change. Don't give them any slippery stuff like philosophy. . . .[4]

The inevitable rebel of *Fahrenheit 451* is a fireman who reads some of the books he must destroy, and then asks too many questions. He becomes an outcast, and finds, along the abandoned railroad tracks, a good many other rebels who are equally concerned with the life of the mind. Once this has been established, the action is resolved by a convenient atomic war, of which previously, there had been no mention. The plot is not particularly important, however, nor are the characters, except as a medium for some sharp comments on contemporary society. Although distinguished as a writer of science fiction, Ray Bradbury also has a sure hand as a social critic. Much of what he describes is all too familiar; it is not reassuring to project some of our attitudes and traits another few hundred years into the future.

George Stewart's skillful volume, *Earth Abides*[5], is the first of several novels, including the sensational best-seller, *On the Beach*[6], which suggest the quick loss of our civilized veneer in the event of nuclear or germ warfare. Two 1963 novels, *The Wanting Seed*[7] and *The Planet of the Apes*[8], the one English and the other French, also fit into the dystopian pattern. *The Wanting Seed* deals sardonically with overpopulation and with several off-beat attempts to resolve the problem. *The Planet of the Apes* assumes a group of cosmic explorers who reach a distant star and find there the role of man and ape reversed. The implication of the novel is clear enough: in a society so largely motivated by other-directed behavior, man had better be concerned about his human status. A mind attuned to the half-life of the television set scarcely distinguishes its owner from his closest anthropoid

[3] *Ibid.*, p. 53
[4] *Ibid.*, pp. 55, 56.
[5] George Stewart, *Earth Abides*, New York, 1949.
[6] Nevil Shute, *On the Beach*, New York, 1957.
[7] Anthony Burgess, *The Wanting Seed*, New York, 1963.
[8] Pierre Boulle, *Planet of the Apes*, New York, 1963.

relatives. These novels have a morbid fascination. The pessimist has the uneasy feeling that these men may be understating their case—that civilization may be trembling in the balance—that it is later than we like to think.

Although the dystopians have been numerous since 1945, and more in tune with the frustrations and uncertainties of the cold war, there have also been utopians; the work of Skinner, Hazlitt, Ayn Rand, and Louis Halle has attracted considerable attention. Their utopian formulae are different and inconsistent, but one man's ideal may represent the worst possible world to another. No doubt most of what they dramatize is completely impractical, but that charge may not seem entirely convincing today when we consider the dilemmas created by thoroughly practical men.

Three of these post-war utopias follow traditional patterns; two others reflect the heavy shadow of communism, Ayn Rand's *Anthem*[9], and Henry Hazlitt's *The Great Idea*.[10] Ayn Rand would not appreciate the label utopian, and certainly she has little in common with others who draft such schemes. This Russian-born novelist makes a fashion of being different; she enjoys the role of iconoclast, she gives a set lecture on "the folly of faith", and frequently wears a gold brooch in the shape of a dollar sign. "For money", she insists, "is the root of all good."[11]

Anthem is less a novel than a parable in which she insists upon the principle, later elaborated in *Atlas Shrugged,* that selfishness is the chief duty of man. She believes that any sort of social welfare legislation is wrong, and that only when each man puts himself first is there any chance of progress. Egotism and selfishness, she feels, mean progress; and, conversely, the more welfare legislation in a state, the more retrogression. In *Anthem* she not only dramatizes the follies of the collective state, but also unfolds her vision of what might be if only there were undiluted selfishness.

Miss Rand writes dramatically, and in *Anthem,* for once, she is brief. Her style is deliberately Biblical as she seeks to give her subject some

[9] Ayn Rand, *Anthem,* Caldwell, Idaho, 1946.
[10] Henry Hazlitt, *The Great Idea,* New York, 1951.
[11] Quoted in *Time* Magazine, February 29, 1960.

mystical overtones. The parable is well told, but the narrative is little more than an outline. Everything is in black and white. There are no grays. One must accept on faith the deadening uniformity and sterility of the society she sees awaiting the social welfare state. Beneath the critic lies a woman without a social conscience. She will accept no responsibility for the welfare of others. She will not serve as her brother's keeper.

In both theme and plot *Anthem* shows a considerable debt to Eugene Zamiatin's bitter and prophetic novel *We*[12], which was written in 1920 as a protest against the increasing pressures for conformity within the Soviet state. Zamiatin's novel assumes a devastating war that has obliterated all but a few great cities. These have set themselves apart by glass walls—so that there will be no contamination from the green belt beyond. Every detail of life is determined by a Table of Hours, which has theoretically evolved from the time-motion studies of Frederick Taylor. The plot of *Anthem* rests on an identical framework. Its citizens are numbered; their lives are planned from birth; no number may think for himself, or indeed, think at all, apart from his institutionalized role. Both volumes depend on the diary technique; the major characters of both fight their individualism and wonder why they are sick, why they are different. In both novels there is a forgotten past with secrets to be probed. And in both there is an attempt to dramatize the personal pronoun—Zamiatin does this more imaginatively when he refers to the square root of minus one, and wonders whether he, too, is an imaginary number.

Although Miss Rand is an insistent atheist, the rebellious symbols of *Anthem,* Equality 7-2521 and Liberty 5-3000, play the role of an Adam and Eve, as the founders of a better world based on individual effort. When Equality 7-2521, the individualistic street-sweeper, rediscovers electricity, his discovery is rejected by the World Council of Scholars, and he is to be executed for his intransigence. He escapes, retreats into the great forest, and there, later, he is found by Liberty 5-3000. Together they explore their new world, together they find a mountainside retreat which has survived the years since the "unmen-

[12] Eugene Zamiatin, *We,* New York, 1924. Translated by Gregory Zilboorg.

tionable times." Here, in ancient volumes, they discover a treasury of the past, and here, too, they discover the magic of a symbol, the first person singular. And in this one word lies the key to Ayn Rand's utopia. For the unsophisticated, who are not burdened with a social conscience, *Anthem* has appeal. It is a book for the aggressive, the self-confident, the arrogant, and for those who are sure of their own abilities and somewhat contemptuous of their intellectual inferiors. No nineteenth century apologist put such ideas more baldly. For those whose social ideals came to fruition before nineteen hundred, and have not grown beyond, she is the perfect philosopher.

Henry Hazlitt, the financial columnist for *Newsweek,* seems an unlikely author of a self-proclaimed utopian novel. The plot of *The Great Idea* is thoroughly improbable, and yet familiar enough. The cold war is projected through the twenty-first century, with the assumption that communism has won, and that the West has been thoroughly humbled if not completely buried. As the novel opens, the dictator of Wonworld, Stalenin, brings back to Moscow his son, Peter Uldanov, who has been isolated since childhood and has been educated in an old-fashioned way, on a diet of mathematics, music, and the sciences, with no history, no economics, and no dialectics. He is briefed in the brutal realities of a society motivated by fear, and Peter and the reader learn together what Hazlitt wishes to explain about the shortages, the brutality, the incredible blunders of the communist state.

The dictator's health begins to fail; he softens, in a most bourgeois fashion, and manipulates the power structure so that his son can succeed as dictator. Stalenin's number two man, Bolshekov, the head of the army and navy, refuses to acknowledge the authority of Peter. Civil war erupts; those who fear Bolshekov side with Peter, and, with the help of the air corps, the forces of virtue retreat from Moscow, across Europe, to England and eventually to America. There they make a stand in a revitalized and renamed Freeworld.

Hazlitt's theme is the transformation of Freeworld's economy. Tediously and meticulously, in careful dialogue, he rationalizes the inevitability of capitalist theory. He demonstrates the logic of the present competitive system—that a man will work harder for his own benefit than he will for the benefit of society; that self-interest and the law of supply and demand will satisfy human needs far more accurately than the planning of any group of experts. Most of this is convincing enough to any well-adjusted capitalist, but Hazlitt makes it all too perfect, too inevitable. The reader becomes suspicious.

The Great Idea does not follow the pattern of More and Bellamy, but it does provide a sort of textbook illustration of classical economic theory, and may properly be called utopian. And it does emphasize the need to make capitalism function as efficiently as possible.

Walden Two[13] fits more easily into the utopian tradition. B. F. Skinner, the author and Harvard psychologist, recognizes that we already have the essential ingredients of a functioning utopia. In *Walden Two* Skinner has his apologist and alter-ego argue:

The one fact that I would cry from every housetop is this: the Good Life is waiting for us here and now. . . . It doesn't depend on a change in government or on the machination of world politics. It doesn't wait upon an improvement in human nature. At this very moment we have the necessary techniques, both material and psychological, to create a full and satisfactory life for everyone.[14]

Indeed, a Walden Two might exist in any agricultural area in the country. Skinner describes his community as entirely self-sufficient, and dependent for its livelihood on a variety of agricultural and industrial products. *Walden Two* makes the economic basis for utopia seem rather simple; but given sufficient capital, and a group of dedicated members, such a society might easily survive for a long time. In the nineteenth century, the Oneida Community and the Amana Society enjoyed considerable economic success for many years.

Skinner appears to have absolute faith in behavioral engineering, and in his ability to condition people for the good life. Perhaps we should all accept his doctrine. If hidden persuaders can be manipulated to make us buy what the hucksters choose, why should similar persuaders not be used to make us believe what is supposed to be good for us? Should the tools of the advertising man be forbidden to the state? According to Skinner, the members of Walden Two "are practically always doing what they want to do—what they 'choose' to do—but

---

[13] B. F. Skinner, *Walden Two*, New York, 1948.
[14] *Ibid.*, p. 161.

2

we see to it that they want to do precisely the things which are best for themselves and the community. Their behavior is determined, yet they're free."[15] What degree of freedom is this, however? Some vexing questions remain.

The success of Walden Two has supposedly bred imitation. Other Waldens are being established. The chief figure of the novel predicts "Suppose it's possible to grow and subdivide once every two years. Then in ten years Walden Two and Six will give birth to some sixty-odd communities."[16] Such optimism seems an echo from the past. Similar predictions were made for some of the utopian communities that evolved and collapsed at the end of the nineteenth century. Utopian zeal comes easily to grief during hard times.

Early in *Walden Two,* Skinner emphasizes that behavioral engineering will work even with sheep, and explains how the sheep have been contained first with an electric fence and then only with string. The implication is that if sheep can be so easily manipulated, how much easier it must be to manipulate humans. Later in the novel it is conceded that the string fence was effective only as long as the sheep dog was effective. Actually, the example was unfortunate; any farmer knows that sheep cannot be contained by an electric fence—or even by barbed wire. Once sheep panic, emotion takes over, and they will go through any fence. No doubt humans are similar. In normal circumstances we follow the guide lines, the fences, that our society imposes upon us. However, once the social fabric has changed, once the guide lines are broken, our patterns of behavior become unpredictable, and volatile. In other words, the psychologists on Madison Avenue may manipulate our purchases of soap or clothing, but in other circumstances we may be more difficult to deal with than sheep. We may disregard our advisors and search out our own goals in unpredictable fashion.

Walden Two may represent the psychologist's ideal, but a good many individualists would dislike the well-organized activities of such an institution. Even the best of utopias cannot be all things to all men.

[15] *Ibid.,* p. 247.
[16] *Ibid.,* p. 190.

Island[17] is the sort of utopian novel one might expect from a member of the lunatic fringe that seems to be irresistibly dawn to Southern California. It is not what one would expect from the man who had written *Brave New World*. The Huxley of *Island* seems more nearly a Southern Californian than an Englishman. In this last volume he dramatizes the life of the isolated island of Pala, where, by avoiding progress, the people had managed to achieve a reasoned utopia, based on an enlightened form of education, a sophisticated and very modern approach to sex, and a religion of faith, without belief, drawn chiefly from Buddhism. Pala's educational system is heavily biological in emphasis, as befitting a society which relies upon the yoga of love, and makes frequent use of the *moksha*-medicine, a sort of super-soma, designed to enhance the sense of reality.

Despite Huxley's skill as a writer, this is a talky, ineffective novel. Most of what he has to say about life, love, and the balance of nature is simply tedious, and it takes a stubborn reader to pursue the plot to the end. When, on the last page, revolution has come to Pala, so that oil and progress may make her citizens conform to the standards of the rest of the world, the reader's only reaction is one of relief that so much aimless discussion has been resolved by action. As a novel, *Island* is a failure, a tired anti-climax to a series of more effective volumes.

Sedge[18], a slim volume by Louis J. Halle, is the most recent utopian novel. Sedge cannot be pinpointed on the maps of the National Geographic Society, but some of the physical details of this country bear a marked resemblance to Switzerland. The fact that Halle is a professor at the Graduate Institute of International Studies in Geneva may explain his partiality for mountainous terrain, for the *téléphérique* as a means of transportation, and may also explain his delightfully dispassionate approach to American foibles.

Perhaps his primary target is our predilection for progress, our obsession with bigness. As he explained, "the word for *bad* and the word for *big* in Sedgian are the same, and . . . the common word for *little* is the same as the word for *good*." And he cited the American city, very likely Los Angeles, which was already growing short of water, but

[17] Aldous Huxley, *Island,* New York, 1962.
[18] Louis J. Halle, *Sedge,* New York, 1963.

was, none-the-less, advertising for more industry so that the city could find more jobs for more people. Many of us are guilty of such inconsistent reasoning; we are also guilty of insisting upon better roads and more freeways so that people can travel more rapidly from city to country, and skyscrapers or hamburger stands can replace the unblemished landscape.

Pluvis, the dispassionate philosopher who explains the Sedgian way of life, cannot understand why Americans are so much concerned with tables of organization and with the high art of administration—with getting things done. Apparently we confuse action with progress. And if the administrator is efficient enough, then there is no need for "that troublesome element called 'mind', with its propensity for deviationism." The computing machines can solve our problems; they will be "objective, dispassionate, and mindless." Our organizations need only grow rapidly enough so that machines can be used efficiently. They can even do our research for us, and "because they have been quite mindless from start to finish, may be accepted as absolutely objective."

Halle has a deceptively easy way of posing the dilemmas of our sophisticated age. In a section dealing with "the disappearance of limits," he explains one of the most frustrating and devastating forces of American life.

The limits on the size of our communities disappear, so that our cities spread and multiply their cells without control. The same thing happens to our governments, which go on growing even after their growth has reduced them to floundering helplessness, like dinosaurs in a swamp. It happens to our population when the limits that disease and the food-supply have set to its growth are removed. It happens to the jurisdiction of government when the limits of natural law disappear from among us. It happens to scholarship when the limits of mind are removed. It happens to publication when new processes of duplication overcome the limits on the production of the written word. It happens to musical composition when the limits set by traditional scales and harmonies disappear; and to art when the limits set by the requirements of representation disappear. . . .[19]

Halle's charges have a bite, and their essential truth is clear enough. *Sedge* is an ironic commentary on the United States; it also suggests

[19] *Ibid.*, pp. 93, 94.

the outlines of a utopian scheme of existence which details, in shadowy form, a system of government, a hierarchy of courts, and a religion which fits the needs of a happily agnostic society. But law, government, religion are surprisingly accommodating to the moods of an unhurried way of life, in which economic pressures are slight, and contemplation, travel, music, and pleasant human relationships are all-important.

The dilemmas which *Sedge* considers are known to all of us. Resolving the dilemmas, however, is more difficult than recognizing them. But perhaps we still need to be reminded that growth does not solve every problem, that attracting new industry to a town is not the only solution to economic woes, that building freeways may create as many traffic problems as are solved, that driving bigger cars with greater horsepower does not make driving safer, cheaper, or more simple. Halle did not write a how-to-do-it book on the utopian state, but he did write a provocative book, and in the process demonstrated wit, verve, and subtlety. For these qualities he deserves recognition among American utopians.

In spite of many changes in our intellectual climate, the germination rate for utopias continues high. Neither our skepticism nor our real achievements has slowed a concern for social experimentation. Most of us learn slowly, if at all, and utopian schemes, even the most impractical of them, have a valid place in a world which places so much importance on the dreams of practical men.

BIBLIOGRAPHY

PART I. GENERAL SOURCES

Adams, Frederick B., Jr. *Radical Literature in America*. Stamford: The Overbrook Press, 1939.

Beard, Charles A., and Mary R. *The Rise of American Civilization*. New York: The Macmillan Company, 1927, 2 volumes.

Brisbane, Albert. *Social Destiny of Man; or, Association and Reorganiza- of Industry*. Philadelphia: C. F. Stollmeyer, 1840.

Brooks, Van Wyck. *The Flowering of New England, 1815-1865*. New York: E. P. Dutton & Co., Inc., 1936.

————. *New England: Indian Summer, 1865-1915*. New York: E. P. Dutton & Co., Inc., 1940.

Calverton, V. F. *Where Angels Dared to Tread*. Indianapolis, New York: The Bobbs-Merrill Co., [c 1941]

Faulkner, H. U. *Economic History of the United States*. Revised edition. New York: The Macmillan Co., 1937.

Gronlund, Laurence. *The Cooperative Commonwealth in Its Outlines; an Exposition of Modern Socialism*. Boston: Lee and Shepard; New York: C. T. Dillingham, 1884.

This was one of the most influential American books on Socialism. The point of view is Marxian. G. B. Shaw helped revise later editions.

Hartwick, Harry. *The Foreground of American Fiction*. New York, Cincinnati [etc.]: The American Book Co., [c 1934]

Hertzler, J. O. *The History of Utopian Thought*. New York: The Macmillan Co., 1923.

Hicks, Granville. *The Great Tradition; an Interpretation of American Literature Since the Civil War*. Revised edition. New York: The Macmillan Co., 1935.

Hicks, John D. *The Populist Revolt; a History of the Farmers' Alliance and the People's Party*. Minneapolis: The University of Minnesota Press, [c 1931]

Hillquit, Morris. *History of Socialism in the United States*. New York and London: Funk & Wagnalls Co., 1903.

Laidler, Harry W. *A History of Socialist Thought*. New York: Thomas Y. Crowell Co., [c 1927]

Miller, Perry. *The New England Mind; the Seventeenth Century*. New York: The Macmillan Co., 1939.

Miller, Perry, and Thomas H. Johnson. *The Puritans*. New York, Cincinnati [etc.]: American Book Co., [c 1938]

Morgan, Arthur E. *Edward Bellamy*. New York: Columbia University, Press, 1944.

——. *The Philosophy of Edward Bellamy.* New York: King's Crown Press, 1945.

Morison, Samuel Eliot, and Henry Steele Commager. *The Growth of the American Republic.* Third edition. New York, London [etc.]: Oxford University Press, 1942, 2 volumes.

Mumford, Lewis. *The Story of Utopias.* New York: Boni and Liveright, [c 1922]

Nevins, Allan. *The Emergence of Modern America, 1865-1878.* New York: The Macmillan Co., 1927.

Parrington, Vernon Louis. *Main Currents in American Thought; an Interpretation of American Literature from the Beginnings to 1920.* New York: Harcourt, Brace and Co., 1927-1930, 3 volumes.

Sullivan, Mark. *Our Times: The United States, 1900-1925.* New York [etc.]: Charles Scribner's Sons, 1926-35, 6 volumes.

Taylor, Walter Fuller. *The Economic Novel in America.* Chapel Hill: The University of North Carolina Press, 1942.

Van Doren, Carl. *The American Novel: 1789-1939.* Revised and enlarged edition. New York: The Macmillan Co., 1940.

PART II. THE UTOPIAN NOVEL IN AMERICA

[This bibliography is far from complete. Some of the volumes listed are not novels, but these are explained by notes.]

1659

Eliot, John. *The Christian Commonwealth; or, The Civil Policy of the Rising Kingdom of Jesus Christ.* London: Printed for Livewell Chapman, at the Crown in Popes-Head-Alley.

    This is a religious tract, but it does try to prescribe for an ideal society.

1670

Denton, Daniel. *A Brief Description of New York: Formerly Called New-Netherlands.* London: Printed for John Hancock, at the Popes-Head-Alley in Cornhill at the three Bibles.

    This is a colonization tract, published for the purpose of encouraging new settlement in New York.

1819

[Clopper, Jonas]. *Fragments of the History of Bawlfredonia: Containing an Account of the Discovery and Settlement of the Great Southern Continent; and of the Formation and Progress of the Bawlfredonian Commonwealth.* By Herman Thwackius [pseud.] Translated from the original Bawlfredonian manuscript, into the French language, by Monsieur Traducteur, and rendered into English, by a citizen of America. [Baltimore?] Printed for the American Booksellers.

1827

[Tucker, George]. *A Voyage to the Moon: With Some Account of the Manners and Customs, Science and Philosophy, of the People of Morosofia, and Other Lunarians.* By Joseph Atterley [pseud.] New York: Elam Bliss.

1828

[Sanford, Ezekiel]. *The Humours of Eutopia; A Tale of Colonial Times.* By an Eutopian. Philadelphia: Carey, Lea & Carey, 2 volumes.

1836

[Griffith, Mrs. Mary]. *Camperdown; or, News from our Neighborhood:* being Sketches by the author of "Our Neighborhood." [anon.] Philadelphia: Carey, Lea & Blanchard.
    "Three Hundred Years Hence," pp. 1-92, the longest story in the volume, is pure utopian fiction.

1845

[Judd, Sylvester]. *Margaret, a Tale of the Real and the Ideal, Blight and Bloom; including Sketches of a Place Not Before Described, Called Mons Christi.* [anon.] Boston: Jordon and Wiley.
    The first edition was charged with being too frank. The 1851 edition is much less vigorous, somewhat less polished, and not at all earthy or frank.

1847

[Cooper, James Fenimore]. *The Crater; or, Vulcan's Peak. A Tale of the Pacific.* By the author of "Miles Wallingford," "The Red Rover." [anon.] New York: Burgess, Stringer & Co.

1852

Hawthorne, Nathaniel. *The Blithedale Romance.* Boston: Ticknor, Reed, and Fields.

1860

Lookup, Alexander, [pseud.?] *Excelsior; or, The Heir Apparent. Showing the Adventures of a Promising and Wealthy Young Man, and His Devoted Friends; and Presently Entwined with the varying Story, the Key to a Diamond United States, or, a Vitally Consolidated Republic, a Perfect Union, Otherwise Kingdom of Heaven.* New York & London: Kennedy, Publisher.
    This is primarily satire.

——. *The Road Made Plain to Fortune for the Millions: or, The Popular Pioneer to Universal Prosperity.* Edited by Thos. Ward, M.D. New York & London: Kennedy, Publisher.
    This is in the same vein as *Excelsior.* It is more nearly satiric than utopian.

1863

[Anon.] *Equality: or, A History of Lithconia.* Boston.
> This is listed in the bibliography of F. B. Adams's *Radical Literature in America.* I have found no other record of this volume. Mr. Adams adds this note: "A curious utopian story, probably written during the Civil War and predated. If the claim of the preface were true, that this tale first appeared in Philadelphia in 1802, it would deserve to be called the first American Utopia. It is apparently unknown to bibliographers."

1868

Freelance, Radical, [pseud.] *The Philosophers of Foufouville.* By Radical Freelance, Esq. New York: G. W. Carleton; London: S. Low, Son, and Co.
> This is a satire on Fourierism, and perhaps also on Brook Farm.

1869

Hale, Edward Everett. *Sybaris and Other Homes.* Boston: Fields, Osgood & Co.

1875

[Twain, Mark]. "The Curious Republic of Gondour." *The Atlantic Monthly,* October, 1875, (36: 461-3).
> This was reprinted in 1919 by Boni and Liveright, in a collection taking its title from this story.

1876

Collens, T. Wharton. *The Eden of Labor; or, The Christian Utopia.* Philadelphia: Henry Carey Baird & Co.

1879

George, Henry. *Progress and Poverty; an Inquiry into the Causes of Industrial Depressions and of Increase of Want with Increase of Wealth— The Remedy.* Author's edition. San Francisco: W. M. Hinton & Co., Printers.
> Henry George's work was almost the standard text on taxes and economics for the utopians of the late nineteenth century.

1883

[Macnie, John]. *The Diothas; or A Far Look Ahead.* By Ismar Thiusen [pseud.] New York and London: Putnam.
> The plot of this novel is similar to that of *Looking Backward.* Macnie and Bellamy had known each other, and it is very probable that they had discussed together their ideas about utopianism.

1885

Casey, James. *A New Moral World, and a New State of Society*. Providence: Printed for the author.
These are essays which seek to show that universal education could produce utopia.

1887

Dodd, Anna Bowman. *The Republic of the Future; or, Socialism a Reality*. New York: Cassell & Co., ltd.
Paper bound, and selling for ten cents, it is one of a series printed under the label of Cassell's National Library. Utopian in form, it is satiric in purpose.

1888

Bellamy, Edward. *Looking Backward, 2000-1887*. Boston: Ticknor and Co.
Hale, Edward Everett. *How They Lived in Hampton; a Study of Practical Christianity Applied in the Manufacture of Woollens*. Boston: J. S. Smith & Co.
This is a moral essay designed to illustrate the virtues of cooperation, profit-sharing, and a Christian life. The date of publication is not certain.

1890

[Bachelder, John]. *A.D. 2050. Electrical Development at Atlantis*. By a former resident of "The Hub." San Francisco: The Bancroft Co.
[Donnelly, Ignatius]. *Caesar's Column. A Story of the Twentieth Century*. By Edmund Boisgilbert, M.D. [pseud.] Chicago: F. J. Schulte & Co.
Fuller, Alvarado M. *A.D. 2000*. Chicago: Laird & Lee.
This is an adventure story, but there is some utopian planning.
Michaelis, Richard. *A Sequel to "Looking Backward," or, Looking Further Forward*. London: William Reeves.
There is no date of publication for this edition, but there are three other editions, all in 1890, published in the United States by Rand McNally & Co. Two of them are listed as volume 1, no. 129 of the Globe Library, but the titles are different. One is called *Looking Further Forward; an Answer to Looking Backward by Edward Bellamy*. The other title is *Looking Forward* etc. Under the heading of volume 1, no. 133 in the same Globe Library is a German edition: *Ein Blick in die Zukunft, Eine Antwort auf Ein Rückblick Von Edward Bellamy*. Chicago and New York: Rand, McNally & Co. Michaelis was editor of the Chicago *Freie Presse*.
Reynolds, Thomas. *Prefaces and Notes. Illustrative, Explanatory, Demonstrative, Augumentative, and Expostulatory to Mr. Edward Bellamy's Famous Book, "Looking Backward."* By Thomas Reynolds, a much abused and ridiculed twentieth century man of thirty years' standing. Printed with *Looking Backward*. London: Thomas Reynolds.

Shipley, Mrs. Marie Adelaide (Brown). *The True Author of Looking Backward.* By Mrs. John B. Shipley. New York: John B. Alden.
    Mrs. Shipley attempts to prove that Bellamy took his ideas from August Bebel's *Die Frau und de Sozialismus.* She is not convincing.
Stone, Mrs. C. H. *One of "Berrian's" Novels.* New York: Welch, Fracker Co.
    This is an attempt to answer, by means of the novel of the future, the charge that life in Bellamy's world would be very dull. It is "sorrowfully dedicated to all who believe 'competition' to be the only incentive to progress."
Vinton, Arthur Dudley. *Looking Further Backward. Being a Series of Lectures Delivered to the Freshman Class of Shawmut College, by Professor Won Lung Li (Successor of Prof. Julian West).* Albany: Albany Book Co.
    This is an attempt to show how utopianism must fail. It is mostly a lecture on the oriental menace.

1891

Fiske, Amos K. *Beyond the Bourn, Reports of a Traveller Returned from "The Undiscovered Country," Submitted to the World.* New York: Fords, Howard & Hulbert.
    This is a novel on spiritualism, but there is a faint utopian twist to it.
Geissler, Ludwig A. *Looking Beyond. A Sequel to "Looking Backward" by Edward Bellamy, and an answer to "Looking Further Forward," by Richard Michaelis.* New Orleans: L. Graham & Son.
Harris, Thomas Lake. *The New Republic. A Discourse of the Prospects, Dangers, Duties and Safeties of the Times.* Santa Rosa, California: Fountaingrove Press.
[Simpson, William]. *The Man from Mars: His Morals, Politics and Religion.* By Thomas Blot [pseud.] San Francisco: Bacon & Co., printers.
    Another edition, in which Simpson is listed as the author, was printed in San Francisco in 1893 by the Clemens Publishing Co.
Thomas, Chauncey. *The Crystal Button, or, Adventures of Paul Prognosis in the Forty-Ninth Century.* Boston: Houghton, Mifflin & Co.
    This was written before *Looking Backward,* but it was not published until Bellamy's success inspired revision.
Wilbrandt, Conrad. *Mr. East's Experiences in Mr. Bellamy's World. Records of the Years 2001 and 2002.* Translated from the German by Mary J. Safford. New York: Harper & Bros.

1892

Chavannes, Albert. *The Future Commonwealth, or What Samuel Balcom Saw in Socioland.* New York: True Nationalist Publishing Co.
[Crocker, Samuel]. *That Island.* By Theodore Oceanic Islet [pseud.] A Political Romance. Oklahoma City: C. E. Streeter Co.

The Library of Congress catalog lists another edition published in the same year by the D. F. Woody Printing Co. of Kansas City, Missouri.

Donnelly, Ignatius. *The Golden Bottle, or, The Story of Ephraim Benezet of Kansas.* New York and St. Paul: D. D. Merrill Co.

Everett, Henry L. *The People's Program; the Twentieth Century Is Theirs. A Romance of the Expectations of the Present Generation.* New York: Workmen's Publishing Co.

1893

[Anon.]. *The Beginning, a Romance of Chicago as It Might Be.* Chicago: Charles H. Kerr & Co.

Miller, Joaquin. *The Building of the City Beautiful.* Cambridge & Chicago: Stone & Kimball.

Five hundred paper bound copies were printed. Another edition was put out in 1905 by Albert Brandt of Trenton, New Jersey. In the preface to this last edition, Miller wrote: "Three small editions of parts of this book appeared in 1894, when the plates were melted. It was never really published till now so far as press and public are concerned, the small and unfinished editions being absorbed mainly by personal friends."

Olerich, Henry. *A Cityless and Countryless World; an Outline of Practical Cooperative Individualism.* Holstein, Iowa: Gilmore & Olerich.

Roberts, J. W. *Looking Within. The Misleading Tendencies of "Looking Backward" Made Manifest.* New York: A. S. Barnes & Co.

Russell, A. P. *Sub-Coelum; a Sky-built Human World.* Boston and New York: Houghton, Mifflin and Co.

This is a series of essays on the possibilities of a utopian world. It can almost serve as a catalog of the reforms current in the nineties.

Swift, Morrison I. *A League of Justice, or, Is It Right to Rob Robbers?* Boston: The Commonwealth Society.

This is a paper-bound pamphlet of ninety pages. It is a political satire disguised as fiction.

1894

Harben, W. N. *The Land of the Changing Sun.* New York: The Merriam Co.

This novel is more concerned with adventure than with utopianism. It tells the story of a people living in a vast cave, much as in Bulwer Lytton's *The Coming Race.* There is emphasis on scientific heredity and the body beautiful.

Schindler, Solomon. *Young West, a Sequel to Edward Bellamy's Celebrated Novel, Looking Backward.* Boston: Arena Publishing Co.

Welcome, S. Byron. *From Earth's Centre, a Polar Gateway Message.* Chicago: Charles H. Kerr & Co.

1895

Bishop, William H. *The Garden of Eden, U.S.A., a Very Possible Story.* Chicago: Charles H. Kerr & Co.

Chavannes, Albert. *In Brighter Climes, or Life in Socioland. A Realistic Novel.* Knoxville, East Tennesee: Chavannes and Co.

The Library of Congress catalog lists this as being published in 1897 as the first volume in The New Thought Library.

Howells, W. D. *A Traveler from Altruria. A Romance.* New York: Harper & Bros.

Lloyd, John Uri. *Etidorhpa: or the End of Earth. The Strange History of a Mysterious Being and the Account of a Remarkable Journey as Communicated in Manuscript to Llewellyn Drury Who Promised to Print the Same, but Finally Evaded the Responsibility, Which was Assumed by John Uri Lloyd.* Author's ed., limited. Cincinnati: J. U. Lloyd.

Another edition was published in 1901 by Dodd, Mead and Co. It deals mostly with scientific marvels.

1896

[Anon.] *Man or Dollar, Which? A Novel.* By a Newspaper Man. Chicago: Charles H. Kerr & Co.

This is listed as No. 55 in the Unity Library.

1897

Adams, Frederick Upham. *President John Smith; the Story of a Peaceful Revolution.* Chicago: Charles H. Kerr & Co.

The cover lists this as No. 24 in the Library of Progress.

Bellamy, Edward. *Equality.* New York: D. Appleton and Co.

This is the sequel to *Looking Backward.*

[Caryl, Charles W.] *New Era; Presenting the Plans for the New Era Union to Help Develop and Utilize the Best Resources of This Country. Also to Employ the Best Skill There Is Available to Realize the Highest Degree of Prosperity That Is Possible for All Who Will Help to Attain It. Based on Practical and Successful Business Methods.* Denver, Colorado.

This was published by Caryl as a trustee for the New Era Union. No date of publication is given, but it was copyrighted in 1897.

Sheldon, Charles M. *In His Steps. "What Would Jesus Do?"* Chicago: Advance Publishing Co.

The story was first published in 1896, in *The Advance*, a Congregationalist weekly. Sheldon tried to get it published in book form elsewhere, but after several tries allowed the Advance Publishing Co. to bring it out in a ten cent, paper-bound edition. Almost immediately it was brought out by sixteen other publishers, the copyright having proved defective. Edward A. Weeks of the *Atlantic Monthly* figured in 1934 that by that year it had sold some 8,000,000 copies in America, and probably 24,000,000 copies over the world.

1898

Craig, Alexander. *Ionia, Land of Wise Men and Fair Women*. Chicago: E. A. Weeks Co.

Farnell, George. *Rev. Josiah Hilton, the Apostle of the New Age*. Providence: Journal of Commerce Co.
This is an attempt to explain the transition period to Bellamy's world. The solution is monetary reform.

Forbush, Zebina. *The Co-opolitan; a Story of the Co-operative Commonwealth of Idaho*. Chicago: Charles H. Kerr & Co.

Sanders, George A. *Reality, or, Law and Order vs. Anarchy and Socialism. A Reply to Edward Bellamy's Looking Backward and Equality*. Cleveland: The Burrows Brothers Co.
A collection of indignant essays.

[Wellman, Bert J.] *The Legal Revolution of 1902*. By a Law-Abiding Revolutionist. Chicago: Charles H. Kerr & Co.
The cover lists this as No. 27 of the Library of Progress.

1899

Merrill, Albert Adams. *The Great Awakening, the Story of the Twenty-Second Century*. Boston: George Book Publishing Co.

189?

Hovorre, M. Auburre. *The Miltillionaire*.
A thirty page pamphlet on utopianism. No date or publisher is given, but it seems to be a product of the late nineties.

1900

Bayne, Charles J. *The Fall of Utopia*. Boston: Eastern Publishing Co.
An oriental romance laid in a perfect country where all wealth is held in common, this is utopian only in background.

[Caswell, Edward A.] *Toil and Self*. By Myself and Another. Chicago and New York: Rand, McNally & Co.
This is supposed to be a collection of essays written in 2400 A.D., and dealing with the labor problems of the nineteenth century. It contains the usual objections to utopian or socialist experiments.

Edson, Milan C. *Solaris Farm, a Story of the Twentieth Century*. Washington, D.C. Published by the Author.

[Grigsby, A. O.] *Nequa; or, The Problem of the Ages*. By Jack Adams [pseud.] Topeka: Equity Publishing Co.

Peck, Bradford. *The World a Department Store; a Story of Life under a Coöperative System*. Lewiston, Me., & Boston: B. Peck.

Persinger, Charles Edward. *Letters from New America; or, An Attempt at Practical Socialism*. Chicago: Charles H. Kerr & Co.

1907

Howells, W. D. *Through the Eye of the Needle*. A Romance. New York and London: Harper & Brothers.

1911

Swift, Morrison I. *The Horroboos.* Boston: The Liberty Press.
A parody on the ways of government, the plot is partially utopian.
A "missionary" devotes himself to an African tribe, the Horroboos,
and proves to them "that the noblest aim of being is to make someone else rich. . . ."

1912

[House, Edward M.] *Philip Dru: Administrator; a Story of Tomorrow,
1920-1935.* [anon.] New York: B. W. Huebsch.
Colonel House became President Wilson's closest advisor. Many
of Wilson's policies are similar to those outlined in this novel. Similarities to the New Deal may also be found.

1913

Hayes, Jeff W. *Paradise on Earth.* Portland: F. W. Baltos and Co.
A separate edition, also in 1913, was titled *Portland, Oregon,
A.D. 1999.*

1920

Shanks, Edward. *The People of the Ruins; a Story of the English Revolution and After.* New York: Frederick A. Stokes Co.

1932

Martin, Prestonia Mann. *Prohibiting Poverty; Being Suggestions for a
Method of Obtaining Economic Security.* Winter Park, Florida: The
Rollins Press.
This is an outline of the National Livelihood Plan. By September,
1939, thirteen editions had been published.

1933

Hilton, James. *Lost Horizon.* New York: William Morrow and Co.
This is American only in terms of its enthusiastic acceptance in
this country—both as a novel and as a movie.
Sinclair, Upton B. *I, Governor of California, and How I Ended Poverty;
a True Story of the Future.* Los Angeles: Published by the author.
No date of publication is given, but it was certainly 1933. This is
fiction, but not a novel.

1935

Long, Huey Pierce. *My First Days in the White House.* Harrisburg: The
Telegraph Press.
This is an account of what he would have liked to do as president.
He may have taken the idea from Upton Sinclair.
Sinclair, Upton B. *I, Candidate for Governor: and How I Got Licked.*
New York: Farrar & Rinehart, Inc.

These are the facts which clarify the fiction. It is an interesting supplement to the earlier volume.

1936

Sinclair, Upton B. *Co-op; a Novel of Living Together.* New York; Toronto: Farrar & Rinehart, Inc.

1939

Churchill, A. T. *The New Industrial Dawn.* Seattle: Press of Lowman & Hanford Co.
The plot follows *Looking Backward.* The main point is that there can be no poverty if everyone is kept working.

1940

Hicks, Granville, and Richard M. Bennett. *The First to Awaken.* New York: Modern Age Books.
This is another modernized *Looking Backward.*

1942

Wright, Austin Tappan. *Islandia.* New York; Toronto: Farrar & Rinehart, Inc.
This is the best written of American utopias. It is more concerned with ideas than scientific marvels.

1946

Werfel, Franz. *Star of the Unborn.* Translated by Gustave O. Arlt. New York: The Viking Press.
This is a strange mixture of mysticism, scientific jargon, and prophecies about the world of the future. It is utopian in terms of the accomplishments of the future, but not in terms of philosophical satisfaction from those accomplishments.

INDEX

Index